D1290040

International Express

International Express

New Yorkers on the 7 Train

Stéphane Tonnelat and William Kornblum

Columbia University Press
New York

Columbia University Press
Publishers Since 1893
New York   Chichester, West Sussex
cup.columbia.edu
Copyright © 2017 Columbia University Press
All rights reserved

Library of Congress Cataloging-in-Publication Data

Names: Tonnelat, Stéphane, author. | Kornblum, William, author.
Title: International express: New Yorkers on the 7 train / Stéphane Tonnelat
and William Kornblum.
Description: New York : Columbia University Press, [2017] | Includes
bibliographical references and index.
Identifiers: LCCN 2016040218 (print) | LCCN 2016054020 (ebook) |
ISBN 9780231181488 (cloth : alk. paper) | ISBN 9780231543613 (e-book)
Subjects: LCSH: Multiculturalism—New York (State)—New York. |
Subways—Social aspects—New York (State)—New York. | Ethnic groups—
New York (State)—New York. | Immigrants—Cultural assimilation—
New York (State)—New York.
Classification: LCC F128.9.A1 .T66 2017 (print) | LCC F128.9.A1 (ebook) |
DDC 305.8009747—dc23
LC record available at https://lccn.loc.gov/2016040218

Columbia University Press books are printed on permanent and durable acid-free paper.
Printed in the United States of America

COVER IMAGE: © VINCENT LIN
COVER DESIGN: JORDAN WANNEMACHER

In memory of Isaac Joseph,
whose pioneering research inspires this volume.

To begin, it would be useful to examine the validity of two understandings. The first is to say that a public space is an order of visibilities destined to accommodate a plurality of uses or a plurality of perspectives, which implies a considerable depth; the second states that a public space is an order of interactions and of encounters and presupposes, therefore, a reciprocity of perspectives. These two understandings make public space a receptive space in which bodies advance, perceptible and observable, and a space of competencies, that is to say, of practical knowledge confined not only to the operators and architects but to the ordinary users as well.

Isaac Joseph, *La ville sans qualités*

Contents

Acknowledgments

This book originated with our late colleague Isaac Joseph, whose ambition was to conduct a comparative study of the 2 train in Paris and the 7 train in New York. Both lines, he surmised, were used by a large number of immigrants as a local transportation link, a form of *ligne de cabotage*, a naval metaphor for small boats moving from port to port, never far from the shore. How did these lines bring all these ethnic neighborhoods together in a single city? Unfortunately, Isaac did not live long enough to conduct the Paris side of the study. It is partly in his memory, therefore, that we decided to go ahead with the New York side of the project. This is a posthumous thanks for his inspiring vision.

Michèle Jolé also was with us from the start and even before. We thank her for her unwavering support and nudges. Michèle invited us to her seminars at the Paris Institute of Urban Planning, and we often sat around her table for great meals and discussions with friends and colleagues. She visited New York numerous times and basically adopted us and our families.

Virginie Milliot was part of the original Paris team. Even though her research took her away from the metro, she stayed close to put together a small team to study the Goutte d'or neighborhood near the Barbès metro stop in Paris. In addition, she organized a conference at the Maison de l'ethnologie at the University of Nanterre, where we were able to present for the first time the idea of the "community in transit."

We owe much as well to our team of research assistants closer to New York, whom we were able to hire through a Professional Staff Congress Grant and a CUNY collaborative grant awarded in 2005 and 2006. Richard E. Ocejo, now an assistant professor at the CUNY John Jay College of Criminal Justice, was an efficient and dependable colleague, helping us manage the team of high school students and make sense of their diaries, all while working at the same time on another urban ethnography.[1] Amalia Leguizamon, now an assistant professor at Tulane University in New Orleans, was a great colleague as well. Besides bringing Spanish to the languages spoken by the research team, she had great interview, transcribing, and note-taking skills, especially when studying the station at 74th Street and Roosevelt Avenue. Finally, Chi-Hsin Chiu, now an assistant professor of landscape architecture at Fu Jen Catholic University in New Taibei City, joined the team to help us talk to Chinese immigrants not yet comfortable in English. Thanks to him, we were able to better understand the dynamics in Flushing.

Both Stéphane and Bill benefited from the support of their colleagues at CUNY. At the CUNY Graduate Center, Stéphane had the enthusiastic support of Setha Low for many years even before this project started. Among other things, she invited Stéphane to brainstorm with a group of distinguished colleagues in the Public Space and Diversity research group funded by the Max Planck Institute. Cindi Katz, we suspect, may have been the originator of the 7 train idea in 2003. We were having a drink celebrating Stéphane's dissertation defense when Isaac asked her: Which subway line do many immigrants take in New York City? Cindi also put us in contact with a teacher who helped us recruit the high school students who kept the diaries. Ida Susser was also supportive from the beginning, believing with us that institutions should have more trust in ordinary people.

While at the College of Staten Island, Stéphane was able to take advantage of Jeffrey Bussolini's advice and support, and Rafael de la Dehesa translated the informed consent forms into Spanish.

We wrote most of this book in 2014 and 2015 when Stéphane was a fellow at CIRHUS, the joint research center between New York University (NYU) Center for Research in the Humanities and Social Sciences and the French National Center for Scientific Research (CNRS), not far from the CUNY Graduate Center. This visiting position allowed him and Bill to work more closely together than they could when they were separated by an ocean. Nicolas Guilhot, as the center's deputy director, was a welcoming colleague. William Rendu and Solange Rigaud, both paleoanthropologists and office mates, were very supportive as well, and William Kornblum also wishes to thank the staff at the Marseille Institute of Advanced Studies (IMERA), where he was able to work on the manuscript during his residency.

Fabienne Malbois, a specialist in feminist theory and a lecturer in Lausanne, Switzerland, read the chapter on gender relations. Rashmi Sadana, an ethnographer of the Delhi subway and an assistant professor at George Mason University, participated and contributed to many panels on subway ethnography with Stéphane and Bill.

Christina Mitrakos, Stéphane's life companion, has been a patient listener concerning all aspects of this book and proofread much of it. Peter Kornblum, William's brother, also proofread the final manuscript and drastically improved its legibility.

This book took its final shape thanks to the editorial team at Columbia University Press. Eric Schwartz showed early interest and warmly welcomed us to the press. Lowell Frye and then Caroline Wazer helped us complete the paperwork, and the design department, with redrawing the maps. Irene Pavitt and Margaret Yamashita carefully edited the whole text with countless corrections and changes. Such professionalism is a treat that we feel very lucky to have had.

Finally, no ethnographic project is possible without the people in the field. We would especially like to thank the twelve high school students who worked with us to document and examine teenagers' experiences of the subway. We also thank the Metropolitan Transportation Authority (MTA) workers, the street workers, and other professionals who agreed to talk to us about their work and their environment. Neysa Pranger, at the Straphangers Campaign, was the first to share ridership data and more with us when we were met only with silence from the MTA. Richard Barone and Emily Roach at the Regional Planning Association later gave us the data from the years 2008 to 2012.

Riders can be thanked properly only in an anonymous way. Thanks, Riders!

International Express

1 Becoming New Yorkers on the 7 Train

That the subway will run tomorrow as usual is for him of the same order of likelihood as that the sun will rise.

Alfred Schutz, *Alfred Schutz on Phenomenology and Social Relations*

We become New Yorkers on the subway. An overstatement? A gross simplification? Perhaps so. But much of a New York City dweller's life is spent "in transit." Climbing the stairs to the station platform, knowing where to get on and off or to transfer, and feeling relief as the train rumbles over impossible geographic and social distances, the competent transit rider practices the art of getting along with a mass of others mainly by pretending to ignore them entirely.

Rider competence is increasingly vital to the overall resilience of the city's subway system. As more and more New Yorkers crowd the subway to travel across the city, the network comes under increasing stress. Aging tracks and equipment, staff reductions and workers under pressure, maintenance delays, fare hikes, and crowded conditions all present a recipe for the system's breakdown. Even though the New York subway is struggling to hold up, it is so successful in attracting riders that it has become the city's largest and most diverse public space.[1] City residents and visitors of every conceivable origin mix in tight subway spaces for limited but repeated intervals. Against all odds, only a few injurious incidents occur during the millions of daily rides.[2] Nonetheless, over a full transit year, through winter storms and sweltering summer heat, daily subway commuters endure many rides when the service is far from perfect, with delays sometimes the consequence of situations and imbroglios involving passengers.

One of our goals in this book, therefore, is to explore how the riders' conduct affects the system's operation and, in turn, how different aspects of the subway's physical and social environment influence the riders' attitudes and behavior.

What constitutes "subway savoir faire," and what can the subway savvy New Yorker teach us about the essential qualities of urbanism? Many of the skills urbanites practice as subway riders are universal, applying in any city with an extensive system of mass transit. Other forms of subway behavior and knowledge, including the geography, are specific to New York City. New Yorkers who become familiar with the metro in Paris or in Santiago, Chile, or that of any great city, feel less strange and vulnerable when they know where to buy a ticket and how to find the right trains. Similarly, newcomers to New York who start learning the ways of our transit system also begin to feel more confident in other ways about their presence in the city. And over lifetimes of subway travel as urbanites, how could mass public transit not somehow shape our feelings about the city and help stamp our identities as New Yorkers?

We, Stéphane Tonnelat and William Kornblum, the authors of this volume, have been riding subways in Paris and New York for our entire lives. For the past few years, however, we have been conducting systematic studies of aspects of the mass transit experience in New York. These studies draw on the work of many other scholars who have written about mass transit, and they reflect our experiences in other mass transit cities of the world. Tonnelat usually lives in Paris and conducts his research at the French National Research Center (CNRS) in Paris, but he frequently visits and works in New York as well. Likewise, Kornblum has lived and taught in New York for many years, but he has also spent time in Paris. Accordingly, although we limit our discussion to the New York mass transit system and its endlessly fascinating sociology, our observations draw on our experience with the Paris metro and that of subways in other major world cities.

What child of the city does not recall her first solo subway ride or her parents' instructions about how to behave on the subway, where to get on and off, how to avoid trouble, and how to "be careful"? As parents and teachers, we are continually reminded by our observations of life in the subways that we

must learn a great deal about getting around before we can t
as competent New Yorkers. In *International Express*, we
analyses of these mass transit competencies by documenting ι
of young immigrants. We frequently refer to the transit diaries
group of high school–age students of immigrant background and to our conversations with them about their experiences. We also know from personal
experience how important it is for a young person to feel some mastery of
the city's vast public transportation system. For Bill Kornblum, a native
New Yorker and the chronologically senior author of this volume, that first
solo subway ride came during a minor family emergency in 1950:

> My mother stopped me as I was leaving for school and explained that my fa-
> ther, who was already at work in his Manhattan office, had run out of batter-
> ies for his hearing aid. They had decided I was old enough, at age eleven, to
> bring them to his Manhattan office from our home in Queens. My father was
> calling from his office in the Municipal Building. He was involved in difficult
> labor negotiations; perhaps it was over the contract with the subway workers
> themselves. Without his hearing aid, he could not continue his work. Our
> family home was in the Murray Hill neighborhood of Flushing, and I had
> been to the city by subway from Main Street Flushing [station] many times
> with my parents. They had taught me how to change trains from the 7 at
> Grand Central to the downtown 6 train in order to go to 33rd Street where
> our family dentist practiced the arts of oral torture. But I had never contin-
> ued on the Lexington Avenue line farther south. The assignment worried me
> but also made me feel charged with an adult responsibility.
>
> The long stairway from the Brooklyn Bridge Station reaches the street level
> under the arches of the Municipal Building itself. Generations of New Yorkers
> have come here to apply for marriage licenses or to pay traffic fines in nearby
> court buildings. But I was on a more urgent mission to a floor well above the
> endless green offices where strangers stood in lines to be married or licensed. I
> was ascending high in the building's Victorian-style upper towers. From my
> father's office I saw tugs plying the East River and barges filled with construc-
> tion materials. A line of subway cars slid in silence across the Manhattan
> Bridge. In the distance I saw the familiar dark span of the Queensboro Bridge.
>
> My mission accomplished, I retraced the ride back to Grand Central, and
> then on the 7 to Flushing Main Street. I felt proud, a kid beginning to "know
> his way around the city."

The 7 Flushing Line: Aboard the "International Express"

Ridership on the 7 train that Bill took to Manhattan as a child has grown even more than ridership for the system as a whole has, in both numbers and diversity. In the 1950s, Flushing and most of the other communities in northern Queens along the subway line were still predominantly populated by people of European origin. But by the turn of the twenty-first century, these communities had become home to immigrants from all parts of Asia and Latin America, with Main Street, Flushing, emerging as a major enclave of Chinese and Korean global commerce and population mobility. No wonder that in 1999, the White House Millennium Council designated the 7 as a landmark "National Millennium Trail," a monument to the American immigrant experience.

Readers not familiar with the detailed geography of New York City should know that the 7 train crosses the northern expanse of Queens from Main Street, Flushing, to Times Square, the subway hub of the entire city and, since 2015, to Eleventh Avenue and 34th Street, next to the newly developed Hudson Yards (figure 1.1). The 7 runs local trains that stop at each of the twenty-two stations on the line, and express trains that skip numerous stations. Along its path, the 7 crosses some important transfer points and destinations such as Citi Field (home of the New York Mets) and the Billie Jean King National Tennis Center (site of the U.S. Open Tennis Championships). It also runs through many ethnic neighborhoods, each representative of several waves of immigrants into the country. According to a 2005 brochure printed by the Queens Council on the Arts, "The International Express [7 train] is a trip around the world in one borough."

From Main Street in Flushing to Eleventh Avenue in Manhattan, the 7 train serves an enormously diverse range of neighborhoods and populations. Yet its riders often call it the "Orient Express" or the "Hong Kong Special" because it ends its long run eastward across Manhattan and northern Queens at Main Street, Flushing, now one of the city's largest centers of East Asian immigrants and second-generation settlers. Old Flushing was known for its expanses of nurseries and open wetlands. Thanks in large part to the centripetal effects of subway construction, by the booming 1950s Flushing had become an urbanizing commercial hub built around the last 7 station, Flushing–Main Street/Roosevelt Avenue. Its avenues retained

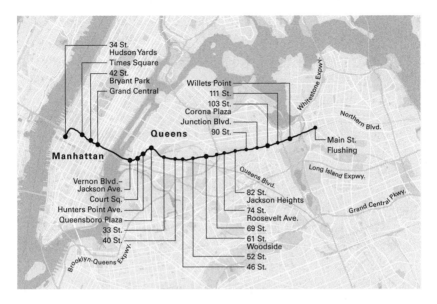

34 St.
Hudson Yards
Times Square
42 St.
Bryant Park
Grand Central

Willets Point
111 St.
103 St.
Corona Plaza
Junction Blvd.
90 St.

Queens

Whitestone Expwy.

Northern Blvd.

Main St.
Flushing

Manhattan

Long Island Expwy.

Queens Blvd.

Vernon Blvd.–
Jackson Ave.
Court Sq.
Hunters Point Ave.
Queensboro Plaza
33 St.
40 St.

82 St.
Jackson Heights
74 St.
Roosevelt Ave.
69 St.
61 St.
Woodside
52 St.
46 St.

Grand Central Pkwy.

Brooklyn-Queens Expwy.

Figure 1.1   Map of the 7 train line. Express stops are indicated by large dots, and local stops by small dots.

their shady canopies of gracious elms, and its low-rise apartment buildings and private homes were interspersed with Dutch Reformed and other Protestant and Catholic congregations. Today, Main Street, Flushing, looks a great deal like a congested section of Hong Kong. Flushing's downtown commercial district is a city within the city, abuzz with local and global commerce, a node of the Chinese and Korean global economies. It also boasts a density of street life worthy of an Asian city, which helps account for the heavy use of bus and subway mass transit at Main Street where the 7 train begins and ends its 35- to 40-minute trip to and from Manhattan.

New Yorkers are proud, even boastful, about the city's diversity, and in this study we seek to know more about the actual experiences of diversity as it occurs in daily life, primarily on one subway line, the 7 train. We look at how social diversity affects the riders and the functioning of the system itself. In our descriptive analysis, diversity refers to many social variables, including race, ethnicity, gender, age, and social class. Length of residence and experience in the city also are critical aspects of rider diversity. How do these many differences actually present themselves on a specific subway train? How do social contexts change along the subway line? Does who is riding the trains make a difference? Stéphane Tonnelat's field notes on the 7 train present a typical scene of subway interaction showing unexpected dimensions of diversity:

7 train to Flushing. Wednesday March 30, 2005. Warm and Sunny

1:39 P.M. Queens Plaza. The sparsely populated train car where I had a comfortable seat fills up with people mainly of Latino and Asian origin. I am jammed in on both sides by other passengers. A few more people stand in front of me, their hands on the metal bars. As the train departs, an elderly Latino man holding a stack of small black and red fliers starts awkwardly navigating his way through the car. A red stained baseball cap hides his eyes and forehead. He is a "flyboy" working a classic off-the-books cheap entry-level job. Most likely he is a newly arrived immigrant.

I am curious to see that not everybody gets a flier and even more curious to see how insistent he is when he does offer one. He won't take no for an answer as he tosses a flier on the newspaper that a woman is reading two seats to my right. He hands another flier to a middle-aged Latina woman sitting directly across from me. He then moves to a group of five teenage high school girls who also boarded at Queens Plaza. He juts his hand in the middle of the group, holding four fliers. They look at him, surprised. He shakes his hand a bit, and they take the fliers. He then pulls two more from his stack and hands them to the group. The girls show little interest in what he is offering. They giggle and resume their animated conversation. Three appear to be white Latinas, one is a black Latina, and one is East Asian. They all are dressed in the same fashion: long black hair tied up or not, tight pants, exposed midriffs, and tight tops that outline their figures. They are much louder than everybody else on the train and do not seem to care if others stare at them. They regularly scan the car to see who is looking at them, yet they carefully avoid eye contact. Two of their fliers fall to the floor. The girls ignore them. They scan the car again, but they do not meet my eyes. Another passenger sees me watching them and gives me a nod of acknowledgment. Another bump in the ride, and another flier drops to the floor. Then, a girl leaning against the door crumples her flier and throws it to her feet. She does it matter-of-factly, as if it were normal to throw garbage on the floor.

The man with the red cap comes back from the end of the car. Without a word, he kneels down by the feet of the girls and picks up the three uncrumpled fliers. The group stops talking for a few seconds. A few bystanders watch the scene. Without a word, he merges back into the crowd and disappears. The girls giggle even more now.

2:01 P.M. 90th Street Elmhurst. The girls have been moving toward the nearest door, ready to exit. The one nearest the doors gets off first. She waits for the others as they push their way out. "Say sorry!" she shouts to her friends. Regrouped on the platform, one of them throws a crumpled flier at them. It bounces and ends up on the train floor.

2:15 P.M. Flushing. Last stop. I pick up the crumpled flier: "Plastic and Vinyl Slip Covers," "Hablamos Espanõl." This is apparently for women only, but hardly of interest to teenage girls. On the platform, a black MTA [Metropolitan Transportation Authority] employee with a broom waits for the last passengers to exit before starting to sweep the car.

In this episode from his field notes, Stéphane was observing the subway as a public realm where riders are free to observe one another and make distinctions based on the widest range of human social categories. At times, his notes show that they act on their observations in a curious and sociologically revealing fashion. For the most part, as we will document throughout this book, riders do not act on social categories because they are expected to treat one another as anonymous, nondescript passengers. And when social categories are summoned,[3] as when the flyboy hands out fliers only to women, the motivation comes from a local furniture store, outside the subway's realm. According to Alfred Schutz's phenomenology, in some "zones" the usual categories can be "relatively irrelevant";[4] such differentiation is a characteristic trait of the subway's social order. That is, people on the trains are riders before they are women, black, young, Hispanic, or rich. As a result, what one ought to do as a rider takes precedence over the discriminating features of fellow passengers. But as we also emphasize, this does not mean that diversity is of no consequence. Women, for example, do not have the same subway experiences as men, adolescents do not behave like older adults, and people of different racial and ethnic groups do not feel they are treated in the same way as white, middle-class New Yorkers are. The overriding challenge of the subway and for all the individuals it carries at any given moment is to move forward through the city.

Everyday Cosmopolitans

Stéphane's notes also suggest that the subway is a city-spanning public space in motion through all the city's territories. Through that space, as we show in chapter 2, the trains carry a shifting cargo of passengers who represent the peoples of the world. Thus, in northern Queens, each station of the 7 Flushing line sends the residents of its nearby neighborhoods (and those who arrive by bus from more distant ones) into an ever-changing subway public. The trains empty and fill according to the city's temporal rhythms of work, leisure, and shopping. In the common spaces of mass transit, the multicultural qualities of life in a world city may attain their fullest expression in daily experiences. On the subways and buses and while negotiating their way through the stations and down platforms, urban newcomers must develop the getting-along and going-along skills and attitudes that constitute a form of quotidian cosmopolitanism. These skills' outward presentation may be a blank stare or mindless involvement with a cell phone. Throughout this book we use the term "cosmopolitan" as a quality of the response to both particular contexts of social diversity and one's experiences in diverse environments.

The quotidian cosmopolitanism of the subway, for example, refers to riders' mundane experiences with, and tolerance of, the differences perceived in other riders. To be cosmopolitan in this sense differs from the more elite connotations of this term.[5] We show that subway cosmopolitanism is often accompanied by small but significant changes in personal values and behaviors, by documenting how immigrants and their children become more comfortable with strangers on the trains who represent the city's different subcultures. Newer arrivals to the city learn to be subway riders by balancing civility and instrumentality. In this way, they start to feel at home as they adapt to the stress of American urban life.

Our focus on urban newcomers on the subways highlights the challenges of mass transit for all city dwellers. Indeed, our overall aim is to better understand the contradictions and paradoxes of the mass transit system's social world and its ever changing moral order. Although the demands of gaining mass transit competencies are not unique to immigrants and their children, their experiences call attention to overlooked aspects of life in the public transit system that are usually taken for granted. It is also true that many native New Yorkers have to learn, or relearn, the skills of ridership as their life situations change. Again, Bill's personal experience with public transit is relevant in this context:

From our apartment in Jackson Heights to my midtown office is a relatively easy commute on the 7 train from 82nd Street, with options to change to the E, F, M, or R trains, at the next stop, 74th and Roosevelt Avenue, one of the major transit hubs in northern Queens. One problem I share with the exploding proportion of my fellow urbanites is an aging body. Senior citizenship in New York City conveys the benefit of a half-price MetroCard with what seems like an elderly stranger's face on its front. On that stranger's legs I climb the four flights of stairs to the elevated 7 at 82nd Street and Roosevelt Avenue. The climb counts toward aerobics, and for a reward, it delivers a panoramic view of midtown Manhattan, whose weather and light are always changing.

During rush hours the platform is jammed. People gather near where they think the coming train's doors will open. This small bet they make each morning can make the difference between getting on a crowded train or having to wait until another arrives. A winning bet about where the train will stop could even be rewarded with a seat, at least for the first two or three entrants. This morning I had my eye on an open seat, but my path to it was blocked by a youth equipped with a backpack who stopped as he entered the car. He was satisfied that he was on the train and ignored those of us waiting our turn to board. As a younger man, I might have lowered a shoulder and nudged my way past him to hustle toward that open seat. I hesitated and lost. A young woman next to me in the doorway sliced though the crowd like a speedy halfback to win the seat. Finishing an awkward second in our unstated race to sit, I stood above her as she fiddled with her iPhone.

If crowded buses and subway cars create competitive situations that demand skills at balancing civility with aggression, they also present us with innumerable other dilemmas and moral choices. Against the background of mass cooperation and consensus on moving forward, acts of selfishness or hostility or generosity and human connection stand out for the ethnographer. Observed carefully, a seemingly quiet subway car can be the stage of a multitude of micromorality plays: here a woman gives up her seat to a mother and child; there a group of teenagers hold open the doors while shouting to a friend still on the platform. Does anyone speak up? Are the young people aware of the delay they cause?

Anonymity and Community in the Subway

Manhattan-bound 7 at 82nd Street, a weekday morning.

A well-dressed white woman is pressed in the crunch of rush-hour passengers who have just pushed desperately onto the train car. She sees space toward the middle of the car. She knows that most of those around her will want to exit at the next stop to hurry for other trains. They have little incentive to move farther away from the doors. The woman intends to stay on the train. She expects there will be a few empty seats as everyone exits. She needs to move toward the center of the car. A tall black teenager wearing a hoodie is directly in her way. She speaks to him. "If you just take a deep breath, I'll just squeeze past," she smiles. He stares at her for a second. Then he says, "I'll move that way. I'm a New Yorker. I know how it works."

Field notes, 2015

This is not a typical subway interaction. When we analyze our data and field notes from the 7, we do find such examples of rider competence, but they are fewer than one would wish for. Far more commonly, there is no interaction at all. Riders remain bunched up near the doors while the space toward the center of the cars often remains available. In this instance, our female passenger displayed advanced subway skills. She read the social context quickly and accurately. She probably decided that the young man was a student on his way to school. Tactfully, she tried to reduce the tension of the situation in which strangers of different genders, ages, races, ethnicities, and social classes are pressed against one another. She did not demand that the young man move farther into the car, as a crankier rider might have. Nonetheless, she made her needs known. And the student? Once jarred from the safety of his anonymity, he invoked his own knowledge of "how things work" in the subway. The alert teenager shifted from thinking about his own situation, to thinking about "how you act on the New York subway." In later chapters, we see that this represents a characteristic mental "code switching" from the subjective voice to the public explanation of shared notions about what constitutes appropriate subway behavior. We further explore this finding with supporting data in chapter 3, showing that such code switching is a competence gained through experience with the system. More significant is that these ideas about norms of subway conduct are essential to the existence of community in the seemingly anonymous mass of subway riders.

Community? On the subway? The subway is often appropriated as a symbol of urban stress, alienation, and mechanical disciplining rather than community. The mass transit rider, usually presented as a scurrying rush-hour commuter, is anxious or lost in endless waiting. George Tooker's bleak vision of furtive strangers in the New York subway in 1950, on display at the Whitney Museum, is one example among many that come to mind (figure 1.2). At the opposite extreme, subways are represented as the heroic product of a people's will to modernize. With its sculptured station spaces, the Moscow subway system stood for the victories of Soviet socialism, just as the more recent systems in Asian cities are touted as national achievements.

Neither of these extreme views of the subway guides our inquiry. New York's subway system, like those of other aging cities, requires constant

Figure 1.2 George Tooker, *The Subway*, 1950 (tempera on composition board, 18½ × 36½ inches; the painting is in color). (Collection of the Whitney Museum of American Art, New York; purchase, with funds from the Juliana Force Purchase Award. © The Estate of Georg Tooker. Courtesy of DC Moore Gallery, New York)

effort to prevent it from becoming overcrowded and dangerous. To that end, the MTA's work to modernize bleak subway stations and trains also includes a significant public-art program. While regular riders have plenty of reasons to grumble over delays and dirt, they also have welcomed the MTA's efforts. The art and music programs add welcome touches of humanity to the system.[6] Nor are atomized commuters an accurate representation of the universe of subway passengers. On the 7 train and throughout the system in early morning when the trains are crowded with adult working people, there are mothers taking small children to day care. When the cars are less crowded, mariachi performers or other spirited buskers may appear. After school, teenagers arrive in boisterous groups, as well as seasonal baseball and tennis fans, middle-school children on class trips with their teachers, and at all hours, shoppers with their carts (figure 1.3). Add to this list occasional peddlers, performers, partygoers in the evenings and on holidays, entire families on weekend outings, lovers lost in each other's eyes, homeless people fitfully sleeping and outreach workers seeking to assist them, and so many more. This is a decidedly livelier world than the usual representations of alienation.

Each time we walk into a subway car, we merge with a sample of New York's population. It's almost as if we were drawn from a deck of cards containing all the most common and also the rarest human possibilities. For the most part we are strangers, but occasionally, by chance, we do see neighbors and friends. We also see familiar scenes enacted by people whose language we understand and less familiar ones enacted by people who may dress differently and whose language we do not know. Some of these situations will test our rider competencies. We may confront trouble and need immediate assistance. Or we may be asked to help others, even for such modest requests as directions. At other times, passengers may annoy us or even appear threatening. And sometimes we may find ourselves included in a clutch of tipsy partygoers. How do we deal with all these situations and possibilities? Isaac Joseph, our dear and late colleague who specialized in the spaces of transportation, including the Paris metro, continually noted in his pioneering subway research the importance of rider competencies to the smooth workings of any mass transit system. He argued that rider competency involved "contextualization skills," or social skills, including

Figure 1.3 Teenagers in motion at the 74th Street/Roosevelt Avenue station. (Stéphane Tonnelat, 2006)

- The ability to interpret, from a course of action or communication, the relevant contextual clues one should act on, including directions but not limited to them
- The ability to code switch while moving one's personal space from a more private to a more public realm
- The ability to justify one's behavior toward other riders[7]

Using a variety of methods, we explore the issue of rider competencies throughout this book and tie it to the more general concept of the subway community. Each ride offers a wide variety of possible situations and encounters that reflect the way the system functions as what we have called a "situational community in transit," even if we most often feel that we are merely part of the anonymous subway crowd. For insight—albeit with some caution—we also draw on an increasingly important subway public created in social media. In the book's middle chapters, we examine the special qualities of the subway community and the important role of trust in maintaining it. We devote entire chapters to gender and age, as they feature in subway interactions that shed a specific light on the subway's social order and its violations.

Women and Teenagers in the Subway System

Too often, women are the recipients of unwanted male attention on the subway, and teenagers who burst onto the trains after school are frequently raucous producers of annoyance. An analysis of how women experience groping and other abusive affronts during subway travel reveals gender-specific aspects of rider competencies. This also takes us into the tendentious politics of gender relations in public spaces. Similarly, our students' travel diaries and our extensive observation of teenagers' behavior on the trains affords insights into how young male and female riders on the 7 develop subway competency.

The diaries of students in two Queens high schools who participated with us in a subway seminar reflect many of the typical experiences of young New Yorkers on the trains, especially those with immigrant backgrounds. We use these and other firsthand accounts of subway interactions and feelings throughout the chapters where they are most telling. We recorded many conversations about subways with these and other students and with adult riders, which also document the interactions we examine. Diversity was often a personal issue for our young diary keepers because they do not entirely identify as Americans or New Yorkers. This feeling of immigrant marginality varied among them, highlighting issues of diversity. Who was rubbing against whom, or who started pushing, became even more salient for this group of foreign-born students. Young people in late adolescence are anxious as well about their public presence, and we see in some of their accounts of subway interactions that they are learning the competencies of more veteran subway riders.

Some of our young female riders wrote about offensive male behavior and incidents of lewdness or groping. For example, seventeen-year-old Connie, a Latina high school student, wrote a diary entry early in our semester about being stroked on the leg when squeezed among a group of men at a subway door. She described how her anger and feelings of humiliation stirred her determination to learn from the experience. The expressive candor of Connie and other young women regarding their experiences enabled us to discuss their feelings and reactions in more depth than would otherwise have been possible (for more on our research methods, see the appendix). Other accounts of gender relations on the subway that we gathered ourselves or gleaned from subway blogs suggest that the trains and stations are not infrequently the site of romantic encounters. Gender relations on the trains are further complicated by never-ending possibilities of mutual attraction and the steady modern effacement of binary gender presentations.

A reading of subway histories, in New York and other major cities of the world, suggests how difficult it can be in some cultures to create a subway environment that is safe for women. Even in its early years, the New York system experimented with gender-segregated trains, a situation common in India and elsewhere today. In these histories, we also see the contribution of mass transit to the increasing tolerance and cosmopolitanism of urban populations.

Subway Citizens and Subway Cities

In chapter 4, about the busy station at 74th Street and Roosevelt Avenue, we show how the station operates within the institutional framework of the

MTA and also becomes a significant fulcrum for the surrounding community of Jackson Heights. We turn again to questions about the subway and its surrounding communities in chapter 8, where we explore the importance of the 7 line to the past and present stability of the communities along its elevated tracks. There we focus on how the subway and, particularly, the 7 train have contributed to urban growth and the resilience of communities like Jackson Heights and others along the 7 route. From this more macroecological perspective, we begin to understand the history of the subway as an engine of urban growth. We show that the subway itself has facilitated demographic balance and diversity. Communities along the 7 line, initially parts of the medium-density "subway suburbs" built along lines opened in previously inhabited areas,[8] avoided the worst effects of the white middle-class exit from the city during the difficult decades of the twentieth century. These suburbs also rebounded more quickly than others during the 1990s and 2000s when the city economy soared. The neighborhood of Jackson Heights, for example, changed from an exclusive, white, upper-middle-class, Protestant community into a much more multiethnic and multiclass area, heralding the no-majority diversity typical of Queens today. African Americans, however, never gained much access to the garden city apartments built in the 1920s along the new subway line. While they maintain a presence in the famous Corona neighborhood around 107th Street, home to the Louis Armstrong House and Museum, in the Bland Houses in Flushing, or interspersed among tenants of Corona's Lefrak City, African Americans and West Indians do not appear as a significant part of the heterogeneity we describe on the 7 train.

Given its centrality to the city's development, how should the subway figure in theories of urban social change? In addressing this question, we review some of the important social scientific literature on the growth of urban communities. The empirical facts we seek to explain involve an understanding of how the ridership has changed and steadily increased over the decades. What this has contributed to the city can hardly be overstated, as the resilience of communities and institutions is clearly enhanced in the middle density of bustling Queens neighborhoods. We argue that the increasing competencies of riders and their sense of trust and security in the subway has a role in these recent trends.

As more cities of the world invest in major mass transit infrastructures, the lessons learned from older systems like those of New York, Paris,

London, and Moscow become part of an expanding literature of "subway studies" like ours. Such research, we believe, can inform ongoing transportation planning throughout the urbanizing world.

Most new subways are promoted as tools of not only efficient transportation but also modernity aimed at civilizing vast populations into sophisticated residents and disciplined urbanites. Our study of the New York City subway, and the 7 train in particular, shows that despite similar intentions at its opening, the system gradually became a symbol of decay, dirt, and ruthlessness. New Yorkers may have never fit the image of the restrained urbanite. Still, over the generations of life on the subways, they have made their steady contribution to the daily efficiency of the city's transit system, by developing their own ways of getting along. In this way, riders are essentially collaborating with the transport authority to jointly run the system.

The MTA, however, operates in a political fishbowl and tends to avoid collaborating with its patrons. It does not sponsor or support public research in the interest of furthering knowledge about the role of riders. The MTA has a restrictive culture and long-standing policies for dealing with its internal affairs. Although it has increasingly made its rider statistics available to the public, we have no idea if it has conducted assessments of its own informed efforts to address issues of subway competence. In Paris, in contrast, executives of the Régie autonome des transports parisiens (RATP) routinely hold seminars and sponsor research on the issues discussed in this book. In New York, the same executives would more likely appear before a legislative committee at City Hall or in Albany. In this regard, the influence of web-based groups like the Straphangers Campaign, Hollaback!, and others we introduce to readers are an important part of the city's subway competence story. These groups and the numerous serious and well-written blogs about subway life and related matters we draw on are creating a new form of mass transit public sphere, one based on the experiences, values, and expressive skills of riders. They are turning up the democratic volume in ways the MTA executives and elected officials must hear.

Over the years that we have been working on this study and even while writing the book itself, the New York City subway system has been changing. As we noted earlier, the 7 Flushing line no longer concludes its run at Times Square and 42nd Street. Instead, it continues into a booming new, high-rise, upscale district at Hudson Yards on the western edge of midtown Manhattan. On the Queens sections of the line, however, during the same period, riders have become inured to constant delays because of the seemingly endless process of modernizing the signal system. Our study generally shows that the city would have much more to gain by expanding the 7 line east into the far reaches of Queens than into already hyperdense Manhattan. These are reminders that the mass transit system is an arena of major political decisions: Where to invest? Where to cut? Should the subway spur real-estate investments, or should it solve congestion issues? How to disturb the riders in the least distressing way? When to police versus when to insist that riders exert self-control? These decisions seem most often out of the reach of riders, who are rarely consulted on issues of service disruptions and fare hikes. Despite the active work of the Straphangers Campaign, an arm of the nonprofit New York Public Interest Research Group (NYPIRG), in evaluating the quality of service and advocating against fare hikes, the MTA's legal organization does not make itself easily accountable to New Yorkers.

The subway is already a public space with its own particular type of community, thanks largely to its riders. If New York City is to meet the challenges of urban life and transportation in the twenty-first century, the subway system must become a more widely recognized and adequately funded public service. We invite the reader to join us on the 7 train, where we hope the lessons that subway patrons have taught us will become evident.

2 Coping with Diversity Aboard the "International Express"

I took out my wallet, slid out the card and swiped it through, all done in three seconds. Sometimes you can tell if a person is a New Yorker by the speed he/she swipes her/his MetroCard. A clumsy swiper is usually a foreign tourist or a newcomer. But it is not an absolute sign. It's an indicator.

Ting, sixteen years old, Sunday, June 4, 2006

In 1999, following the nomination by the Queens Council on the Arts, the 7 train was designated a "National Millennium Trail" by the White House Millennium Council, the U.S. Department of Transportation, and the Rails-to-Trails Conservancy. It joined fifteen other trails, such as the Underground Railroad, that are deemed "emblematic of American history and culture." Nicknamed the "International Express" by the City Planning Commission, the train was advertised to New Yorkers and visitors as a symbol of the American immigrant experience and a celebration of cross-cultural encounters.

Aboard the International Express

A report by the New York City Department of City Planning, *The Newest New Yorkers, 2000*, helps us understand the situation better.[1] Briefly, it states that the city gained fewer than 100,000 people between 2000 and 2003 because of the massive flight to the suburbs or to other states in the United States (−475,000). However, the strength of the city's natural increase (+200,000) and immigration flows (+340,000) massively compensated for the loss, actually saving the city from depopulation. The result of these in-and-out movements is a city that in 2003 had reached an extraordinary level of diversity, in which the foreign-born accounted for 36 percent of its residents, close to the peak of 41 percent in 1910, when the city stood at 4.8 million (in 2015, 8.5 million). The next report, released in 2013, confirmed this trend toward greater diversity.[2] The borough of Queens is the main destination of immigrants in the nation (Brooklyn is second), with almost half of its population being foreign-born. If we add the second generation of immigrants, well over half of New York City's dwellers have recently adopted "hyphenated identities."[3] In terms of race, no single group can now claim a majority. In a landmark study of Elmhurst, a neighborhood along the 7 line and at that time the nation's most ethnically diversified neighborhood, anthropologist Roger Sanjek and his colleagues revealed the slow but seemingly inexorable emergence of interethnic cooperation on local community board committees and political forums during their fifteen years of fieldwork. Sanjek focused on "whites," and his coresearchers studied "blacks,"[4] "Chinese,"[5] "Hispanic women,"[6] and "Indians,"[7] attempting to identify the spheres of political encounters. Citing these signs of comity and intergroup understanding, Sanjek observed that diversity was growing everywhere in the nation and that white Americans would soon lose their majority status. In that regard, Elmhurst, with its tensions and its breakthroughs, was a laboratory for the "future of us all."[8]

Following the landmarking of the 7 train, the Queens Council on the Arts put out a brochure listing museums, arts centers, and restaurants located at the different stops in Queens. The council's advertising campaign was part of an effort to enhance the image of the borough, which trails behind Manhattan and Brooklyn as a desirable place to visit. The brochure was directed to both cosmopolitan New Yorkers and tourists curious about the cultures (especially the food) of the borough's inhabitants: "The International Express is a trip around the world in one borough. People from approximately one hundred and fifty nations have settled in Queens. Communal memories permeate the streets: stores and restaurant names recall a variety of native lands."

The 7 train was thus used as the link to all the many-flavored places below its tracks, though the train itself seemed to offer no specific interest.[9] In addition to declaring the 7 train a landmark, or celebrating intergroup local leadership, we argue that studying interactions on the 7 train offers a neglected view of daily life in the New York melting pot: the experience of the 7 train reflects a cosmopolitan environment mixing people of many origins and cultures. As opposed to restaurants, where New Yorkers and tourists look for exotic flavors and experience, the subway requires a different skill in order to get along with riders with whom they haven't chosen to spend time. Indeed, the subway environment can be overcrowded, harshly competitive, and enervating. The gritty cosmopolitanism of the 7 train is not for everyone.

The most famous denunciation of the subway was that of Atlanta Braves pitcher John Rocker, talking to a local sports reporter in 1999. The reporter asked Rocker if he would mind being traded to play in Flushing for the Mets:

> I would retire first. It's the most hectic, nerve-racking city. Imagine having to take the [number] 7 train to the ballpark, looking like you're [riding through] Beirut next to some kid with purple hair next to some queer with AIDS right next to some dude who just got out of jail for the fourth time right next to some 20-year-old mom with four kids. It's depressing.

Of course, Rocker never became a regular rider on the 7 train. An even more serious problem for him was the city and the train's cultural heterogeneity:

> The biggest thing I don't like about New York are the foreigners. I'm not a very big fan of foreigners. You can walk an entire block in Times Square and not hear anybody speaking English. Asians and Koreans and Vietnamese and Indians and Russians and Spanish people and everything up there. How the hell did they get in this country?[10]

The 7 line is one of the system's busiest lines, accounting for more than 10 percent of overall traffic. More than 400,000 riders take this train every day, and their number is growing.[11] The ride from Flushing to Times Square draws a range of passengers whose origins are truly global. The densely crowded train treats them daily, for better and sometimes for worse, to an experience peculiar to New York. Since most trips on the subway are from home to work, home to shopping, or home to leisure activities, much of the actual diversity of daily life in New York is on display day and night on the subway and on the streets around the stations.

More than that, as increasing numbers of New Yorkers ride the subway trains, they end up spending a significant amount of time in their life in motion throughout the city. For many of these riders who maintain ties to foreign countries and cultures, their "home" may seem merely a temporary point in a network of links and movements. They are neither totally American nor foreign. Their lives may make them feel what anthropologist James Clifford called "dwelling in travel," an increasing phenomenon on our urbanized planet.[12] Clifford asked: "What skills of survival, communication and tolerance are being improvised in today's cosmopolitan experience? How do people navigate the repressive alternatives of universalism and separatism?"[13] The fleeting interactions on the 7 train are part of an urban middle ground between the parochialisms of family and neighborhoods, and the larger horizon of America. On their way to becoming American, riders of all origins are helped by the subways to first become "New Yorkers."

In their remarkable collective study of second-generation immigrants to the city, Philip Kasinitz, John H. Mollenkopf, Mary C. Waters, and their colleagues described the ways that their young respondents "balance notions of foreign-ness and native-born entitlement, of 'insider' and 'outsider' status"—a tension that, as they often point out, makes them very much "New Yorkers."[14] By looking at the daily subway commute, we aim to show that becoming a New Yorker can also entail a set of values and skills, some of which are more or less universal aspects of life in urban public spaces, and others are peculiar to New York. Indeed, one of the main satisfactions in mastering the subway system is to gain access to the entire city territory, which may in turn help inhabitants identify with New York City. As Kasinitz and his colleagues wrote, "The changes necessary to become a 'New Yorker' are not nearly so large as those required to become an 'American.'"[15]

This assertion rests on the assumption that sharing the experiences of daily life in the city, including daily subway ridership, builds a common stock of competences and attitudes necessary for inhabitants of New York. In fact, our data show that as young people and newcomers to the city gradually gain these "getting-around" skills, they also increasingly identify themselves as savvy New Yorkers. It may take time to cherish the New York City they come to know on the 7, and some never will, but veteran riders often mention the feeling of pride and belonging they experience when standing on one of its elevated platforms toward sunset, they watch a silver ribbon of train cars against the city's gleaming skyline.

While real and significant, such moments remain infrequent. Riders more commonly mention having to endure crowding and uncertainty and that relief comes with having secured a seat and the opportunity to lose themselves in self-involvement such as reading, listening to music, or doing homework. Nor do our conversations with riders indicate that they celebrate ethnic and racial diversity for its own sake, contrary to the hopes of the city's boosters. "People who don't take the 7 train sometimes have a tendency to romanticize that train," said John Liu, a Flushing-area city councilman and later city comptroller and mayoral candidate, in an interview in 2007. "Getting on the train, there is nothing romantic about it; it's just the only way to get to and from work, to and from school."

During his tenure in the City Council and as Flushing's first elected official of Asian origin, Liu established a reputation as a plain-talking and effective urban innovator. He often clashed with Metropolitan Transportation Authority (MTA) officials about the pace and scheduling of repairs along the 7 line. Indeed, it was his ability to put the issues in class terms, avoiding any sentimental references to diversity, that also helped him become the first New York politician of Chinese origin to develop a strong citywide reputation in New York's populist-leaning political culture:

> The rich kids have the express buses. When I was a kid, it was $3 to take the express bus. It was a 20-minute ride from Flushing to Bronx Science. It was a 1-hour-and-45-minute ride taking the subway into Manhattan and then to the Bronx.
>
> People don't get up in the morning thinking, "I got to ride the International Express!" No one thinks of it that way. People wake up and say "Shit, I got to get on that train again!" And as much as they hate the train, when they take it out of service, it's even worse! 'Cause then they cannot get to work. Or they get to work 45 minutes late and they risk losing their job.

It is helpful in this regard to ask who, precisely, are the 7 daily riders to whom Liu is referring? What do we actually mean by diversity as a daily experience on the subway? Do the 7 train riders represent all the groups living along the line? How do physical and social aspects of the subway environment shape riders' experiences of diversity? We structure our inquiry by looking for answers in the scenes that occur every morning during the weekdays. We begin at the Flushing–Main Street terminus of the 7 train and continue to examine the changing ridership as the train proceeds to Manhattan.

Boarding the 7 Train in Flushing: Who Gets On, Who Gets a Seat, Who Cares?

Main Street, Flushing, and the Flushing–Main Street subway station have never offered subway riders a pleasant start to their workday. Even before the 1970s, when it began its transformation into a major urban hub of North Shore Queens as the influx of Chinese and Korean immigrants accelerated, the Main Street station was cramped and antiquated (for more on this subject, see chapter 8). Today the streets around the station are congested and noisy, and the air is laden with the fumes of bus, truck, and car traffic. Although downtown Flushing is often termed "Little Hong Kong," it would not be unfair to say that parts of the Main Street area make Hong Kong seem like a city in Switzerland.

Flushing–Main Street is a major bus-to-subway transfer station serving a large area of northeastern Queens. Commuters from College Point, Murray Hill, Bayside, Whitestone, Beechhurst, Little Neck, and other neighborhoods east of Flushing leave their homes early to catch a bus to the Main Street station, where they have the option of a free transfer to the 7 train (figure 2.1). According to the 2006–2010 American Community Survey (ACS), compiled by the U.S. Census Bureau, the population in the catchment area of the Main Street subway station in Flushing was slightly more than 300,000 inhabitants during this five-year period and growing.[16] More than twenty bus lines bring commuters from the confines of northeastern Queens to Main Street, where they can choose to forgo the transfer and take the more expensive but faster Long Island Rail Road (LIRR). This singular situation in New York City makes Flushing–Main Street the busiest station in Queens and one of the top ten stations (in 2007) in the entire system, despite being served by only one subway line.

In order to compare the 7 train riders with the population of the Queens neighborhoods it serves, we looked at the census data on the ethnicity and

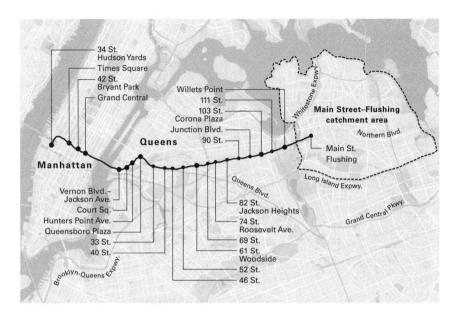

Figure 2.1 Catchment area of the Flushing–Main Street station.

race of the residential neighborhoods around the major stations and the census data on the means of transportation to work. We also conducted our own turnstile counts of riders according to gender and race/ethnicity for 1-hour periods at the Flushing–Main Street and 74th Street/Roosevelt Avenue stations during weekday morning peak times and compared them with the relevant census data.

In Flushing, about 39 percent of the working population relies on public transportation (U.S. Census 2010). Fifty-two percent drive to work in automobiles, a proportion lower than that of the city overall (56%). Table 2.1 shows that the racial and ethnic characteristics of the population living in the area and of those using public transportation to get to work are largely consistent. That is, the riders who begin their mornings on public transportation are largely representative of the residential population in the area.

The segments of the population not well represented in public transportation, based on our counts, are children and people older than sixty, which is hardly surprising given the preponderance of commuters. People of Asian and European (white) origin make up 46 percent and 31 percent,

TABLE 2.1

Population Living in the Flushing Catchment Area Compared with Population Using Public Transportation to Go to Work

	Population of Flushing Area	Percent	Population Using Public Transportation
Total population	302,789	56,460	
Male	146,382	48.34	49.91%
Female	156,407	51.66	50.09%
RACE			
White	132,079	44.43	41.31%
Black or African American	8,067	2.71	3.08%
Asian	137,617	46.30	46.53%
Asian Indian	11,115	3.74	
East Asian	121,417	40.85	
Hispanic or Latino (of any race)	48,379	15.98	18.96%
White non-Hispanic	10,4737	34.59	31.09%

Source: United States Census Bureau, American Community Survey, 2006–2010, https://www.census.gov/programs-surveys/acs/.

respectively, of the population taking public transportation to get to work, proportions very close to their share of the overall population. But since these census numbers combine bus, subway, and LIRR riders, they cannot be used to estimate the composition of riders that enter the Main Street station.

The 7's Adult Game of Unmusical Chairs

The morning rush hour at Flushing–Main Street starts for many riders as a competition for a seat or at least a good standing spot on the train. Of course, competition for seats is ubiquitous in the subway system and accounts for many positive and negative interactions. The stakes are elevated when riders looking for seats face a 35- to 40-minute daily commute—as is the case at Main Street—as opposed to a brief ride of a few stations.

Our own turnstile counts of subway riders at Flushing–Main Street showed that an average of 8,000 people entered the station in the morning rush hour between 8:00 and 9:00 A.M. on a weekday. At this time, local trains were scheduled to run every 4 to 6 minutes and express trains, every 2 to 5 minutes. On average, this is a train departing every 4¼ minutes, amounting to a total of fourteen trains between 8:00 and 9:00 A.M. The 7 train is one of the longest (600 feet) in the New York City system, with eleven cars each seating 42 or 44 passengers. Even if riders were split evenly between express and local trains—and they are not—that would amount to 570 passengers per train, or 52 per car. This is already 10 more than the number of seats. In addition, we know that a preponderance of daily riders who fail to find a seat then seek to stand by the same doors, in the same car, in order to exit at the most convenient location.

These elevated stakes help explain the volume of negative comments about older Chinese women that we've heard and that abound in the social media, which emerge from the specifics of demographic diversity on the platforms and train cars on weekday mornings in Flushing.

Pushy Little Old Chinese Ladies, Debunking a Subway Stereotype

Owen (his English-language name) is a thirty-one-year-old computer technician. He emigrated with his brother and mother from Taiwan thirteen years ago, settling in Flushing in an apartment provided by his uncle, who was already living in the neighborhood. Owen usually takes the Q28 bus to Main Street. Like most commuters, he complains about the station's crowded conditions in the morning:

> **Owen**: It's very crowded in the morning. People are like monsters. They don't yell at each other. They just run to grab a seat like crazy.
> **Stéphane**: They don't say "sorry?"
> **Owen**: No. no. They just grab a seat like little children.

Interview, 2007

This remark echoes many posts that riders leave on websites such as yelp. com, where the 7 train was rated in 167 posts. In these posts, amazement at the diversity of riders vies with their aversion to crowding and the rudeness of riders. "Chinese women" seem to have acquired a reputation of ruthless efficiency in the competition for a seat:

> Hundreds of little old Chinese women with red shopping bags who will push you down, or rudely jump in front of you, to get a seat when the train

doors open. Now, subways are always every person for themselves, but Flushing takes it to a new level of utter rudeness and chaos.

Luca M., Kew Gardens Hills[17]

One thing I always hate is getting off Flushing Ave., the last stop, people there, especially the older Chinese women always try to push me back onto the train as I was stepping out. They are so afraid they are not able to get a good seat! Really people! Let the passengers off first! Thank you =)

Ling Z., Jackson Heights[18]

Are these representations of a stereotype, a reflection of cultural proxemics and gender norms, or are they mainly an effect of overcrowding associated with the nature of the population at Main Street?

East Asian women are a predominant demographic rider group during the later part of the morning rush hour. Our turnstile counts show that more women (55%) than men were taking the 7 train at the morning peak hours, a proportion higher than that in the census data. We also found that the proportion of whites and Hispanics entering the subway was lower than that of the residential neighborhoods. Conversely, the proportion of East and South Asians also was substantially higher than census figures indicate. Only the proportion of African Americans, low in any case, did not vary much. The underrepresentation of white riders is undoubtedly due to the alternative offered by the LIRR, an ethno-racial preference linked to income levels, since whites tend to live in the more suburban and well-off neighborhoods of northeastern Queens, farther from the subway. Indeed, only in the census tracts immediately around the station does the proportion of non-Hispanic whites fall to 10.5 percent, much closer to their representation on the train.

Finally, we also observed that most passengers of East Asian origin board the express train, making it crowded from the first stop, whereas most riders of Hispanic origin board the local train. Only the local train stops in the Corona neighborhood, a stronghold of Hispanic residency. And only the local 7 stops at the key transfer station at 74th Street/Roosevelt Avenue, where many riders switch to the express E and F trains. After the morning rush hour, all the 7 trains run as locals. On those trains, the unintentional racial and ethnic sorting during rush hour is absent, and the competition for seats is not as fierce.

The 7 morning express train is the most crowded train to depart from Flushing–Main Street and likely the most crowded train to depart from its terminal in the entire city. It is populated by a majority of riders of East Asian origin, more than half of whom are women of predominantly East Asian origin. Based on mere probability, therefore, Main Street is the New York subway station where riders are most likely to be in competition with "Chinese women" for a seat. Moreover, since they are the most numerous group, it seems statistically logical that they would win out overall.

Beyond demographics is the implicit or explicit notion in the blogs, in our students' diaries, and in our interviews, that "Chinese women" are particularly aggressive or otherwise adept at winning seats in the competition. Notions of cultural proxemics are no doubt at play here: "they" come from a culture in which densities are greater, so "they" have become used to pushing and darting. But the "Chinese woman" category is not homogeneous. It lumps together women from very different regions and cultures, so that references to, say, the Beijing, Shanghai, Taibei, or even Seoul subway are risky. The density in all these places, however, is extremely high, and jostling is common. Aside from opportunities to create ethnic stereotypes, what Flushing–Main Street may give its riders is a foretaste of how the increased crowding in public transit is challenging subway norms of conduct and heightening levels of commuter stress. Indeed, such crowding as we experience on the subways may also be the "future of us all."

The Main Street station also offers ways to master the system. Some riders, including many "Chinese women" with an intentional strategy, do not have to push to get a seat. Instead, they exploit the peculiar configuration of the station, where every other express train, running on the middle track, opens its doors on both sides; first on the local platform and then on the express platform. This means that the most savvy passengers hoping for a seat on the express will be waiting instead on the local platform in order to increase the likelihood of getting a seat.

Ting, a high school student from China, described the problem:

There are always more people on the express platform. You would think they'd figured this a long time ago. Usually, the express on the middle track opens the doors on the local side first, letting the passengers out. We express passengers stand beside and around the closed doors, watching people exit the other way and, worst of all, watching some enter the other door with ease. At that moment, it seems like we just lost a big battle.

Tuesday, June 6, 2006

Riders of the express train leaving Main Street are thus left with a choice. They can either save a few minutes' travel time by waiting on the express platform but lose out on seating, or wait on the local platform and have a better chance of securing a seat if the express leaves before the local. In the end, who gets a seat has less to do with cultural background or proxemics and much more to do with riders' individual needs and local skills. Riders who have not yet figured this out may see it as a problem with "Chinese women." Those who have figured this out are far more likely to see it as a consequence of "subway smarts" involving specific choices between time and comfort.

Willets Point: The Mets Games, the U.S. Open, Fans, and Commuters

A few minutes after its departure from the Flushing–Main Street station, the 7 train emerges from a dark tunnel under Roosevelt Avenue into the light. It climbs up to a bridge deck, which is itself elevated over the Roosevelt Avenue Bridge; crosses Flushing Creek into the most highly urbanized section of Flushing Meadows; and pulls into the Willets Point station, where passengers have access to Citi Field (home of the Mets baseball team), the United States Tennis Association (USTA)'s Billie Jean King Tennis Center (home of the yearly U.S. Open tennis tournament), the World's Fair marina, and the facilities of Flushing Meadows Park on the site of the city's 1939 and 1964 World's Fairs. All trains stop at Willets Point, where some riders transfer from their cars to the train, but hardly anyone walks here from home. Indeed, in 2007, there was only one official resident in the surrounding census tract, but there were 255 auto-parts and repair businesses.[19] This traffic is likely to increase as a Bloomberg-era condo development replaces this remnant of the area that F. Scott Fitzgerald's *Gatsby* narrator called the Valley of Ashes.

The Willets Point station is elevated above Roosevelt Avenue, and its exits allow fans access to the tennis complex south of the tracks and Citi

Field on the north side, toward Flushing Bay. Often deserted and bleak, on game days or during festivals in Flushing Meadows Park, the station suddenly becomes extremely animated. The MTA adds special trains to bring spectators back to Manhattan, so as not to disrupt the already tight schedule of regular commuter trains.

The MTA recognized the need to accommodate thousands of extra passengers who must move through the station in relatively quick time bursts before and after events. Accordingly, it reconfigured the old station in ways that facilitate fans' access to the venues and to the trains, including the adjacent LIRR. In a 2008 interview, the deputy line general manager for the 7 train explained that during the construction of the new Citi Field, which replaced the older Shea Stadium in 2008, the original station rotunda where passengers went through the subway turnstiles was demolished:

> We had to move the turnstiles into the confines of the station, and what that did is that it allowed Long Island Rail Road riders and people parked on the other side of Flushing Meadows Park to use what had previously been the pay zone in the station as a free passageway across Roosevelt Avenue and onto the passerelle [bridge] that led into the park.
>
> That in itself is not remarkable in any way, but it caused us to have to introduce a new service that we never had before. We had always handled the crowding there with a local service only. We would just increase the pulse. Diminish the headway. That is how we would manage the crowding.
>
> Well, with the turnstiles inside the confines of the station, that created unacceptable levels of crowding within the station. We were pressured to do it by the Mets to provide a more attractive alternative to driving and parking. We did not want to do it as an agency, but we were forced to do it. So we introduced the "Mets Express." It is a limited-stop express: three stops in Queens, transfer points, and three stops in Manhattan.

The Mets Express runs only after games or tennis matches. On their way to the stadium, many baseball fans join the usual rush-hour crowds. These changes in rider demographics on game days, which are even greater during the U.S. Open, reveal much about the class differences characteristic of the 7 train. Subway professionals are practical social empiricists and keen observers of human behavior. They tend to use coded references and intentional ellipses regarding issues of class, race, and national origin. "The Mets game injects a whole other element . . . into the usual mix of age, gender, ethnicity," the deputy line general manager observed:

> And you know, the Mets fans economically are much more homogeneous, and ethnically they are more homogeneous. But Mets fans are also pretty reflective of the line. People are affiliated with that, and those people tend to mix on the line. Like at 6 o'clock, when the trains are coming out here [to Willets Point, Queens], you have people that have met their friends in Manhattan and they have a couple beers in hand, even though that's against the rule, they're in cups or bags and they are surreptitiously having a party on the train. And they can be disruptive. The noise level on the trains, from the conversations, is very loud. There is an incredible amount of socialization going on within the groups, but then you see it among groups that are strangers. A bunch of guys, and a bunch of girls, and it's interesting because they overlay on the daily regular riders.

On regular workdays, when there is no game, the 7 train is filled predominantly with people going to and returning from work, so there are fewer violations of the subway's normative order, although, as the deputy line general manager pointed out, they can happen at any time:

> We have a good deal of what we call unruly customers. Inebriated people. It is around payday, Wednesday, Friday, Saturday. It could be disruptive to the line. It's not just at night. I am always amazed at the time of day. Someone who has worked all night, their night time is morning.

It would be extremely unusual to spot a rider of immigrant background drinking from an open can of beer at any time on the 7 train. In fact, the contrast between the boisterous, well-off white men and women continuing their party on the subway and the 7 train's generally cautious, polite riders of Latino or Asian origin is itself a commentary on the distance between subway citizenship and identification as an American. The more minimal sense of being a New Yorker may start with acquiring skills at effectively getting around the city. This achievement remains in stark contrast to the behavior of bold but boozy young Americans on their way to a night baseball game after work in the office towers of Manhattan.

The Mets Express is an extra service for riders that is implemented by the new line general manager, a position first created in 2007 on the L and 7 lines in an attempt to improve communication among the different departments of the MTA's subway division. The popularity of the Mets Express has been measured yearly through a subway report card filled in by the riders:

> The idea is that the vice presidents are really out of contact with the employees. The idea is to flatten out the organization. As a line general manager, I am only one step away from the frontline people. There are supervision and management there, but all those people, I can interact with them. They know me.

The main challenge for the 7 train's new line general manager was to accommodate a growing ridership while setting up a new real-time signalization system that would allow the MTA to know where all the trains were at any moment and to post waiting times to passengers on the platform:

> This is a train where the scale of operations is deceiving, because we are probably on track to carry 450,000 people a day, which is huge. And it's very short, only a 19-mile route. So it is like a metronome. If you miss a beep, you are in trouble. One of the old timers said to me: "If you spit on the rails, you have delay." To a certain extent, there is some truth to that. So it tends to be very demanding in that regard. But it's quite an opportunity. It's the fourth largest transit system in the United States all by itself.

One of the remarkable achievements of the program was to recruit voluntary bilingual information staff during the many disruptions incurred by breakdowns and upgrade work. This was one of the first attempts to consider the actual diversity of the ridership. In 2009, the line general manager program was judged successful by the subway administration and was extended to all the lines in the system. But in 2010, following the nomination of a new president, the program was cut, and attention to the diversity of the ridership receded.

Corona and Elmhurst: Hispanic New York
Meets Asian New York

The next four stations after Willets Point—111th Street, 103rd Street, Junction Boulevard, and 90th Street—are elevated over Roosevelt Avenue and trace the border between Corona on the north side and Elmhurst on the south side. Here the 7 rumbles over tracks that are above the roofs of three-story row houses where a majority of immigrant families and workers live.[20]

At 111th Street, according to the ACS (2006–2010), the population boarding the local train and a local bus line largely reflects the population of the neighborhood. Here, almost 70 percent of the population relies on public transportation to get to work. It is overwhelmingly male (61%) at peak time and of Hispanic origin (78%), mainly Ecuadorian, Mexican, and Dominican with a minority of Chinese (7.5%). These numbers remain basically the same at the following stop, 103rd Street, except for a small proportion of African American riders (about 10%) mostly living in the Lefrak City area of Elmhurst.

After the morning rush hour, all trains leaving Main Street are local. This is when the mostly Chinese and Korean populations of Flushing meet the Hispanic population of Corona on the train. Another episode on the local off-peak train narrated by Ting illustrates this point. This time a "Chinese woman" offered her seat to a young "Mexican mother":

> A Mexican mother in her mid-thirties, short, dark skin came in with her two daughters. She carried one of them, a two- or three-year-old. The other, five or six years old, following her into the train, crying "Mommy! Mommy!" . . . It is mild but loud enough to catch attention in the train. I looked to my left and see the big sister crying. I just spaced only for a moment. I did not respond immediately by giving them my seat. Then, at the corner of my eye, I saw the Chinese lady expressing to give up her seat. She said, "Excuse me" and made an inviting hand gesture. . . . Something struck me. I woke up. I gestured to the mother, "Do you wanna sit?" "Thank you," she said. The Chinese woman and me got up almost at the same time."
>
> Wednesday, June 14, 2006, 11:30 P.M.

The "Mexican mother" whom Ting observes may just as well be Ecuadoran, the other dominant ethnic group in Corona. Somehow, just as "Chinese" is a proxy for "East Asian," "Mexican" is often a synonym for "Hispanic" or "Latina." What is at play here is at the same time a norm about helping women with young children, a general idea that this norm is widely shared in the city, no matter what the ethnic identity of the other is, even if it is by no means observed consistently.

Another of Ting's example shows the formalization of yet another norm shared by "Asians" and "Hispanics":

> I doze off. Sitting to my right was a Spanish macho-looking mid-aged man. I guess my head fell to the right a few times. He poked me and said, "Excuse me." I don't remember other English words he said. I noticed what happened and tried hard to stay alert. I remember my head fell to the right once. But I am not sure. After all, I was dozing off. I was kind of pissed off because he continued talking about it to some other Spanish men across from us in a loud voice. He talked in Spanish but I understood. He was saying something like: "I'm not his father or mother. Why he fell on my shoulder?" I guess he was very acute to his personal space. The problem is he talked about it the next 5 minutes. I knew it was my fault, so I didn't say anything.

Tuesday, June 13, 2006

Junction Boulevard is the only express stop in Elmhurst and Corona. Apart from a small proportion of people from Colombia (4%), the composition of riders entering the station is basically the same. By now, the local train is entirely filled with riders speaking Spanish, while the express train is a mix of East Asians and Hispanics, plus a small white minority. Again, we see that that the actual experience of "diversity" depends on opportunities structured in part by the unintentional effects of train service.

At 90th Street, in Jackson Heights, the crowd coming in is two-thirds Hispanic and one-third East Asian. Ecuadorans still make up the main group, with Colombians, Mexicans, and Chinese close behind. The stream of riders from India (about 6%), the Philippines, and, to a lesser degree, Pakistan grows as the train moves west. White non-Hispanic riders also gradually become more numerous. This trend is confirmed at 82nd Street with a new addition of white (non-Hispanic) riders, mostly of Italian, Irish, and Jewish ancestry. While the proportion of Hispanics gradually diminishes, the main group is now Colombian, with Ecuadorans a close second.

74th Street/Roosevelt Avenue: Queens Masala

The second busiest station in Queens, after Flushing–Main Street, is 74th Street/Roosevelt Avenue. This station offers passengers the greatest number of possible transfers, since it also serves the F, E, R, and G (in 2007) trains. Six bus lines also converge on the congested streets outside the station. Yet 74th Street is only a local stop on the 7 line, as the express bypasses it, angering many riders. This problem dates back to the separate construction of the Roosevelt Avenue IRT (7 train) and IND (now the F, R, and A trains) stations in 1916 and 1933, and the subsequent municipalization of the IRT in 1940. The 7 train's Roosevelt Avenue stop was not built as a transfer point, and the platforms are located on the outside of the tracks, giving no access to the express tracks.

For riders on the local 7 train, 74th Street/Roosevelt Avenue is a major transfer point to the faster E and F express trains that also serve midtown and downtown Manhattan, whereas the 7 serves only midtown. At rush hour, about half the train empties out here, only to fill up immediately with riders going to Long Island City or to Grand Central or Times Square in Manhattan.

At 74th Street, Latin America meets South Asia. The streets around the station form one of the main commercial centers serving the city's rapidly growing Pakistani and Indian populations. Descending from the elevated 7 to the station's street level, the largely Hispanic flow of people is representative of Corona and Jackson Heights, as well as a significant minority of Asian and Korean riders from Flushing. This human current then meets African Americans and South Asians, especially Indians and Pakistanis. Here the interactions among passengers of different races and ethnicities may invite multiple layers of misunderstanding and ignorance, as we see in the following excerpt from a discussion among three high school students we worked with: Indira and Aisha, two South Asian women, and Tao, a female immigrant from China. Aisha wears a head scarf that completely covers her hair, as well as a traditional Pakistani tunic that comes to her knees, covering only half her blue jeans. She explains to the others that her head scarf always draws stares on the subway, but when she is with her mother, who "covers herself completely," there are often more testy encounters. Recently she had an encounter with a

"Chinese lady" who said something like, "Go back to your own country. . . . You terrorists!"

Indira: For real?

Aisha: She did not even speak English well and she was saying that. I almost said to her, "You go back to your country."

Tao: How do you know that she was Chinese? Sometimes there's Korean.

Aisha: Maybe she's Korean. I don't know. I don't know. The difference between a Filipino and a Chinese is that their skin is darker. Like your skin is of the Chinese. I don't know the difference between Chinese and Korean. Maybe Korean. And I'm like . . . and I said to my mother, "What did she say?" and she's like, "You heard her." [Then] My mother is telling her, "You go back to your country."

The unstated assumption and the very New York aspect of this interaction is that after paying the fare, we all have an equal right to be on the subway, to be in the city dressed however we please, and to be ready to defend ourselves against stereotyping and bigotry. Far from becoming intimidated by the attention she attracts when she is on the subway in her burka, Aisha says that her mother enjoys riding on the subway. The stares they receive sometimes make them feel more foreign and different, but they still are proud to be in public in the city wearing clothing appropriate to their religious beliefs.

The transfer at 74th Street/Roosevelt Avenue often brings Connie, a Colombian high school student who usually gets on at 82nd Street, close to people of color. She comments in her subway diary on the discomfort caused by this proximity:

When I take the E train, there was a black man that was looking at me in the all trip and I was scared because I don't like the way that he look at me. When the train stop at 23 Ely Avenue, I get out from the train and walk faster to the exit.

Subway diary, 2006

Connie's anxieties about navigating her way in the subway are compounded by her fear of people who seem to be looking at her, especially when they are dark-skinned men. She takes the measures that she feels will make her safer, and each time she does so successfully, her confidence and ability at reading subway situations will gradually replace her fearful reliance on racial stereotypes. Or it won't. When young women like Connie experience actual, rather than imagined, negative encounters with men on the subway, they may withdraw and cease to ride underground, a subject to which we return in detail in chapter 6.

Riders remaining on the 7 local are met at 74th Street by a diverse throng of people who have entered the station from the street or who are transferring from the underground lines. According to our turnstile counts, people entering the station between 8:00 and 9:00 A.M. are demographically representative of the surrounding neighborhoods. Hispanics are still the main group, along with a substantial number of East Asians, whites, and South Asians. This population then separates into the many subway lines as it passes the turnstiles. It is then met by a different flow of people walking up from the lower train lines. Accounting for the people walking up the stairs and taking the main escalator to the 7 train, including riders transferring and excluding those taking other trains, we found that ethnic diversity increases at 74th Street. This is especially true because more black riders from southern Queens board the train (Jamaica, at the end of the E and F trains, is a mostly African American neighborhood), creating on that line the same interracial and interethnic groups found on the E and F trains.

Hélène, a young, dark-skinned woman and a studious high school student from Haiti, rides the E train from Jamaica and transfers at 74th Street to the 7 train. In the following diary entry, she is annoyed by what she finds to be the blatant gaze of boys of different races and ethnicities. Even though she roughly identifies the boy's ethnicity ("Hispanic"), she does not claim their behavior to be a consequence of their culture or racial difference. Instead, Hélène insists on her right as a rider to reject unwanted attention and prefers to generalize more abstractly about "people":

> Can you believe I got a seat in the morning? That doesn't happen very often. . . . There was two Hispanic males sitting right across from me, looking at me like they know who in hell I was. I didn't say anything to them and turned my head to my right. Then I heard them giggling. I don't know what it was at all to tell you the truth. They are lucky I was in a good mood that morning because I got a seat. If not, I would have cursed their asses out real

bad. By the time they were looking at me again, I was already at my stop, which is the 33rd St. station. Yo, people can be really stupid at times.

June 6, 2006

After 74th Street, the 7 train stops at all the neighborhoods between Jackson Heights and Long Island City. By then, its ridership has become more representative of the true diversity of Queens and is no longer predominantly the Asian–Hispanic train. In fact, the mix gets increasingly more diverse as the train continues its course toward Manhattan. At 69th Street, a significant Filipino and Korean minority gets onboard. At 61st Street, a stream of white passengers transferring from the Long Island Rail Road joins them. Their proportion increases gradually to about 60 percent of the population boarding the train at Long Island City's Vernon–Jackson station, the last stop before the train enters the tunnel under the East River.

Woodside–61st Street and Queensboro Plaza are the other two main transfer points. At 61st Street, riders on the express train who are not going all the way to Manhattan transfer to the local train, and vice versa. This station thus contributes to mixing the riders who boarded in Flushing (mostly Asian) with those from the rest of the borough. This continues at Queensboro Plaza, where riders, much as they did at 74th Street/Roosevelt Avenue, get another chance to transfer according to their final destination in Manhattan. A small minority of inhabitants originally from the Dominican Republic also lives near the station, resulting in additional black and Hispanic riders on the train.

The Queens Mix: Immigrants Meet Immigrants

The mix of riders on the 7 train reflects their different socioeconomic backgrounds as much as their ethnicity and race. This is changing quickly, though, as Long Island City rapidly converts from an industrial area to a neighborhood of expensive residential towers.[21] Nevertheless, the train's ridership right now is disproportionately composed of less affluent riders, reflecting the temporal organization of work in the city. Census figures consistently show that workers in the service and construction sectors leave their homes earlier than do office workers. Although they may not be in the same train cars, they all use the 7 train. The average income of people who live in the Queens neighborhoods served by the 7 train (as well as the E and F trains) is much lower than the income of people who live in the wealthier neighborhoods of Manhattan and farther out in the suburbs. The competition for room on the subway is therefore reminiscent—at a more microlevel of interaction—of the interethnic competition among immigrant groups with a similar socioeconomic status for the same jobs and apartments. On the subway, however, expressions of tensions or overt prejudice are relatively infrequent as a proportion of the total number of interactions during a given time period. Only certain groups, such as young people or inebriated sports fans, seem to act routinely in ways revealing intolerance and prejudice. When overt conflicts or incidents of bigotry do occur, they tend to reflect ways in which the subway community in transit resists the imports of parochial rivalry.

When riding in groups, some high school students may have fun by acting out the racial prejudice that they most often suppress. Here again is Connie, the recent Columbian immigrant:

> I enter the 7 train at 1:40 P.M. [coming back from school] with 7 friends. A man was standing, looking to the map of the train, and one of my friends was sitting. And he raises his hand and he starts to smell very bad and my friend stand up and said "Ese man huele a cebolla" [That man smells like onions], and all my friends start to look at him. I think the man was Hindu. He was old. He had a blue shirt and blue jeans. His skin was like brown and he smelled like onion.

Journal, June 9, 2006

As time passed, however, we began to see Connie's increasing tendency—especially when alone on the train—to observe subway encounters that lead her to revise some of her stereotypes:

> In the train that I take today was many black, Chinese, white people, and I was the only Spanish in that train. These people were reading newspapers in English and listen[ing] to music. I was standing in the door and I saw that a man give his seat to a woman that she was with a kid and I saw that he was the only person that stand and give the seat. This man was skinny, short, black and the clothing look dirty. He had a gray shirt and blue jeans. This man start to look at me strange, and I was scared because he walk and

stand next to me. But finally he get out in Queensboro station and I calm down.

June 10, 2006

When high school students are not in groups, they may even extend a helping hand and look for ways to revise their prejudice:

> Today, on my way to work, one of my friends was waiting for me at 46th St. Once I entered the station, he was there. The train came but at the same time I observed that he ask a girl around 17 to 20 years old if she was OK. So, I thought he was flirting with the girl. Then he told me that the girl had had an accident on the R train. He said, "The train was too fast and when the train stopped the girl was moving and she got hit hard on her nail on the foot. The accident was that her nail come off." He said, "No one pay any attention to her. So I helped her. I put a bandage on her toe."
>
> Then after a while, he was joking about it. He said, when she gets home, she is going to tell her parents and friends what has happened to her. And she is going to say: "You know how much I hate Mexicans, and one of them helped me today." He also said she might say, "An immigrant helped me." He didn't know how to speak English.

Vasco, journal, June 24, 2006

Manhattan: Queens Meets the Other Boroughs

By the time it enters the tunnel under the East River, the 7 train has collected an impressive medley of Queens inhabitants, most bound for the offices, restaurants, and stores of Manhattan. Finally after about a 30-minute ride (the express and the local take almost the same amount of time), the 7 train lets its riders off first at Grand Central–42nd Street, where they can transfer to the uptown and downtown 4, 5, and 6 trains. At the Fifth Avenue–Bryant Park stop, they can transfer to the lettered trains F, B, D, Q, and M. At Times Square–42nd Street, passengers may transfer to the West Side 1, 2, 3, E, and A trains. Times Square and Grand Central are the busiest stations in the entire system. Both stations are a world of passenger flows, each worth a separate study.[22] At these stations, the immigrant riders brought by the 7 train now mix with riders from the other boroughs and the suburbs, including more affluent regional rail commuters from Westchester County and Long Island. There are no more neighborhood demographic groups entering the trains. Riders are now strangers in travel, immigrant or not. In September 2015, the line was finally extended by one additional stop into Manhattan's Far West Side, where it serves the offices and luxury condominiums going up in the Hudson Yards district at the northern end of the celebrated High Line.

From Flushing–Main Street to 34th Street–Hudson Yards, the 7 train journey is an experience in blending human diversity of all kinds. It starts off with adjacent neighborhoods meeting on the train and gradually morphs into an experience of the entire borough of Queens before finally blending into the full New York City mix. Depending on the time of the day, it is also an experience in crowding, forcing all these different bodies, cultures, and personalities together in a small space for an involuntary daily get-together. The tensions and cooperation between all these riders of different origins revolve around practical issues of bodily copresence, comfort, and the efficiency of the trip. The daily miracle is in how riders find ways to tolerate and manage their way in the crowd, whether they like it or not. The tricks and implicit social agreements that allow them to get to their destination day in and day out are not very difficult to acquire, but they do demand some adaptation, and for many newcomers to the city, they require the acquisition of some new values and orientations.

Contrasting Differences and Highlighting Similarity: The Riders' Competences

The 7 train riders experience a succession of contexts of copresence representative of distinct neighborhoods coming together from the borough of Queens and the entire city. Accordingly, riders have to adapt to different situations requiring the enactment of actions specific to the subway. First they must master the subway's technical hardware, including buying and swiping a MetroCard (more about this in chapter 4) and finding their way. In addition, the main competence required, regardless of each rider's origin, is the ability to read the many different social cues and situations that subway life presents. Such a challenge is characteristic of large cities, where immigrant populations are numerous, and flows crisscross territories. Isaac Joseph, who pioneered the study of urban sociability in the United States and France, with a special focus on the spaces of transportation, including the Paris metro, referred to the competence shared by all urbanites as requiring "contextualization skills."[23] In this chapter, we have seen how young immigrant riders develop some of these competences, especially in their growing ability to read subway situations, thereby transcending their initial stereotypes and gaining a deeper understanding of what they see and encounter. Their diaries show how they learn a technique used by veteran riders as they search for empirical confirmation of their initial impressions. For example, they often begin to discern the language of the papers and books that people are reading. But rather than data reflecting the differences among riders, such perceptual details confirm the reassuring fact that despite their differences, riders have similar expectations regarding the trip and generally accepted subway rules.

Mike, an Indian American around fifty years old, has been living in Queens for twenty-five years and in Jackson Heights, near the 74th Street/ Roosevelt Avenue station, for eight years. He describes this technique with great enthusiasm:

> **Mike:** This is a world community as you can see. Ha? (*door beep*). You can see all kinds of populations here. The Orientals, the Chinese, the Koreans, Indians, Hispanics, everybody.
>
> **Stéphane:** You can see that?
>
> **Mike:** Yeah! Right now! How do you identify which community they belong to? From the newspaper they read, you know. It is a lot of Chinese and Koreans . . . carry their own language papers. Ha?
>
> **Stéphane:** Do you sometimes meet people on the train?
>
> **Mike:** Hmm . . . Sometimes. But most of the times when I get inside the train, to be honest, I am buried in my newspapers. Except when I see somebody familiar, I am buried in my newspapers. And except when I am traveling with somebody.
>
> **Stéphane:** Do you feel comfortable in this train?

Mike: Not just comfortable, very comfortable. Because I like this train ride (*station-stop noises*). Like I said, I see so many different people and I continue to marvel.

Ethno-racial categories do not need to be precise. It does not matter whether the person standing by the door is really "Chinese," "Mexican," "black," or "white." She may, in fact, disagree with that label in the first place. What matters is that the observable difference contrasts with the more subtle behavioral similarity that riders gradually expect. This big difference/small similarity is an effect often noted in literature on the subway to illustrate the elusive togetherness of its population:

> They rock in unison, at least they agree on that one small thing. Check their wallets—the denominations won't jibe. Review their prayers—the names of their gods won't match. What they cherish and hold dear, their ideas and shopping lists, are as different and numerous as their destinations. But all is not lost. Look around, they're doing a little dance now in the subway car and without rehearsal they all rock together. Shudder and lurch together to the car's orchestrations. Some of them even humming. Everybody's in this together until the next stop, when some will get off and some others get on.[24]

Riders are fascinated by the diversity they experience and take pride in learning to read cues regarding the identities of strangers on the trains. A most remarkable characteristic of the process whereby one becomes an urbanite on mass transit is that the ethnic and racial categories that might seem to distance one from fellow passengers are usually and quickly dismissed as secondary. As Roger Sanjek observed, people need to be "color-full" before they can be "color-blind."[25] This process of knowing-yet-ignoring whereby riders become "blasé" New Yorkers on the subways is essential to the establishment of a community in transit. In such a process, the heterogeneous crowd of subway riders is united in its desire to keep moving forward with skillful deliberation. In the next chapter, we will discuss this community in transit through riders' accounts of their walk from home to station and onto the trains. In these accounts, we will again see evidence of subway skills and competences in action.

3 Walking to the Stations, Code Switching, and the I-We-You Shift

Nothing is more characteristic of urban life than the fact that we often gain extreme familiarity with the faces of a number of persons, yet never interact with them. At my railroad station, for example, I have stood at a commuter station for several years, often in the company of people whom I have never gotten to know. The faces and the people are treated as part of the environment, equivalent to the scenery, rather than persons with whom one talks, exchanges greetings.

Stanley Milgram, "The Familiar Stranger"

In this chapter, we explore the shifts in perceptions, feelings, and behaviors typical of New Yorkers who travel regularly from the private spaces of their homes, through their familiar neighborhood streets, and then into the quintessentially urban world of the New York subway system. For most of us, the walk to the subway station becomes a humdrum trajectory in which we normally lose ourselves in personal thought. In this chapter, we report on interviews in and around the 74th Street/Roosevelt Avenue station, in which we asked our respondents to relate what they were seeing and thinking as they left their homes and took their usual path to the station, and then as they waited on the station platform and ultimately boarded the subway. In doing so, we gained insights into the mental life of urbanites in a subway city, using a social scientific interview technique known as the "go-along"[1] or the *parcours commenté* (walking interview).[2] To introduce the method and the quality of responses that our interviews elicited, we begin with this one with Jack, a single, thirty-eight-year-old New Yorker, born in Brooklyn.

Jack's parents immigrated to the city from Peru. When asked about his educational background, Jack explained:

I didn't finish college. I went to B.M.C.C. [Borough of Manhattan Community College (CUNY)] and I went to the City College [CUNY] in upper Manhattan. I had a year or two left and I ran out of money.

He now works for the city as a clerical administrator and commutes from the station at 74th Street and Roosevelt Avenue in Jackson Heights to nearby Kew Gardens. After work, he often rides the 7 train to Flushing to visit the public library there. The following excerpts from his go-along interview highlight his perceptions of both his local neighborhood and the subway. As in all our interviews, however, Jack offers vignettes that also reveal his own way of acting and expressing himself.

The interviewers, Richard Ocejo and Amalia Leguizamon, conducted this interview while they were graduate student assistants on this project. They are now university professors themselves. They began the go-along at the doorway to Jack's apartment building in Jackson Heights, Queens. As they began walking, Richard first asked Jack to describe the area. Amalia then took over, asking most of the questions while Richard recorded their conversation and gestures with a video camera:

> **Jack**: This is multicultural, multiethnic, should I say, neighborhood. You have a lot of Spanish, Asian, Indian. . . . That's one of the reasons why I chose this neighborhood. Well, why I decided to stay because I grew up in Bushwick and Bushwick is predominantly . . . [black, although he does not want to voice this thought]
>
> . . . well, the main reason I moved from there is because it is a much more hostile environment, hostile meaning that it is a lot of drug activity going on around there, lots of violence. Meanwhile, this area is more family oriented, it's quiet. So you don't have any . . . it's away from here . . . so, that's why I've decided to stay. [There are birds chirping in the background as Jack hesitates to voice his full feelings about street drug traffic.]
>
> **Amalia**: Do you live with your family, or do you live alone? Because you said it [the neighborhood] is family oriented and thus it's safe . . .
>
> **Jack**: No, I feel safe because of me [he does live alone] (*laughs*), because no one here bothers me. Everyone, when you are here, basically, you know, it's more of the family neighborhood . . . there is a lot more . . . I don't know what the word is . . .
>
> **Richard**: What do you think of the people here? [There is a group of people sitting in the front yard of a nearby building as we pass.]
>
> **Jack**: These are people who live there. I don't know them personally; I say "hello" to them when I pass by. . . . I see the wife; every morning we cross paths.

Amalia: So you know them . . .

Jack: I don't know them personally, I just say "hello" . . .

Amalia: I mean, you're used to seeing them every day . . .

Jack: Yeah . . . the husband I see, like when I get home, I see the husband, we talk a little bit, you know, he tells me about stuff, what's going on with his family . . . well I don't know his name, or anything about his family . . .

Amalia: Are they Spanish?

Jack: They are Spanish.

Amalia: Do you talk to them in Spanish or English?

Jack: Depends, depends on the person . . . if it's Asian, it has to be English (*laughs*).

Amalia: [How can you tell?]

Jack: Guess. . . . when you look at a person you can tell; you can guess whether they are going to be a Spanish or not . . . like you . . . like him [pointing to Richard, who is from Staten Island and not Latino], not Spanish, no offense (*laughs*). You can tell based on . . . I don't know . . . but some people you can't tell whether they are Spanish or not, something about the features, like being around, I don't want to pinpoint, but being around certain people you can, I can say "OK, this person may be Ecuadorian" because I know a person that is Ecuadorian and that looks just like the person or this person is probably Colombian because I know someone Colombian looks like the person. OK. Or if I don't, if I can't guess correctly, maybe the accent . . . living here I learned to distinguish say like Spanish accents: Mexican, Ecuadorian Colombian, Argentinian . . .

When he steps out of his building, Jack notices people whom he considers part of his neighborhood. He may not socialize with them around a lunch or dinner table, but over years of sidewalk chats he knows who their children are and how they are doing. Even if they have never exchanged names, they are among his familiars. They populate his notion of "who we are in the neighborhood." But as he gains distance from his own building and corner, Jack sees strangers of different races and ethnicities. He is especially fascinated by the many different Spanish accents he hears and tries to identify. We understand from his observations that in its density and cultural diversity, no single ethnic or racial group gives the area an overall identity. In this regard, Jackson Heights is a hyperdiverse community even if the dominant language spoken in Jack's immediate neighborhood is Spanish. This became apparent to Jack as he and his interviewers approached the elevated tracks of the 7 at 74th Street and Roosevelt Avenue:

Jack: This area, I think it's a mixture, this area of Roosevelt, it's a mixture of Filipino and Indonesia, I think Indonesia. Restaurants. Never been into them, never tried them. I think over there . . . this place right here, "Su Realty" [?], OK, got close, I don't know if it got closed down, but there was the word spreading that it was prostitution going on there.

Amalia: When?

Jack: Couple of years ago. Because guys would walk back and forth and there'll be some Spanish guy sitting on top of the bar, like saying "girls, girls, girls," and you would see people going in and out of that building. That was about a couple of years ago.

Amalia: And what happened?

Jack: I don't know.

Amalia: Because they didn't close it up . . .

Jack: No, they didn't, because it's still there.

Amalia: . . . [D]o you notice that this place is different from what it was [in the past]?

Jack: It's all the same people. Again, it's a mixture of Asian, Indian, Spanish; that's what you see here. Now, this area right here, I wait till the train passes by (*train noise*). All right, this little area right here, in any given morning, you'll find guys hanging out here, OK, all looking for manual labor. So if you ever need like help with gardening or construction and you don't know where to hire someone to work, and you need someone to work for you, all you have to do is come here. And do you see them like sitting down, and as soon as you announce that you're looking for work, they come out of the woodwork. It's almost like if they are hiding, as soon as they know that you are hiring, they come out and they say, "Pick me, no, pick me! I do the job for you."

Jack is animated as he speaks about the casual labor market he has pointed out. His satisfaction in voicing his local knowledge vanishes, however, when Amalia shouts in surprise at something falling from above their heads:

Amalia: WHAT'S THAT?

Jack: Pigeon poop!

Amalia: Does it bother you?

Jack: I've been hit a couple of times (*laughs*). That's how you know to walk around . . . say, if you look at this, and there's nothing here [no pigeon poop in the floor] but there's a lot here, because they all [the pigeons] sit here [under the rails].

This is 73rd, 74th. In this area right here is where the heaviest concentration of Indian people is, in relation to the rest of the neighborhood. You've got 74th Street, what we are going to hit up, is full of nothing but Indian stores. Thirty-seventh Road, right there, is also Indian stores, predominantly Indian, practically all of it, maybe like, I don't think there's anything else there. But on that little strip over there on 37th Road, you can get phone cards at a discount. Maybe four cards, get four cards buying, get one free, or three cards . . . depending on the card. But you can get, usually you get, a good deal there.

Amalia: To make international calls?

Jack: Yeah, to make international calls. Because right there, that's all they sell, long-distance phone cards.

Amalia: And do you buy them?

Jack: I buy, ahmm, well, I don't buy them for myself. I buy for my parents because they call to Peru quite a lot, so when I'm about to go to the house, they call me and they say, "Listen, since you're coming, pick us up like $20 worth in cards."

As they approach the entrance to the newly built subway station at 74th Street and Roosevelt Avenue, Amalia asks, "Would you mind describing the area here?" Note in his response that Jack has switched his commentary to the more impersonal and generalized "you" form. Clearly, his thoughts have shifted from a ruminative perspective on the neighborhood, residential and commercial, and its inhabitants, to the ways in which an experienced subway rider enters the station. Through these packed passages, the rider merges into the even more crowded and impersonal environment of buses, elevators, escalators, station platforms, subway trains, commuter trains, and airports:

Jack: Well, this is where you are going to see a lot of people going back and forth because you have the train station right there, the main entrance . . . the train is coming (*train noise*). So you are going to have . . . another train . . . (*train noise*) a lot of people going in and out in this station . . . (*train noise*) they either go into the main entrance or into one of the other entrances because this station has three, three other alternate routes of getting out or getting in. You can go in through this stairway to get the 7 train or you can go, there's another entrance over there, you got one over there and then the one that we went in. So you can get into this station through various ways. And since you got the five trains, a lot of people look for this area to live just because of that one fact, because you can get any train, you can even get to the airport from here, 'cause that's with a Q33 bus it's only a minute, no, 30-minute ride to get to the airport.

As social scientists, we seek in the interviews the general, or even universal, aspects of the respondents' perceptions and their ways of expressing them. Much of the richness of what they yield, however, is found in the particular ways that each person experiences the environments of neighborhood, community, and subway. The transcripts of these "go-alongs" include many deeply personal experiences, often demonstrating urbanites' strong attachments to and associations with the mass transit system. Jack's interview offers one of these:

The interviewers stand with Jack on the elevated westbound platform of the 7 train. An incoming train causes them to suspend their talk momentarily.

Amalia: Does it bother you that the train is noisy?

Jack: I'm used to it. Once I had this, I had a friend one time who was, without going much into it, she was going through a major depression because things were going too wrecked in her life, and we were talking, and I sensed that what she needed was to vent, but vent hard . . . vent, like release, 'cause she was like, she was going through these problems, she wasn't, she was holding it in and she had no way of releasing. 'Cause you know, people deal with stress with exercise or other ways . . . so here she was, she was going through problems, but she never had an opportunity to release all that, all that, her problems. So I had an idea, I took her to 74th Street, right, we got on the tail end of the platform, waited till the train pulled up, right, like this . . . waited till the train pulled up, and as soon as the train was going in, as it was pulling in, before it even got to the station, I just told her, "All right, imagine you are the only person, you got all these problems, you have no way of solving them," right, so she was going like this, right, and I said, "OK, as soon as the train pulls up, yell like crazy!" And she did. As soon as the train pulled up, she let out this tremendous scream and she started crying because it was the first time; she felt free after that and she never had felt like that before. So in that way, the train helps. Because we couldn't have done that underground.

Amalia: How did the other people react?

Jack: No one knew. Because the train was louder than her.

Amalia: So no one looked?

Jack: No, no one looked, at least that I know, no. I mean, no cops came, so . . .

Amalia: Well, not the cops, but . . . ?

Jack: I know, but we weren't concerned about that . . . she cried and we stayed there for a little while and I took her home.

The Go-Along Interviews, Sampling, and Coding

Jack's interview offers a good introduction to the "go-along" interviews we conducted in the 74th Street/Roosevelt Avenue and Flushing–Main Street stations (for more about this method, see "Walking Interviews" in the appendix). While Margarethe Kusenbach, a pioneer of the method, was conducting interviews in two different neighborhoods of Los Angeles, she uncovered five themes that go-alongs are particularly suited to explore: "environmental perception, spatial practices, biographies, social architecture, and social realms."[3] The way that commuters perceive the social realms they traverse on their routine trips from home to the subway is precisely what we set out to explore. The other themes that Kusenbach identified also are relevant. In Jack's transcript, the architecture of the subway, his own biography and history in the neighborhood, his spatial practices (such as where to walk to avoid pigeons overhead), and his observations about the urban environments he encounters all help shape his perceptions and feelings. For Kusenbach, the "go-along" method permits ethnographers to examine "naturally occurring patterns and variations in social encounters which they could not fully access as outside observers, nor as practitioners."[4] For example, while walking along, one can observe instances of "friendly recognition," indicating that the informant considers the environment as familiar, or "parochial."[5] In contrast, demonstrations of "civil inattention" indicate a public social realm. Thus the go-along can help identify the significant changes in perception and behavior that occur as people make the transition from their private spaces, through their immediate neighborhoods, to their larger community areas, and then into the mass transit environment.

We conducted twenty-one walking interviews following a standard procedure. One of us filmed the walk and its surroundings while the other asked questions. We met in front of the interviewee's home and inquired first about his or her residential career, including immigration, and then about that person's occupation and how often he or she took the subway. We also asked for a description of the neighborhood, at which point the resident generally explained his or her idea of diversity, which we then compared with how that person acted when we started walking. The interviewee then took us to the train station, and we boarded the 7 train to Manhattan for one stop, got off, and walked back under the elevated track to the departure station. During the walk, we asked the informant to describe the immediate environment and to explain his or her orientation choices.

We coded the interviews from each respondent's transcripts and videotapes, paying special attention to verbal clues and observations that indicate a respondent's perceptions of two social realms: the public and the parochial. We watched especially for identifying comments that appeared to mark observable shifts in the respondents' perceptions of others and in the feelings and thoughts they expressed as they moved toward the subway. How did our informants define and recognize their own group in the environment? Did we find switches in language and observations about other people and groups as the respondents moved from their familiar neighborhood to the more anonymous environment of the subway?

Findings: Diversity of Perception and Concerns

Each go-along taken separately reads like a singular narrative organized around a particular concern. Jack's interview, for example, revolved around a series of personal anecdotes that anchored him in the neighborhood in a very familiar way. Other interviewees had other concerns, each one personal and distinct. Safety, knowledge of the neighborhood and its changes, the quality of the physical and social environments, and aspects of mass transit service were a few of the frequently stressed themes. All the respondents made a common and significant linguistic shift, from the " I and we" to the more impersonal and abstract "you" mode.

George, another respondent from Jackson Heights, is a white middle-aged professional living in a co-op building two blocks from the station. He identified himself as part of the white homeowner population of Jackson Heights. On the "go-along," his description of the environment was largely based on his concern for the control of diverse territories, ranging from the whole neighborhood to an eventual seat on the subway. Throughout the walk, George defined his peers as fellow Jackson Heights residents who shared a vision of the "community" based on similar architectural and aesthetic values. George felt that such values should be preserved because they represent an ideal quality of life. A member of the local community board, he often used the pronoun "we" or "us" in an ambiguous fashion, meaning at once "we" as in my family of residents, "we" as in the concerned people of the neighborhood, and "we" as in the community board:

> Well, coming up here is this parking lot that was one of my pet peeves . . . one of the issues that was before our community board recently just this past week. They need a variance to have this place here because it's in a residential zone, so they had to come before us and they have these lights that are in there and they shine into my apartment. So I was trying to make the point that they shouldn't have these lights. They should have some type of shade on them or something so they don't shine into the neighborhood, which is the rule. We have a big problem with that, and we were trying to get them to plant a little ivy here so that it would grow on the fence and it's not the nicest fence in the world.

As a homeowner advocating for certain aesthetic standards for the neighborhood, George seemed to view local social relations as mediated by a particular set of antagonisms pitting resident property owners against some of the businesses. For George, others (or "they") thus appeared in the walking interview more as representative of business owners and their patrons rather than as ethnic groups. This view, however, does not suppress ethnicity but translates it through items defining the quality of life such as street lighting (as seen earlier), parking, and sidewalk congestion.[6] For example, George justified the route to the station that he chose by invoking the norm of speed and efficiency, as opposed to the elbow rubbing of 74th Street ("Indian Street"), a more crowded option in his opinion:

> This is the fastest way. It's the same distance as if I'd gone up 74th Street, but it's less crowded. Seventy-fourth Street's just a bit too many twists and turns to get through there.

In the subway, George mentioned the recent renovation of the station as a much welcome improvement, not so much as a practical means of transportation, but more as the symbolic gate to his community:

> And they're just finishing the station here. They haven't quite finished it. It was a mess. I remember about five years ago or so I went to an event up in Connecticut and on the way back some woman gave me a ride back who was at the conference and there was this little hole in the wall that you used to have to walk through to get in the subway and I was so embarrassed by it because, you know, I'm telling her what a nice neighborhood it is ... but then we got here and it was a total disaster where you had to walk through this little doorway. I don't know if you ever saw what it was like. But they've totally redone everything in here and it's just really turning out to be a very nice station in term of—there's space, you even have artwork, the glass is a certain tinted glass, and such, so it's a pleasure compared to the way it used to be.

In George's description, the pronoun "they" doesn't mean the anonymous other but the institutional forces represented by the Metropolitan Transportation Authority (MTA) and, beyond it, the city and the state. Here the station has come to symbolize the recognition given to the neighborhood by the administration and its leaders.

Finally, when asked in the train to describe the ride, George continued to display concern for his territory, this time not for his peer group of homeowners or neighbors but for his own body:

> Well, no one's bumping into me, so to me it's adequate. This is good. I could read my newspaper if I was so inclined. See this is all right. I've got a pole; this is spacious.

George proudly considers the new station to be an amenity of his local neighborhood, in contrast to the old station, which was a blemish on its status. On the train itself, his concerns for the neighborhood quickly dissolved into a concern for his own body, yet a larger theme, the control of personal territory, remained active in mediating his comments to the interviewers.

Pete, another white middle-aged man, has also been living in the neighborhood for almost twenty years. He is a tenant and does not identify with the co-op owners of the neighborhood. Instead of territory, he is concerned with his part of a vulnerable working class threatened by gentrification. While he readily defined himself as white, he did not describe any signs or features in the environment that denoted his sense of belonging to a specific ethnic group. Instead, he considers himself for the most part a minority in a place newly invaded by the middle class. Throughout the walk, Pete kept pointing at other ethnic groups and emphasizing their jobs. Such a view fit his unwillingness to identify with what he called an "American culture," which he associated with the type of intellectual work that he has decided to leave for a more manual vocation. As we were leaving his building, Pete stopped to say "Hi" to the super of the adjacent building, whom he described as Russian. In addition to indicating that we were in a "parochial realm" and not yet in the public domain, this instance and other encounters along the way, such as the one described next, show that Pete identifies with a multicultural working class rather than with an ethnic group, even though ethnicity remained a salient descriptor of cultural differences:

> **Pete**: I got to know one of the Chinese women that sells things on a table over here, she lived downstairs. They had like a downstairs area here where they had rooms all sharing the same kitchen. They had like six rooms around a

central kitchen and a bathroom. And she had, because one time I was helping her load her stuff down there, carrying it down the stairs. There's a lady
who came here and set up a booth over, not a booth, but a table.

Stéphane: What did she sell?

Pete: Trinkets. You know, just stuff. . . . [S]he goes and buys the things down
in wholesale places and comes back here and sells them.

When we reached a portion of the street occupied by more recent co-ops,
Pete started talking about residents as if they didn't belong to the neighborhood, using an economic rather than an ethnic factor:

Pete: These two are hot properties because they're right around the corner
from the subway, these two co-ops. It looks like usually when you . . . I
met one girl that lives here, Chinese. People I think like it because they
come out of the subway and they walk right around the corner and
they're in their apartment.

Stéphane: You mean they don't like to walk very much?

Pete: I think, to tell you the truth, I think, generally speaking, from just
their appearance, they seem to be more wealthy. And they're not that interested in the neighborhood. They're working in Manhattan, you know.
I shouldn't say the neighborhood, but they're, they just seem to, well, it's
probably, I think most of the time places that are close to the subway cost
more anyway because people will pay more to have the convenience of it.

Finally, on the subway, when asked what he thought about the 7 train, Pete
looked around and declared:

It seems like more of the poor people take the 7. You know what I'm saying?
The immigrants, especially up that way around Jackson Heights, they're
probably, the apartments are a lot more expensive than along the line coming in here. And so I like it because you see more of the immigrants that
are . . . you know like around Jackson Heights you'll see more doctors and
stuff like that, here you'll see more of a menial group. . . . I like to see the
working class.

Throughout the walk, Pete's definition of himself and the social data he
mobilized to describe urban space were based on a differentiation between

tenants and owners tied to a notion of working class versus upper-middle class. The last sentence is the climax of his reflection during the walk. It is almost as if the context had no influence on his earlier comments. There were no more instances of "friendly recognition" once we went inside the station, but we were hard-pressed to find a boundary between the subway and the neighborhood. Indeed, after having said that co-op owners don't belong to the neighborhood but instead buy their apartments because of their proximity to the subway, he pointed us to a Pakistani store right at the foot of the subway steps whose vendor Pete knew. Again, in the subway car, Pete seemed to identify more with the generalized "poor people" around him than with his Jackson Heights neighbors.

All the individuals we encountered described their environment according to a dominant concern defined by one or several of the four themes uncovered by Kusenbach (their biography, their perception or practical knowledge and values, their spatial practice, and their social network). For example, Amala, a middle-aged immigrant from India who lives two blocks south of Roosevelt Avenue, arranged all her descriptions around the possibility that she and her family might successfully integrate as hyphenated Americans in a multicultural society. Jack, as we have seen, is a native-born New Yorker with immigrant parents who live in the city. Living in an immigrant milieu yet moving into the American lower-middle class, he displayed a practical knowledge of the community with his ability to identify accents, ethnicities, and situations. Irina, a middle-aged woman and a recent immigrant from Russia, kept unfavorably comparing the neighborhood (stores, people) and then the subway with their equivalents in Moscow. Paola—a Colombian immigrant, a middle-aged mother, and a restaurant employee—was concerned about security for her teenage daughter, whereas Guillermo, a young man of Cuban descent, reflected on his role as the father of a toddler. This is not to say that they all were obsessed with a single concern. Indeed, in the last example, Guillermo might have offered different perceptions of the trajectory between home and subway had he not been pushing his son's stroller during the go-along.

These are some of the underlying themes that emerged in our review and analysis of the interviews and videos. Despite their diversity, they can help us understand the shared world of the interviewees. Most notably, the linguistic shifts in their replies reveal views that are more communal and personal than the anonymous, coldly urban aspects of the mass transit system.

The "We-You" Shift in the Situational Community in Transit

As we noted earlier, when the respondents walked to the subway station and entered the train, there was a marked linguistic shift in how they expressed their concerns and perceptions. In fact, in many cases, the interviewees were able to express their concerns most clearly when we reached the train. Recall Pete's final declaration that he liked to "see the working class." In the same way, Amala declared in the train car:

A lot of different people. A lot of different nationalities. It is really fascinating. People come to New York City, and they are living in the same neighborhood and traveling together. It's very fascinating. You don't see that often in many cities, I think.

Nearer their homes, their concerns come out as concrete and peculiar to the interviewee's individual situation. Once in the public realm of the subway, these concerns and abstract sensations are expressed in more general terms (for example, "fascinating," "strange," "annoying"). This can sound somewhat distant and make these observations sound like "folk ethnography"—that is, a preoccupation for reading the cues that situations involving individuals and groups seem to offer. What, then, are the markers of the passage from the familiar realm of the neighborhood to the public realm of the subway?

George, for example, told us that he does not often walk along Roosevelt Avenue, preferring the quieter 37th Avenue. It was only when we reached the foot of the staircase to the 7 train on 74th Street ("Indian Street") that he mentioned the actual ethnic mix, as if we had changed neighborhoods and had correspondingly needed to adjust our behavior:

And obviously the stores are all servicing people who are from South Asia, and we're here. And obviously everybody is from someplace else. It's quite apparent if I open my eyes to it. You know, you get used to it after a while.

More common to all the interviews, and evident in this observation, is the switch to the impersonal pronoun "you," as opposed to the "we" that George used nearer his home territory. It is as if, after a personally defined limit, the interviewees began to make observations in a language that more abstractly denoted a common experience. In the station, while George was still describing the place as a part of his neighborhood, his repeated use of the pronoun "you" reflected the publicness of a very familiar location where the paths of innumerable strangers intersect. George thus perceived, in an ambiguous way, the station as a meeting ground between the neighborhood and the city:

> You get run down when too many people are coming, during rush hour and such. But it's a good opportunity to see who's in the neighborhood. And actually it's mostly people passing through. If you go there, then you know that it's mostly people passing through because anyone coming off the 7 will go right out here, they won't go down that . . . well, yeah, they will, depending upon where you're going, you could go down those steps too if you're going that way. So it varies; everyone's got their own reason to go out a certain way.

Here George seems ambivalent about the setting, sometimes taking the position of an observer and sometimes identifying with the flow of people, as shown by his use of the pronoun "you." His commentary indicates that we are still in Jackson Heights, but his demeanor exhibits a more urban and impersonal viewpoint.

This difference is due to a change of "footing," or a change in our frame for events.[7] In this case, the speaker makes a situational code switch as he adapts to a different context, here the public realm. According to linguists Jan-Petter Blom and John J. Gumperz, three kinds of contextual elements can trigger such a switch: the spatial setting, the social occasion, and the social event.[8] For George, the occasion is constant. It is defined as a specific interview, which consists of talking while going to take the train. Events, for their part, can be observed as we walk and thus accounted for separately. An example occurred when a group of Hispanic day laborers whispered a few words to a young lady who was walking with us. Her embarrassment and the way she regarded us as witnesses were clearly a consequence of the event. As a consequence, the switch from "I" or "we" to "you" corresponded

to a change in spatial setting that redefined the conditions of the social occasion, the subway trip.

Anita Konzelman Ziv proposed an interpretation of the way that the
pronoun "you" is used in this impersonal way (*on* in French):

> [T]he singular and impersonal character of the pronoun "you" makes it fit
> to serve as a substitute for the plural and personal pronoun "we" when the
> latter requires a collective interpretation. In such a case, the pronoun "you"
> allows the expression of an intentional state which rests on a relationship of
> affiliation determined by shared conditions.[9]

In our case, the shared conditions refer to the spatial setting. George thus
enacted a situational code switching marked by the shift from "we" to "you"
when we arrived at the bottom of the elevated station at 74th Street. From
this point on, he referred to himself as part of a collective different from
the community of homeowners to which he had been referring since he left
his building.

The switch from "we" to "you" is a clear marker of the shift in perception from the local to the public, from the neighborhood to the city.
Many interviewees use it. Amala, for example, started using it when she
saw the station from the end of a perpendicular street to the tracks of the
7 train:

> It is changing now. Because of this subway station, it changes a lot. Before it
> was very old station. Now they renovated everything, beautiful big station
> like Manhattan Lexington Avenue. This entrance is closed . . .
>   Here one big shopping center. A supermarket. *You* get all Chinese gro-
> ceries there. Vegetable, fresh fish, everything. It is a very beautiful store. *We*
> come here for Chinese groceries. There is an English learning center for
> immigrant people come here to learn English.

She stopped using "we" a little bit farther along, when we reached the multiple bus stops outside the subway station:

> Before it was very old. I like this very much now. It is brighter and very clean
> Very convenient buses will get here. Across the street you get the buses. You
> can go to Queens Boulevard.

Amala also used the word "you" in an impersonal way once before, when she obviously felt we were still in her neighborhood, thus casting doubt on the efficacy of this marker. But she stopped using "we" once we were at the station, also referring more and more to the anonymous "people" in the area. The linguistic shifts relating to the passage from one social realm to another are often somewhat more complex than the simple and easily recognizable switch from "we" to "you" that occurs in many of the go-along interviews.

For example, Jack, like Pete and a few others, never actually used the word "we" during the walk, although he did describe his fellow feeling for his immediate neighbors. We saw, however, that when he boarded the train, he started using "you" consistently:

> Here, it's only one train so is not, you know, if you are here at the stop is because you're getting off or you're getting on, you're not transferring to any other train.

It seems that at this point in the walk, Jack had run out of personal histories to recall and instead resorted to deductions of what would be logical to do in the same situation. His interview is similar to those in which the respondents do not identify with a specific group in the neighborhood but whose language marks a clear shift in their perceptions of the subway and the area around their home.

From Looking to Observing

Another marker mixing both verbal and nonverbal language is the interviewees' tendency to take an observer's stance once in the subway. Kate, for example, considers herself a member of a distinct minority in an immigrant neighborhood. A middle-class African American woman, she described the walk as crossing territory occupied by hostile foreign people. It seems, in fact, that she sees no difference between the area around her house and the subway. We noticed while we were walking, however, that she was describing the environment from the point of view of a car driver, as if she were trying to extend the distance between her body and gaze and the other people around her:

Stéphane: So, what do you see on the weekends?

Kate: You see more people out. More people walking, more people shopping. These streets are not that crowded because they're inside, but on the main boulevard, in Broadway, and Roosevelt, it's hectic. As far as even trying to drive down Roosevelt, it takes about 20 minutes.

Stéphane: You're thinking like you're driving, right?

Kate: Yeah, yeah. I don't really walk a lot, so yeah.

Stéphane: It is funny, when you are talking, I can see you in the car.

Kate: I don't do a lot of walking. It is not like Manhattan where you can walk a lot.

Stéphane: But you walk to the station . . .

Kate: Yeah, I walk to the station and sometimes. . . . [W]ell no, not even to the laundromat. It's just, there's not as much to see, you know, as opposed to living in Manhattan.

When we got to the subway, Kate stopped using this perceptual trick. She looked around and told us the main concern on her mind, that she was isolated as an African American in the city:

Stéphane: If you look around, right in this [train] car, you see there's different people, from different ethnic groups, can you . . . ?

Kate: I don't see many African Americans.

The visual perception "of other riders" was, in fact, the most common marker of a change of footing from the neighborhood to the subway. As we got closer to the station, the interviewees prompted us to look around and see what they were talking about. To George, Pete, and Mike, the subway station feels more like a place to rub elbows with strangers and acquire an almost sociological knowledge of ethnic groups or other social categories. Once past the turnstile, it seems that one can more freely observe and rely on basic ethnic categorizations without having to take into account the complexities previously induced by the neighborhood context.

Pete on the subway mezzanine:

Pete: You see, you see here's another big crowd coming in. And did you notice the ethnic . . . ? I don't know if you're allowed to pan the crowd, but if you noticed, the crowd that just walked by, almost exclusively Asian and very few Caucasians.

Rich: Where are they coming from?

Pete: From Flushing, the 7 line coming from Flushing. Oh here, a lot of Mexicans, here look at this. You're not going to pan the crowd, right?

That Pete isn't sure that we have the right to "pan the crowd" with the camera is telling. During the walk through his and other neighborhoods along the way to the station, he never before questioned the presence of the camera or that we were filming his familiar streets and passersby whom he was identifying as typical of his social environment. Once in the station and on the subway, however, he was concerned that "panning the crowd" could be seen as a breach of the social norms typical of the subway environment. It could be taken as an infringement of the universally recognized right to civil inattention and anonymous circulation in an urban space. In contrast, on the subway Pete felt that he had more latitude to observe and typify people into large ethnic categories as long as we did not single out individuals. Hence the terms "panning" and "crowd" suddenly become incompatible. Instead of individuals and groups, he now pointed at crowds and types of people.

The train and station thus are places not for encounters but, rather, for a mutual, unobtrusive observation and a silent copresence. In this environment, others can be identified in the subway crowd only according to highly visible traits that sort people into types.[10] When the subway doors open at each station, however, the cultural group that one represents is far less important than everyone's need to get on or off the train. Therefore, it is not as a member of a given cultural community that interviewees describe the situation, but as coparticipants in a shared material situation. In this situation, access is (or should be) granted to every anonymous member of society, regardless of his or her social category. The use of the pronoun "you" is a reflection of the dos and don'ts of this new social environment. To be sure, there are occasions when, for example, the "first come, first served" rule is disturbed and when ethnic or racial tensions or stereotypes resurface in anger. However, our observations on the platform, even during busy peak times, show the remarkable evenhandedness of riders' behavior. Whatever members of the anonymous subway crowds may be thinking as they brush against one another on the subway, their behavior makes one believe that despite all its stresses and challenges, the subway is a crucible of urban civility and a shared sense of belonging.

The subway's accessibility as a service provided by the city and as a universal right asserted by the riders themselves establishes what we think of as an accidental or a "situational community in transit."[11] Such a community is revealed in part by our respondents' use of the pronoun "you" in describing ways to behave and negotiate their passage through the subway environment. The impersonal collective to which "you" refers are the behavioral norms, the ways in which to act—what one should and should not do in a given situation in which all riders find themselves and share as part of the transitory or incidental community of fellow passengers. We explore further the norms and their limits of this subway community in chapter 5.

A Transitional Zone Between Parochial and Public Realms

Despite personal variations, all our respondents revealed a switch of perception as they approached the subway platform. For Amala, the doors of the station mark the entrance to the subway. It is a less secure environment than her neighborhood, where she fears for her daughter's safety and wishes for more security personnel. This passage from a comfortable small Colombian community to a social order regulated by routinized anonymity and impersonal institutions marks her perceptual boundary between the parochial and public social realms. Whereas she can rely on, or at least hope for, aid and understanding from her cultural confreres in her local streets, she must resort to a notion of civil rights when in the subway. The passage from one mode of perception to another as interviewees progress toward the train occurs for each at different points in the walk. Rather than a well-determined border, the switch responds to the interviewee's level of comfort in the neighborhood and to visual cues such as the elevated train tracks. For Kate, the anonymity and her position as a racial stranger started as soon as we left the gate of her apartment building; for Mike, it appeared the first time he noticed the elevated subway tracks before going back to "Indian Street" and then again when we entered the station.

Two notable findings emerged from our analysis of these interviews: the perceptual "boundaries" separating the social realm of the subway and the social realm of the neighborhood. First, each interviewee had a space of transition between the two realms. The passage between the realms covered a larger or smaller space, depending on the individual. In the "we-you switch," the length of the threshold between domains is defined by the period when both pronouns are being used. For George, it went from the bit of street at the foot of the subway stairs to the subway platform. For Amala, it spanned a larger space from a block away from the station to the sidewalk in front of the station.

The second finding is that these transitional spaces are not the same for each interviewee. The location of the thresholds between the two modes of negotiating their way across this space varied, showing that both social domains, the public and the "parochial," may constantly overlap. The result is an ambiguity regarding the essential nature of the social and spatial setting in an area extending from inside the subway station to about a block around it. Whereas a visitor resorts to his or her right to be on the street, a norm carried by the social order of the subway into the neighborhood, residents often feel comfort in their sense of belonging to an identified group in the neighborhood. At the liminal zones where the environments of subway and neighborhood overlap, some individuals may feel uneasy or uncertain. Others may enjoy the occasion for greater flexibility in interpreting the norms of behavior. It is also true that places of high foot traffic are known to be the locations of serendipitous encounters with varied consequences, one of the city's defining features.[12]

The Subway, Public Space, and Street Cosmopolitanism

The main finding in this chapter is the collective dimension of the subway experience as a form of situational community. The norms of behavior associated with this elusive collective bring social order to the subway as well as a sense of shared condition. By itself, this finding is a justification for regarding the subway as a field with its own culture. The second finding is that there is no clear limit between the parochial domain(s) of the neighborhood and the more public realm spilling out of the subway. This doesn't mean that the two realms are indistinct. Rather, the walking interviews show a kind of ambiguous superimposition of the parochial and the public realm in and around the subway station. Ultimately, this observation points at the self-defeating task that most studies of public space face when posing as a principle the opposition of the private and intimate, on the one hand, and the public and anonymous, on the other hand. What makes a space public could be the different ways in which parochial and more anonymous social orders mingle while always preserving the possibility of welcoming a stranger, if not with open arms, at least with a piece of the sidewalk.[13]

Much has been said about the factors that allow a neighborhood like Jackson Heights to attain an unprecedented and unplanned diversity.[14] The fact that over the past decades white residents were able to preserve the value of their real-estate property while minorities were moving in is crucial. Instead of producing a white flight, Jackson Heights has retained a substantial proportion of white and now nonwhite middle- and upper-middle-class households. But the walking interviews suggest something more. The subway community extends out from the trains into the streets in ways that vary for different residents in personal ways. The impersonality and universalism of the subway community are not shared by all the ethnic cultures of the neighborhoods. Instead, they seem to occupy the space left free in between the personal and cultural affiliations of the residents, who rely on it when nothing else is at hand. This suggests that general accessibility to the sidewalk, which defines public space, is not a multicultural asset but a day-after-day construction of a common world and shared values. There is thus a double and simultaneous transformative process at work in and around the 7 train in New York City, one specific to pluralism.[15] When individuals are asked to talk about their walk from home to subway, they are obliged to make their thoughts and feelings public in a way that excites their interest and cooperation. Our questions momentarily transformed the humdrum aspects of the daily walk into a special guided tour. In their comments, each respondent displayed a unique identity shaped by distinct influences of race, culture, gender, and other personal attributes. At the same time, and especially as they entered the subway system itself, they displayed their common identities as urbanites and street cosmopolitans. We will see, as we explore the 74th Street/Roosevelt Avenue station in Jackson Heights, what this specific form of cosmopolitanism entails.

4 The 74th Street/Roosevelt Avenue Station

Universalism, Differentiation, and Discrimination

You get run down when too many people are coming, during rush hour and such. But it's a good opportunity to see who's in the neighborhood.

George, walking interview, at 74th Street/Roosevelt Avenue station

In the previous chapter, we learned that for its riders from nearby neighborhoods, the imposing elevated 74th Street/Roosevelt Avenue subway station (hereafter called the 74th Street station) is positioned between two different social realms: the familiar parochial environment of the neighborhood and the situational community in transit that exists on the subway. For arriving subway riders, the station becomes a transitional zone between neighborhood and city. The station thus provokes a mental and linguistic shift that for most people occurs somewhere between the nearby streets and the train platforms. As they approach the station and its platforms, subway pedestrian-passengers become increasingly wary of possible encounters with strangers and prepare themselves to join the crowds of anonymous riders.

The 74th Street station is not only a space of passage whose physical environment is designed and controlled by the Metropolitan Transportation Authority (MTA) but also, less formally, a social institution of Jackson Heights. This station, like many (but hardly all) in the vast New York City subway system, provides many unplanned services to riders and passersby. In doing so, it develops a unique (and always changing) social environment, with its own locally based, working populations occupying the sidewalks, the mezzanines, and the platforms. This includes subway workers, from MTA employees to police officers, as well as vendors, performers, and proselytizers. Operating in regular and visible places amid the diurnal flows of travelers, these workers provide riders with MetroCards, directions, food and refreshments, entertainment, and religious or political messages. For frequent riders in the various neighborhoods that feed into the station, they also provide a predictable human presence, adding another layer of possible sociability to the parochial and anonymous realms that spill out to the street and onto the platforms. They guide, help, and at times may hinder the flow of thousands of riders through the station. Unlike a restaurant or the train itself, where customers remain immobile for varying durations, the station is a space of temporary passage, more analogous to the lobby of a Manhattan apartment building whose doorman must manage intermittent flows, idle periods, and sudden congestion.[1]

All the station's service workers offer occasions to stop and socialize. As they provide services tailored to riders' needs, they also influence the quality of the overall subway experience, although not always as one might wish. The tension created between offering universal standards of service while remaining welcome and open to particular personal requests is at the heart of all service businesses striving to achieve quality in public spaces.[2] A professional commitment to this difficult goal should produce an institutional culture that does its best to makes all customers feel that they are treated with equal fairness. How can this culture and commitment over a long workday marked by innumerable encounters with the public be maintained?

The tensions this fundamental dilemma creates are especially marked in the subway, whose managers must consider individuals as equivalent vehicular units in a mass or flow and at the same time must anticipate needs specific to the riders. The problem becomes especially relevant when train service is disrupted or when escalators break down, as often happens and frequently because of the special needs of individual riders—who get confused, need directions, faint, stumble, or need medical attention—and when station congestion provokes widespread discontent and anger at the failures of "the system." At a busy station like 74th Street, hundreds of interactions—personal/impersonal, intended/unintended, private/public— are taking place at most times of the day and night. These interactions are guided by the particular service workers and by the broader circumstances of subway service in which they occur (normal traffic, disrupted traffic in particular). Each of the four types of subway workers has a different influence on the station's social order:

1. MTA employees have the strongest commitment to universalism. They act within an employer–employee relationship with their supervisor that demands they work to rule and treat riders as equals, sometimes to the detriment of more personal service that might better ease congestion and stress. These work regulations are always subject to formal and informal change as managers and workers adapt to the demands of the subway environment.

2. In contrast, subway vendors work within a server–client relationship that often encourages attention to individual needs and preferences in ways that may help mitigate the effects of congestion and alienation. Most of the vendors at 74th Street are immigrants who represent the different ethnic populations using the station. Although many of their interactions are with coethnics, perhaps just as many are with people best classified as New York subway riders.

3. The police who patrol the station and monitor the crowds adopt a predator–prey perspective. They scan the crowds for their own purposes as they discriminate among the riders. The police's presence may, under varying circumstances, help either alleviate or heighten riders' stress and discomfort. Subway riders also view police officers as those who can offer help, especially with directions. Even though such requests humanize interactions, during a long shift they can also frustrate officers.

4. Proselytizers, performers, and beggars seek attention from passing subway riders and pedestrians. Their goal is to stop the normal flow of physical bodies to engage in personal interaction for their own purposes. Each has something to offer, usually in the way of an emotional reward in return for attention or coins, and each presents passersby with a moral choice that can be momentarily disconcerting or rewarding.

These four categories of workers illustrate different approaches to the conflicting demands of universalism and differentiation common to all service jobs. Each of these occupations also entails a spatial logic that creates, as we shall see, the particular human ecology of the 74th Street station, a public space filled with both felicitous and unhappy encounters, where familiarity and alienation, routine and happenstances, exist side by side.

74th Street/Roosevelt Avenue:
A Legible Elevated Station

The elevated subway tracks stand on steel girders high above the avenues they cover. Daytime sunlight filtering through the railroad ties dapples the streets and sidewalks below. At night, the shadowy elevated structures loom above a bright stream of vehicles' headlights. The vertical girders glow faintly from the passing traffic and the neon colors of nearby storefront signs. Of the New York subway system's 468 stations, about 280 are underground and about 150 are elevated, with the rest in open cuts, at grade, and on embankments. During the second half of the twentieth century, many of Manhattan's elevated tracks were eliminated in favor of underground stations, thereby fulfilling the dream of car makers and real-estate investors along the major avenues of the city's most affluent borough. Elevated lines in contemporary New York roughly track the city's more middle- and working-class neighborhoods, which also house immigrants and other newcomers to the city.

The relationships of underground subway stations with their surrounding neighborhoods tend to be very different from those with elevated stations. In Manhattan and other boroughs with subway service, proximity to an underground station is an advantage for commercial and residential property owners. In Queens, the Bronx, and Brooklyn, however, immediate proximity to the elevated lines and stations is associated more often with noise and congestion, which depress housing property values but may benefit commercial uses. Thus in Jackson Heights, 37th Avenue, which runs parallel to Roosevelt Avenue and its elevated line, one can find more of the community's important institutions: schools, post office, banks, and slightly more upscale stores. The properties under the elevated tracks along Roosevelt Avenue are certainly in demand but more commonly for fast food outlets, cell phone stores, bars, and ethnic nightclubs than are those in the surrounding, quieter shopping streets.[3]

With its three levels extending from the underground part of the station to the entry at ground level to the elevated tracks above, the 74th Street station is unique to New York City's subway system. The station occupies its own, triangular city block, bounded by Roosevelt Avenue on the northern side, 73rd Street on the eastern side, and Broadway on the western diagonal between these two streets. The 7 train tracks are elevated above Roosevelt Avenue, the main commercial artery of the area. The E, F, R, and M trains run underground below Broadway. The ground floor opens to a congested bus station with six lines, including one serving LaGuardia Airport.

Among the system's major transfer hubs, the 74th Street station is the second busiest in Queens, after Flushing–Main Street. It is the fifteenth busiest station in the entire system. From 1998 to 2012 as the neighborhoods of Jackson Heights, Elmhurst, and Corona were gaining residents, the average number of riders passing daily through the turnstiles rose from 35,000 to 50,000 (a 43% increase). In 2007, the year when our fieldwork began, an average of 47,000 riders per weekday swiped their MetroCards at the station. The average Saturday and Sunday ridership rose even more, from 24,000 and 18,000 in 1998 to 37,400 (+55%) and 30,000 (+60%) in 2011, respectively.

The station was under renovation from 2003 to 2006, and it now features a wide ground-floor central area with a high, industrial cathedral-like ceiling, letting in abundant natural light through stained glass. A large staircase connects the ground floor with the upstairs and downstairs mezzanines. This configuration makes the station a visible landmark in this area of Queens. The station has nine separate entry points. The three main ones are located on the ground floor and have large doors that open directly onto the three sides of the station building: Roosevelt Avenue, Broadway, and the covered bus station. One staircase, located on 74th Street, busy with many South Asian businesses, leads directly to the upstairs mezzanine and the 7 train. The other sets of stairs lead down to the ends and the middle of the lower mezzanine under Broadway and 73rd, 74th, and 75th Streets. Inside the station, two sets of escalators link the lower and upper mezzanines, bypassing the ground level. Although the many entrances make the station accessible from all aboveground directions, our observation showed that riders prefer to use the central entrances and immediate access to escalators, elevators, and stairs rather than the passageways at either end of the lower mezzanine. Consequently, the concentration of people at the center of the station can be quite high at peak times. On a weekday between 8:00 and 9:00 A.M. in 2007, we counted 2,011 people entering through the ground floor entrances. These riders then go on to mix with passengers transferring from one line to another. As a public space within the subway system, the station gathers many diverse populations from different parts of Queens (for more on this, see chapter 2).

Tailoring the Service to Individuals: Sidewalk Vendors

Street vendors seeking to capitalize on the converging pedestrian traffic are the first service workers that riders encounter when they reach the station.[4] The vending scene around the station changes often, so the following observations may no longer exactly describe the current situation, but the interactions with different vendors and their location efforts are still relevant.[5]

On the sidewalks of Roosevelt Avenue and Broadway, a total of about twelve street vendors shared the selling spots over a 24-hour period. They sold ethnic fast food, fruits, drinks, books, and newspapers, some out of silver trailers—carts that can fit up to three vendors—and others from small tables with a milk crate for a seat. They shared the sidewalk in an almost always orderly manner and usually could be found at the same spot every day.

Occasionally, the vendors argued over selected spaces on the sidewalk. According to Luis, the large Mexican food cart was the one that more often ran into conflict with the rest, as it sometimes stood in a place that "belonged" to someone else. Although the vendors were aware that no one could "own" the sidewalk, they did agree that if a vendor had been in a spot for a while, she could legitimately claim it as hers. As vendors rotated throughout the day, up to three different vendors could take the same spot in one day without conflict. The problem was that the big Mexican food cart remained at the station for 24 hours each day. It could claim a spot for only one shift a day, so for the rest of the day the cart had to keep moving along Roosevelt Avenue, often taking the spot left empty by a vendor who had taken that day off (and thus if the sidewalk was especially crowded that day, it would conflict with the other vendors). All these norms are, of course, informal. Their existence and the sanctions involved in maintaining them help keep the station as an institution of the Jackson Heights community.

The Station as a 24/7 Community Institution

Street vendors are largely responsible for making the station a round-the-clock social institution of the community. Their "eyes on the street," in Jane

Jacobs's memorable phrase,[6] make the sometimes ominous physical environment feel much more humane, even late at night.

They have three overlapping "shifts": early morning (4:30 A.M. to noon), midday (10:00 A.M. to 7:00 P.M.), and evening (after 6:00 P.M.), providing time-specific services on a 24-hour basis. The first vendors early in the morning sell coffee and bagels and distribute newspapers to riders rushing to work. During the day, the vendors sell books, fruit, or prepared food, targeting people who have time to browse through their merchandise and people strolling through the neighborhood on their lunch breaks or coming back from work. The evening vendors sell mostly food, catering to people who are returning from work and, late at night, patrons of the many bars and nightclubs in the area. The following is a description of what we saw during our fieldwork.

Early Morning: Breakfast on the Go

On weekdays, the morning shift on the sidewalk of the 74th Street station started before sunrise. Irene, an Egyptian woman in her early forties, arrived with her coffee cart at 5:00 A.M. She would like to be there earlier, but it is "just too early in the morning to be up." She set up her cart east of the entrance on Roosevelt Avenue, by the big Mexican food cart, which is parked on Roosevelt Avenue 24 hours a day, seven days a week.

At this hour, huge flows of people were rushing to the station from the east and from the west, emerging from 75th Street and exiting the Q32 bus right in front of the Roosevelt Avenue doors. As the sun began to rise, the sidewalk became progressively busier and noisier. Car engines and honking combined with the rattling of the elevated 7 train running every couple of minutes to produce an almost deafening sound. Hispanics, whites, blacks, Asians, men, and women, many wearing business attire, walked at a fast and steady pace. Some of them grabbed a cup of coffee and a bagel or muffin from Irene's cart to eat on the train. This was part of their daily routine, and they knew the exact amount to pay. Most of the commuters, however, did not know much about the vendor, except that she always had a smile on her face. Many of her customers assumed she was Hispanic. But those customers who spoke to her in Spanish were surprised when they discovered that she did not understand them. Irene said she found this amusing, and after eight months at the station, she had learned some basic words that enabled her to better serve her Spanish-speaking customers: "¿Quiere leche? ¿Quiere azúcar?"

Irene was well on her way to becoming a New Yorker. Regular commuters who took the time to speak with her, and many did, learned that she was a mother of four; that she was happy to be her own boss; and that she dreamed of the day when she could expand her business. Like other vendors around the block, Irene used to work in various chain stores and franchises. At Taco Bell, she did not see a future. Here, however, she had an Egyptian friend who, after twenty years in the United States, owned several coffee carts. Moreover, in this job she got off at noon and could then spend time with her children.

Many of Irene's customers also bought a newspaper from Elisa, an Ecuadorian woman in her late thirties who sat on a milk crate behind a small fold-up plastic table on the eastern side of the Roosevelt Avenue entrance. She sold the *New York Times, Daily News, U.S. Daily,* and, for Spanish speakers, *El Diario* and *Hoy.* On the Broadway side of the station, Elisa's co-worker, Marta, also Ecuadorian and in her thirties, sat on her milk crate and displayed her papers. Marta was a tiny woman, almost lost against the wall, but not unnoticed by her regulars.

Both Elisa and Marta worked for the same employer, who had people working at thirteen different train stations. At 74th Street, they worked in two shifts of two on each side of the station, every morning and afternoon. Elisa and Marta worked the morning shift. They arrived at the station at 6:00 A.M. and left by 10:00 A.M. But if they were able sell all their newspapers before 10:00 A.M., they could go home earlier (they were happy when this happened).

Riders who preferred not to pay could pick up a copy of a free newspaper. At the east side of the Roosevelt Avenue entrance, an Ecuadorian man in his late fifties distributed the *Metro.* He stood there in a bright orange shirt and cap, a white latex glove on his right hand. By the end of his shift, at 10:00 A.M., the front of his shirt and the glove had been completely stained by the ink bleeding from the freshly printed pages. He had been working at the station for five and a half months, but he wanted to stop in order to work in his specialty: French cuisine. At the west side of the same entrance, an old man, with the recognizable Sikh turban, handed out *amNewYork.* He was rather tall, with a big white beard and mustache, and wore the red apron of all *amNewYork* employees.

Distributing these free morning newspapers is an entry-level job for new immigrants.

On the Broadway side of the station, subway riders who arrived in the morning were more likely to be immigrants from China who lived on the southern border of Jackson Heights or in nearby Elmhurst. The free paper distributed to them was the *Epoch Times*, a diaspora Chinese newspaper printed in the United States by members of the city's Falun Gong congregation. John, a middle-aged man from Singapore, handed out both the Chinese and the English version of the paper. He was a volunteer and a member of Falun Gong. The goal of the paper was to educate people about the situation of Falun Gong practitioners living in China. According to John, the Chinese government maintained secret labor camps where Falun Gong practitioners were confined. John didn't mind not being paid for the time he worked at the station, as his mission was to "tell the world the truth of what's going on in China," and he argued that raising awareness "help[ed him] to be part of the Universe, the Cosmos."

Midday: Lunch Break Anytime

By 10:00 A.M., the long and frantic morning rush was over. The newspaper workers and some of the breakfast food vendors had been replaced by peddlers who catered to a slower stream of shoppers, students, and riders facing somewhat less time pressure. Amparo, who owned a fruit cart, was usually the first of the new shift to arrive. A petite Ecuadorian woman, she was dwarfed by her huge cart with its two separate stands. Her husband or her older son usually came with her to help set it up. They pushed the carts and parked them slightly west of the Roosevelt Avenue doors, right by the bus stop. They opened wide and colorful umbrellas to shelter the fruits from the sun and the summer heat, and then they cleaned the surface of the cart and arranged the fruit: grapes, cherries, apples, bananas, oranges, cantaloupes, and avocados. Amparo worked all day until 8:00 P.M. In June, her thirteen-year-old son began coming to the station with her. She explained that now that school was over, he got bored at home, so she brought him to the station, where he entertained himself working as a fruit seller. This, however, had caught the attention of the police, who warned her about exploiting a minor. Amparo shrugged her narrow shoulders and explained that she was not forcing her son to work, that he would keep doing it even if she told him to stay home.

Eduardo, a nut vendor, did not always get all his customers off to a good day. He set up at about the same time as Amparo. A middle-aged Ecuadorian, Eduardo sold nuts in front of the Roosevelt Avenue entrance, between the fruit cart and the coffee cart. He was an employee of a company called Nuts4Nuts, which has carts all over New York City.[7] A huge truck would bring the carts to all the selling spots, so when Eduardo arrived on the sidewalk, his cart would be waiting for him. Around 11:00 A.M., he would light the burner and, in a copper saucepan, begin roasting the peanuts, cashews, and almonds, coating them with sugar. He was not paid by the day but by his sales, with his daily earnings amounting to 40 percent of the money he collected from customers.

Eduardo worked three days a week at the Flatbush Avenue station in Brooklyn and three days at 74th Street. He liked Jackson Heights "much, much better. Because there's people like us [Hispanics]. In Flatbush, it's full of *morenos* [African Americans]."

> **Eduardo:** They don't behave. They try to touch the nuts, to steal from me.
> **Amalia:** You don't have that kind of problem with Hispanics?
> **Eduardo:** No, never. They are not like us.
> **Amalia:** In which way?
> **Eduardo:** Well . . . They are not . . . people. . . . [I try to look cool, but it seems I don't succeed, so he adds:]
>
> It's not that I'm a racist, but you know. . . . When the *morenos* are born, they are born with an inferiority complex. So they try to stand out, but they do it the wrong way: spitting on the train, robbing people, trying to touch the food . . .

May 5, 2006

In addition to his racial prejudices, Eduardo liked to flirt with his female customers "because women like to hear that they look good." So for the price of $1, his female Hispanic customers got a bag of *garrapiñadas* and a comment about their physical appearance, like "You look good today, *mami*." Some women seemed to enjoy this. A Colombian woman standing beside him smiled when he described her as "beautiful and handsome." She lived in the neighborhood and knew Eduardo from the sidewalk. When she was not in a rush, she liked to stop by for a little chat. Even though his cart attended to all kinds of people, his demeanor marked him as Latin American. More than other vendors, Eduardo anchored the space immediately outside the station doors to the Spanish-speaking neighborhood along the avenue. Although his presence was seen as familiar and reassuring for some, it was rather unnerving for others like Amalia, our young Argentine co-researcher:

> While the nuts vendor was having breakfast, he called on me, saying, "Hey *mami*, say hi to my friends," pointing at the driver of huge truck on Roosevelt Avenue, with the letters "Nuts4Nuts" on the side. He flashed me a lascivious smile while the driver and his companion were waving at me, calling me "*mami*." Very nasty. It's going to be hard for me to interview this guy.

At 11:00 A.M., with lunch hour approaching, the hot-food vendors began to set up. A Mexican food cart, attended by two Mexican women, stood on the corner of 75th Street and Roosevelt Avenue. One of them, wearing a white apron with small pink flowers, was rather old, with a wrinkled face. The other woman was in her twenties. Because both were petite, they needed to step on a wooden block to reach the griddle where they cooked tacos and burritos. This was the only cart on the sidewalk exclusively attended by women. On the left side of the food cart, a small seating area with a fold-up table and two stools was used by customers who liked to sit, enjoy the food, chat, and watch pedestrians walk by.

These women paid Oscar's wife to drive their truck to the sidewalk. Oscar was a thirty-five-year-old Mexican food vendor set up on the west side of the Broadway entrance. He was always in a good mood and cooked gyros and skewers. Oscar's wife and their three-year-old son usually stayed with him. This was a family business: he cooked while she did all the errands, driving the cart to the station, buying the groceries and other goods, and taking care of their child. When Oscar was cooking, his wife sat in a chair beside him, under a parasol, and the boy sat in his stroller.

Like the other food vendors, Oscar wore his vending license around his neck, which he earned by taking a class on hygiene and food handling. The class is offered only in English, which is a problem for many Spanish-only speakers. The license, the cart, and the car to move it around together represent a significant investment. Even though the city charges only a modest sum for a food cart permit ($200 in 2014), the number of licenses is restricted and the waiting list is long. Most vendors sublease their license from middlemen for a price well above the official one. When he arrived from Mexico in 1996, Oscar worked for eight years at a deli to save the $9,000 for the cart and the $6,000 for the two-year cart license. At the station, he sold beef kebabs for $2.50 and sodas for $1. Thanks to his amiable demeanor and modest prices, his business was doing pretty well. Oscar added: "If I received money for all the information that I give, I would be rich." Indeed, he had acquired the stature of a "public character" in the area. Even the storeowners in the neighborhood often came to chat with him.

When his wife was hit by a car while she was crossing Broadway on an errand, Oscar was not at the site, and a customer watched over the cart while she was taken to nearby Elmhurst Hospital. For a few months afterward, she was not able to work and Oscar went back to working at a deli and a restaurant. But as soon as she recovered, they resumed their teamwork. By then, their son could walk, and when he got bored, he liked to run around the corner. His parents knew that he was safe around the station, as the other vendors knew him and looked after him.

Around 11:30 A.M., Irene closed up her coffee cart, and in a few minutes, she was gone. At this time, Luis would push his book cart—which he stored nearby for $100 a month—onto the sidewalk. Luis was Mexican too, in his late forties, though it was hard to tell because of his dark hair. Even though most of the books he sold were in Spanish, he aimed at a broad range of clients, from Latin American literature by authors such as Mario Vargas Llosa and Gabriel García Márquez, to translated best sellers by John Grisham and Dan Brown, as well as New Age and self-help books. Luis also sold bilingual dictionaries and methods to learn English, which non–Spanish speakers could buy. His stock included books for children, which he displayed at a lower level. Children who did not yet know how to read and write were attracted to the colors and the characters on the covers that they recognized from popular television cartoons. Ironically, when South Asian women dressed in saris bought a Spanish-language book for their toddler, they may not have been able to read it.

When rush hour started at about 4:00 P.M., people returning from work started pouring out of the station. The sidewalk was as congested as early in the morning. The intervals between trains were shorter, and the noise of the 7 train, rolling overhead every other minute again made a deafening sound.

Evening: Hot Foods to Take Home

The end of the midday shift came at 6:00 P.M. (a little later during summertime). Amparo took her fruit cart home. Luis rolled his book cart to the storage area nearby. The two Mexican women attached their small food cart to the back of Oscar's wife's truck and left until the next day. Oscar, on the Broadway side, also left the 74th Street station and traveled along the line for two stops to the 61st Street station in Woodside for the night. Only two Mexican food carts remained during the night on the Roosevelt Avenue sidewalk.

One large cart, bigger than all the others, stood at the station all day and night, every day. Two people worked standing inside and a third one sat outside, selling sodas from a big cooler full of ice. The cooks were employees, Ecuadorians or Mexicans, working 8-hour shifts, three shifts a day, for a total of six employees. They prepared a variety of Mexican food: tortas, tortillas, flautas, tacos, and burritos. The woman selling sodas outside the cart was the owner. She also was Ecuadorian and looked very young, under thirty-five, with olive skin and dark, straight hair gathered into a ponytail. The cart was always busy. Peak time was around 1:00 A.M., especially on Saturday and Sunday, when many people came out of dance clubs and bars in the area in search of a taco or a burrito to satisfy their after-drinking hunger.

The second Mexican food cart arrived around 7:00 P.M. and stood on the corner of Roosevelt Avenue and 75th Street. Two middle-aged Mexican men manned it. They were tall and muscular, each with a thin mustache and wearing a white apron; they looked like brothers. It took them about an hour to set up, during which time people gathered near the cart. They sold the "best tacos in the area," and the line of customers who waited for more than half an hour gives credence to that claim. Another cart, by the 73rd Street entrance on Broadway, also gained a good reputation when in 2006 it won the Vendy Cup during a competition organized each year by an advocacy group, the Street Vendor Project. Sammy's Halal's chicken over rice, as well, won much praise from neighborhood subway riders. Set up in front of a bank, it brought welcome activity to an otherwise deserted corner.

Foot traffic created by the subway thus provided regular work for about twenty to thirty immigrants. Some of the jobs were low-paying, entry-level jobs, but others held the promise of helping their self-employed owners succeed. Thanks to all these vendors, the sidewalks around the main entrances of the 74th Street station were never empty. In addition to the food, newspapers, coffee, and books they sold, they gave a familiar feel to the station's fringes that helped riders make the transition from their neighborhood to the station and back. Although some vendors catered to specific ethnic groups, all of them displayed a commitment to serve everyone who passed by. The service they offered added a personalized plus to the subway trip, in the form of a coffee, a newspaper, and an occasional pause and chitchat.

In 2007, the MTA opened the bidding for the concession areas included in the design of the new station, but architectural constraints postponed the opening of the main spaces.[8] Finally, after another round of bidding, a large pizzeria opened in December 2013 on the ground floor facing Roosevelt Avenue.[9] Despite the laudable ambition of the owners to create jobs for the community, the opening of the store has now prevented the food and book vendors from settling next to the station doors. Some carts have been pushed farther east on Roosevelt Avenue, where they often come into conflict with stores (and the 82nd Street Business Improvement District) and the police. Farther west on Roosevelt Avenue, a space under the 7 train tracks and over the sunken Brooklyn–Queens Expressway, which separates Jackson Heights from Woodside, serves as an open-air market for casual labor. Male immigrants, mainly of Latino origin, gather there in the mornings. These *jornaleiros*, as they are called in Spanish, hope to be hired by private contractors and homeowners for various construction jobs.

Inside the Station: Universalism and Differentiation Under Pressure

Once inside the doors,[10] subway users enter an institutional realm under the control, to varying degrees, of MTA agents.[11] In the main hall, a sign announces the name of the station manager, Steven X. This position was invented in 1991 to help improve the state of the stations and reduce crime.[12]

Steven is a white, middle-aged, heavyset man. When we met him in 2006, he had already been a manager for twelve years. He explained that he was not often present in this station, as he was responsible for ten stations on the 7 and F trains, including Flushing–Main Street and Lexington

Avenue/63rd Street, both more heavily trafficked than 74th Street. Although his main task here was to keep the station clean, he noted that this station was the worst under his supervision. With only one cleaner per shift because of budget cuts, this manual worker's job was nearly impossible. As the station manager saw it, the problem was mostly with the riders, of whom Steven had a low opinion. They were "careless." He observed that on Roosevelt Island, people had

> stronger feeling of community that helps keep the station clean. Even in Flushing, as busy as here, it is not as dirty.

He pointed at MetroCards littered on the floor, liquid spills, and cups, and added:

> The 7 train transports a lot of drunk people at night and some vomit on the platforms.

Another reason for their carelessness, he believed, was that many riders did not speak English and could not read signs. Rather than offering information in Spanish, he believed that riders "should learn to speak English, if they've been living in the U.S. for ten years." Clearly, the differentiation of customer needs did not rank high in this station manager's conception of professional service.

The Station as a Public Service Provider

Community Service in the Station

One solution to cuts in full-time station cleaners that was being tried during our observations was to rely on people sentenced to community service (and, since 1997, welfare recipients).[13] This program started in the 1980s when the courts were looking for a deterrent against fare beating, and it was quickly expanded to a list of other misdemeanors. Community service is preferable to jail time, as it is erased from the offender's record. At 74th Street, teams of four or five people, usually young, often swept and mopped the floors, under the supervision of an MTA employee. They wore blue jackets marked "New York City Transit. Community Service Program. PARTICIPANT." The supervisors and their participant sweepers avoided contact with riders. As the station manager's observations about litter in the station indicate, whatever this program's benefits were for the persons convicted, the results in cleanliness and sociability in the station were largely negligible.

Giving Directions, Endlessly

The only reliably present MTA staff person in the station was the 24-hour token booth clerk. The centrally located ground floor booth has room for only a single agent. It occupies the center of the grand theater-like space of the station. Turnstiles on either side open onto the large staircases that lead up and down to the mezzanines. On the wall facing the booth, opposite the stairs, MetroCard vending machines (MVMs) stand on either side of the doors to the bus station.

Most riders usually walked quickly through this majestic space, bathed in light colored by the tinted glass two floors above. They swiped their MetroCards and went to the stairs, sometimes under the watchful eyes of police officers, who, when they were in the station, usually stood on the first landing of the stairs going up to the 7 train. This spot afforded them a clear view of the turnstiles, which allowed them to stop any fare beater without being easily accessible to riders seeking directions or information. That responsibility rested primarily on the agent inside the booth, the last human in the station still authorized to sell tickets. Unfortunately, the relationship between the riders and the token booth worker was often fraught with misunderstanding and impatience, as the following scene reveals:

A middle-aged East Asian woman walks through the open gate next to the booth, and immediately the two police officers run down the stairs and stop her. They walk her back through the gate and give her a ticket. The woman complains that her unlimited card is not working, but they do not want to engage her in a conversation.

Visibly upset, she then walks to the teller and asks for her card to be fixed. The African American woman in the booth hands her an envelope to mail her card to the MTA and ask for a new one. But the woman is not happy with that. She yells at the teller in perfect English with a heavy East Asian accent. But she does not get a satisfactory answer. She then asks to see the manager. The teller picks up the phone, but she does not seem to be calling anyone. The woman screams a little more, and the people in the line behind her start to give up and instead walk to the vending machines. Two minutes later, the dejected woman gives up and walks out onto Broadway.

Field notes, 2007

This type of tense interaction between a rider and an MTA booth worker is commonplace in the busy stations of the New York City subway system. Time and time again, riders bring their malfunctioning MetroCard to the clerk, only to be told to try again (and get in line again) or to be handed an envelope without much explanation. Riders get frustrated with the lack of responsiveness to their personal problem and feel like they are being treated inhumanely.

The endless number of claims pressed on them also aggravates the MTA workers. They prepare ready-made answers and usually do not have much patience for offering an additional explanation. As Marvin Holland, a station cleaner and union activist described in an interview in 2007, the sheer number of riders has forced the workers to find a way to protect themselves. "I'm a short-tempered person on the job," he admits. "I mean I don't have time to answer all sorts of questions."

If you come to me and ask "How do I get to Times Square?" I am going to give you the quickest way, the easiest way, for you to get there. Now if you tell me, "Somebody told me if I get this train . . ." I don't have time for that. So it may appear that I have a short fuse, but I have heard this question a hundred times. For the people in the booth, it is even worse. That's all they do. Could you imagine, say you work at Bowling Green and every person that gets off the train asks you "Where is the Staten Island ferry?" When we have a little time, we don't mind. But specifically in Manhattan, they have cut jobs so much that we all are doing so much more work than we were doing five or ten [or] fifteen years ago.

Declining Personnel, Increasing Conflict

Jobs in Jackson Heights were eliminated during our field observations, so feelings about the subject were still quite raw. Until 2005, the station had three token booths; one open full time, 24/7, and two others part time, on the upper and lower mezzanines. After this date, the agents in the part-time booths were reassigned to a newly created position, station customer assistants (SCAs). They were recognizable by their burgundy jackets as they stood by the turnstiles to answer questions and otherwise provide direct personal services to subway customers. As we explain in more detail later, the new positions had been part of a contract settlement with the Transport Workers Union (TWU), which argued that the jobs were merely a transition to an eventual workforce reduction. Indeed, since 2010, these positions have been cut (570 throughout the whole system),[14] and now only one full-time booth worker is assigned for the whole station.

This planned shrinkage of the station workforce is the result of years of financial trouble for the subway, which date all the way back to its opening more than a hundred years ago. As a result, the relations between riders and workers are, at best, mediocre and the perception of the quality of service is poor.

The Transport Workers Union Strike of 2005

Following the MTA's refusal to negotiate a new contract with worker concessions,[15] TWU Local 100 called a strike at the peak of the 2005 Christmas shopping season. Since 1967, however, the Taylor Law has forbidden public employees in the state of New York from striking; the union can be fined and its leaders jailed.[16] In 2005, as the strike effectively paralyzed the city, two questions were repeatedly discussed in the news: How much should the union be fined, and how much is the strike hurting the city's economy?[17] Mayor Michael Bloomberg demanded that the workers be penalized with the largest fine possible.[18] Governor George Pataki, the only elected official actually in control of the votes on the MTA board, refused to negotiate during the strike and kept a low profile, thus avoiding any further involvement.[19] When the strike ended on the third day, the city comptroller declared that it had cost the city economy $1 billion in lost business.[20] Despite a few op-eds in the *New York Times* sympathetic to the workers, the argument was never turned around to ask how much subway workers were helping the economy on each day that the system worked and how much salary and benefits they could decently ask for in exchange.[21] Public opinion was split and, in general, poorly informed about the contract negotiations leading to the strike.

In Jackson Heights, the three days of strike were not much different from the many weekends that shut down the line for work and maintenance,[22] but this time all lines were down. The people who really had to go to Manhattan either vied for crowded Long Island Rail Road trains in

Woodside or shared cabs. When service resumed on December 23, nobody in the line at the token booth mentioned the strike to the MTA worker. A woman who worked in Manhattan and had to walk sixty blocks to Woodside told us:

> I do not want to blame the workers who need a contract, but the strike is not right.

A man who knew more about the dispute between the workers and the MTA told us that he was not going to talk to the MTA employees. He would not know what to say and did not want to start an argument. Subway business resumed as usual, but the distance between riders and the remaining station workers had only widened.

The Station Customer Assistant Program: A Chance at a More Professional Service?

One of the items on the negotiation table between the MTA and the union touched the heart of the complex relationship among the riders, the workers, and the institution that manages the subway. For a few years, the MTA had been pushing the elimination of the job of train conductor (the worker who stands in a booth in the middle of the train, opens and closes the doors, and makes the announcements). The MTA was also pressing for the elimination of most token booth workers. Although the union won the fight for the conductors, the MTA continued to urge closing the booths. In response, the influential Straphangers Campaign, a riders' advocacy group, sued the MTA for not having held public hearings on the issue and won. At the hearings, the public expressed strong concerns for the security and safety of riders, and the union opposed the elimination of jobs. As union activist Marvin Holland recalls:

> The original plan was to close all booths, and the fight that I started with the union kept the booths there. One of the things was the emergency [phone] line to station command. If you remove the booth and the person, who is going to make that phone call? This was after 9/11, so they agreed to leave the booths, but they wanted to move the personnel outside.

This solution eased riders' safety concerns somewhat. It also removed the workers' responsibility of selling fares and transferred this essential mission to the MetroCard vending machines. The union was divided, as it saw this program as a surreptitious way of progressively phasing out agents from the stations. But it also saw it as an opportunity to establish better relationships with the riders.

The Station Customer Assistance (SCA) program started in 2006 and closed 110 part-time booths throughout the system. At the 74th Street station, the lower and upper mezzanine booths were closed. Downstairs, where the peak time traffic is heavy, two agents were initially appointed to work from 7:00 A.M. to 3:00 P.M. and from 3:00 to 11:00 P.M. every weekday. Upstairs, the position was filled irregularly by "extras," or recently hired workers who could not yet apply for a fixed job location.

"They are taking my job!" Tommy said, pointing at the MVMs lining the back wall of the lower mezzanine entrance by 73rd Street. He was an SCA, and he felt ambivalent about his job. Although he felt threatened as a worker, he enjoyed the new contact with the "customers." Like most SCAs, Tommy blamed the tense relations between riders and booth clerks on the glass panel that usually separates them. Marvin Holland, the union activist involved in watching the unfolding of the SCA program, explained how this barrier both protects and exposes the workers to abuse:

> The average person is not violent by nature. They are a little more calm and polite when next to you. Whereas behind a glass, a person is more likely to curse, even a decent person, because you can't get to them. It changes the perspective. The way customers treat workers.

The same is also true the other way around. Another station worker at 74th Street explained that the glass window also forced the workers to exaggerate their facial and body expression in order to better communicate with the customers. Signs of dismissal or deterrence, such as blatantly ignoring the client or raising one's voice to signify the end of a transaction, are used to overcome the communication barrier, albeit at the risk of offending the rider. Conversely, all the SCAs who worked at 74th Street agreed that relations were easier when they stood outside the booth.

Tim, an MTA "extra," came to New York from Bangladesh when he was a child, grew up in Queens, and attended St. Johns University. He had worked both inside and outside the booth and preferred the latter. When we spoke to him, he was working on the ground floor as a support to the main booth worker. He pointed at her inside the booth and said:

> You see her, in 8 hours, she probably sees 700 people coming to her booth. Out of the 700, about 500 are very similar questions, like "Where is that bus, that train, or my MetroCard is not working." You quickly get bored with some questions. Plus people are frustrated and they are a little bit aggressive. It is hard. Outside, on the other hand, it is much easier. People are friendly. Basically, they want directions and help with the MetroCard vending machines [MVMs].

In fact, the riders' demands on the SCAs were just as repetitive, but the SCAs did not find them boring. They regarded each interaction as a brief encounter with actual people, most of the time peaceful and even good spirited.

Riders and SCAs often agreed on the difficulty of using the MVMs or swiping the card through the turnstile. Also, riders in need of help dealing with the automated equipment were often quite grateful for the personal assistance. Clearly, the SCAs were performing a needed service by helping clients deal with the vending machines, saving them both time and money. For example, after an elderly woman had tried several times to swipe her new card at the turnstile without success, the reader announced "insufficient fare." Rather than continue to hold up other passengers, Tommy, an SCA worker, let her through the gate. "The machine ate up the money," he explained. "That's what happens ninety-nine times out of a hundred."

An even more common problem in the automated subway environment is the small amount of change, $6 (in 2007; $8 in 2014), that the MetroCard vending machines could return. This limitation made it impossible for a rider to purchase a single ride with a $10 bill, much less a $20 bill. According to Neil, another SCA working on the lower mezzanine, this problem was much worse at 74th Street than in Manhattan:

> In this working-class immigrant neighborhood, people mostly want to buy a single ride with cash. In Manhattan, the middle and upper class and tourists tend to use a credit card or to buy multiple rides.

An important part of his job was to send riders to buy their ticket at the main booth. But he could not let them go through the station without paying the fare, which meant that they had to go back out to the street, walk two blocks, and cross Roosevelt Avenue to get there. Most of them preferred to get change from the stores and vendors immediately around the station entrance, even if the SCA did not tell them to do so. The MTA thus informally relied on the surrounding businesses to make up for its own inability to provide fares to riders without a credit card. In addition to providing information, this is another free service provided by the vendors to riders and to the MTA. But this limitation made the SCAs feel helpless.

There Is No "Standard Rider": An Experiment in Differentiated Service That Failed

The inability to handle money that came with working outside the booth deprived the station agents of the only measurable task able to evaluate the service they provided. Despite a generally favorable reception of their presence by the public, attested to by a poll by the Straphangers Campaign,[23] the SCA job was never clearly defined by a list of tasks.

This uncertainty produced difficult situations for the workers caught between the riders' demands and their supervisor's orders. In another example, since they had no direct law-enforcement authority, agents were instructed not to directly confront fare evaders for fear of retaliation. They were to let people jump over the turnstile rather than engage in a conflict. Yet they were also instructed to do whatever possible to make sure that every rider paid the fare, creating contradictory instructions that were difficult for most agents to manage. According to Marvin Holland, the union activist, SCA was the only job in the MTA that was not clearly defined by a set of precise tasks and duties. In a culture rife with tensions between supervisors and workers,[24] rules act as a resource on which workers can rely to defend their professionalism:

> For an authority that loves rules more than any other around, they never made rules for the SCA. Define the job. When does a person come out of the booth? When do they allow her to go in the booth? The other jobs, in the booth, the cleaners, all have a set of rules that is set like a bible. They don't have that because they don't know where they are going with the program. They never thought it out.

When they felt unsafe, the SCAs were allowed to stay in the booth. A problem in this case was that many riders approached the window, only to discover that the worker could not sell fare cards, something the customer found difficult to understand.

We do not know whether high-level MTA officials ever wanted to make the Station Customer Assistance program a success. From the start, union officials claimed that their intention was to eventually eliminate jobs. The problem for the customer assistants was that they did not benefit from professional attention or a degree of initiative that would have helped them provide better services to riders. That would have required day-to-day discretion that the MTA was apparently not ready to give to its workers. It also would have demanded specific attention to riders as unique individuals, an approach at odds with the standard image of the rider as an able-bodied, English-speaking person.

The need for more individualized service was never at issue at the 74th Street station or elsewhere in the subway system. At 74th Street, the customer service agents could have provided an invaluable service by helping people with disabilities or those with babies and strollers negotiate crowded elevator lines. They could have been invaluable in directing traffic to alternative escalators in the frequent cases of mechanical breakdown.

One elevator in particular is almost useless to people with strollers. It serves three different levels: the upper mezzanine, the ground floor by the main booth, and the landing to the lower mezzanine. Because of these three stops, the elevator is almost always full of riders transferring when it reaches the ground floor every 2 to 3 minutes. Very little space is left for people waiting. However, there does not seem to be any kind of priority system other than the "first come, first served" rule. As a result, people with strollers must stand in line with single people, some of them with a disability or elderly, and some apparently perfectly able. When the elevator doors open, there usually is not enough space for a stroller, especially if a single person enters first. As a result, strollers end up passing up their turn, time after time, until the rare occasion when the adult with the stroller gets on, even if the elevator is not going in the right direction. Consequently, the adult and the stroller are still on when the elevator stops again at the ground floor, leaving no room for an additional passenger. Usually, most people with a stroller give up after one, two, or three fruitless passages of the elevator. And regular users do not even try but go to the stairs where, fortunately, they usually receive an offer of help from another rider.

The examples abound of what SCAs could have been directed to do by dedicated higher MTA officials. Unfortunately, in Jackson Heights, they were confined to the zone of the station near the MVMs, outside the turn-stiles; they were thus not able to provide needed services elsewhere in the busy station. As a result, SCAs felt that their job was dispensable, aimed primarily at mitigating the effects of the transition to a new technology that would not include them. In essence, they were driven to accept their own growing inadequacy in the subway environment, a trend exactly the re-verse of that of street vendors who cater to individual needs (with little concern, as we have seen, for the overall subway environment).

Despite the potential of the new SCA position to provide the New York City subway stations with a host, the program remained mainly a transi-tional measure to cut more service jobs. Then in 2010, the SCA program was terminated, and the booths were permanently removed. With the crime rate at a low in the subway and city overall, the question of security had subsided, and the MTA was able to quietly terminate station personnel. On the lower mezzanine, high entry and exit turnstiles (HEETs) prevent fare beating with revolving doors that look like prison gates. An emergency tele-phone set on a wall took over the task of providing safety. Unfortunately, as a soon-to-be-phased-out SCA pointed to us, at 3:00 P.M., when the ven-tilation kicked in, the noise was simply too deafening for the phone to be of any use. The race to rely on inefficient security technology rather than human presence, denounced by Harvey Molotch and Noah McClain, goes on unabated.[25] Riders are mostly left to themselves to deal with any challenging situation. Apart from the overworked booth clerk, the station has no effective host.

Predatory Hosts: Distinction That Discriminates

Along with vendors, MTA workers, and riders, the 74th Street station is populated by a range of semimobile surrogate hosts: the police, Jehovah's Witnesses, Scientologists, army recruiters, International Socialist activists, musicians, and other performers. To varying degrees, and for selected members of the riding public, they act as hosts inside the station in the same way as the vendors on the sidewalk do. In this largely immigrant area of Queens, riders are usually wary of both the police and proselytizers of all sorts, as they are somehow thought to be preying on the riders. But they also offer a modicum of order welcome to at least a fraction of the population.

The Police: Targeting Minority Males

New York police officers from the 110th or the 115th precinct or the Transit Bureau of the New York Police Department (NYPD) patrol the station on an almost permanent basis, usually in teams of two. But the station is vast, and they cannot be present everywhere at all times. This is why they usually station themselves in a strategic location, the landing of the staircase to the upper mezzanine, which grants them a panoramic view of the main hall. From this post, they regularly take walks around the station, usually going down the escalator at 73rd Street to the lower mezzanine and platforms and then back up the main staircase to their post. Their principal activity there is to watch the gates and make sure that nobody jumps the turnstiles or walks through the open gate without paying the fare. They also watch for illegal use of discounted fares. Student, senior, and disabled MetroCards cause the turnstiles to flash colored lights different from the normal ones. When the student light flashes on an off-day or if a young person uses a senior card, an officer tickets the rider. If he feels more tolerant, the officer sends the offender back behind the gate to pay the full fare. There are innumerable ambiguous situations and mistakes that frustrate officers and customers alike. One of our student informants was issued a ticket when, as a high school student who was taking an advanced college class at LaGuardia Community College, she tried to use her student pass on a day when the city's high schools were closed. The police simply did not believe her. Another of our students who goes to his job as a mariachi musician, in full regalia with his instrument in hand, was stopped and forced to pay the full fare, even though he was indeed returning directly from school.

Other riders, mostly male, to whom we spoke were simply afraid of random police stops, questions, and being frisked. This fear was confirmed in a study by Brett Stoudt, a colleague at the CUNY Graduate Center (personal communication) and his colleagues, which shows that most such stops occur at and immediately around subway stations, confirming the uncertainty of order in these locations. Moreover, their work showed that along the 7 train, as well as in the city overall, more than 90 percent of the stops never lead to any arrest or even a summons.[26] The data collected by the neighborhood precincts in the 74th Street station confirm this tendency. From 2008 to 2009, the NYPD reported an average of 350 stops per year. They affected mostly men (93%), and 95 percent of the cases resulted in neither an arrest nor a summons. However, 17 percent of the people stopped were subjected to the use of physical force. These numbers reproduce in the subway environment the fraught relationships that many immigrant and poor communities experience with the police in their neighborhoods.

Perhaps even more worrisome is the unreported activity of the Transit Bureau officers. This division of the NYPD, previously the Transit Police, is charged with enforcing the rules and code of conduct of the New York City subway. Since the 1990s, when the chief of the Transit Police, William Bratton, initiated the "zero tolerance" policy,[27] the Transit Bureau has been proactively stopping would-be criminals by focusing on minor offenses, such as fare evasion, unlicensed vending, soliciting, and walking between subway cars. In 2014, with Bratton once again New York City's police commissioner, reporters at the *Daily News* discovered that summonses usually issued for fare beating had been increasingly changed into arrests.[28] In an article based on data from the New York State Division of Criminal Justice, the reporters found that fare evasion was the second cause of jail sentences in the city, after possession of controlled substances. They also found that black and Hispanic men made up the vast majority of people sentenced to jail time after an arrest for fare evasion. In many cases, jail time may be due more to a low-level outstanding warrant from previous encounters with the criminal justice system than to the "theft of service" constituted by the jump over the turnstile.[29] Indeed, more than half the cases are dismissed, reflecting the absence of serious justification for arrest in the first place. Although the police officers also arrested a small number of people for "sexual abuse" (groping), "lewdness" (exhibitionism), and stealing from other riders during these years, the data suggest that a larger proportion of their own measured activity contributes to resentment and insecurity rather than feelings of being protected and hosted by officers in and around the station.

Selling Religion, Politics, and More: Targeting the Vulnerable

Those who wish to "work the crowd" find a rather ideal space in the lower mezzanine of the 74th Street station. It occupies a wide swath of the station's underground footprint. Not yet a successful retail area, it features a Bank of America ATM and a few stores, some usually vacant, as noted earlier. It is well lit but gray and intentionally not equipped for anything but quick passages to the stairways leading to the trains. From its landings, the crowds descend to either the Manhattan-bound trains or the east-bound trains to outer Queens. The E train brings people from lower and midtown Manhattan who are on their way to the Sutphin Boulevard station in Jamaica and the AirTrain to Kennedy International Airport. People going to either LaGuardia or Kennedy circulate through the station and the mezzanine. Crowds slow and often form a line attractive to panhandlers at the long escalator in mid-mezzanine. Another escalator, most popular when that one is broken, as it very often is, requires a walk of about a half an underground block to the western end of the station.

In sum, the mezzanine offers flows of people going in enough different directions—with ample space to work the edges—that it also attracts a representative diversity of those who would seek your glance, hold you for just a moment of your time (or even more if you only knew what was good for you). The Jehovah's Witnesses appear regularly, usually two or three at a time, sometimes with a full display set up as in many New York stations, especially during rush hour. Andean folk musicians and a variety of other performers enliven the space, mostly during peak hours as well. Panhandlers usually stand where the crowd slows. Uniformed military recruiters are a discreet but visible presence quite regularly. Other proselytizers, like the Scientologists and the Larouchites, appear with less regularity but always behind a table with literature to offer. Political groups with newspapers, and often a table with literature, appear less regularly but in a year will have come enough times to say "now and then."

Passengers and station MTA officials often become annoyed with some of those who work the station's crowds. In the early 2000s, the station manager cooperated with the police to remove the Church of Scientology from the station. The Scientologists had set their table and their stress tester on the lower mezzanine. Although the law permits the diffusion of religious opinions and the distribution of free promotional materials, it does not permit sales. The police were able to prove, with a person posing as an interested passerby, that a book, supposedly free, was in fact sold for a set price ($8) and was not given in exchange for a possible donation. Consequently, they expelled the group from the 74th Street station and other stations in the system, including Times Square at the end of the 7 line in Manhattan. But the Church of Scientology is a notoriously powerful organization and was able to challenge the eviction. Its argument in court and the newspapers was that it provided a welcome relief in a stressed-out environment.[30]

In 2006 and 2007, the International Socialists also set up a table on the lower mezzanine, every Monday and Tuesday from 7:00 to 8:00 P.M. François, a chemistry student at Queens College, explained that they were harassed by the police officers who were giving them tickets for obstructing the passage (but not for selling literature). The situation improved once they received an e-mail authorization from the MTA under the umbrella of free speech, but relations were still tense. The International Socialists did not linger long. Their main target populations were immigrants, especially undocumented, whom they wanted to warn against enrolling in the army.

Relations with the different groups and the local managers often become conflicted when the contact with the public becomes more active and the groups directly address prospective clients. This is also often the cause of incidents of conflict with individual subway riders. Vasco, a Mexican student recounted how a Jehovah's Witness once singled him out:

> One day, one of them tried to give me a pamphlet by force, so I told him, this guy was Ecuadorian, and I was very tired, coming from school, and they always try to give you the pamphlet and if you don't grab it, they get mad at you. That time, they were trying to give me the pamphlet. As I am Catholic, I told him, "OK, I grab the thing, but next Sunday you go with me to mass." He said no, because he believes in his own god. So I told him: "And I believe in mine, see you later!" and he got mad.

Juan, a Mexican student, spoke of how tired he was of people telling him day after day that he is "going to hell" and of army recruiters trying to lure him. Hélène, a student from Haiti, had to find the strength to resist the religious admonitions proffered by proselytizers:

> I took a newspaper from the *AMNY* guy, something that I don't always do and walk down to the train station. As I swipe my card to go down on the platform, a Jehovah lady hands me a paper. I felt bad for her so I decided to take it. I took it and was scared to throw it away because I don't want to be the one who sends the word of the lord in the garbage. So I just put it inside my bag and went to school with it. I still have it in my bag. When I was about to take the escalator, there was another Jehovah lady trying to give another

paper. I am sorry, but this time I put my head straight and I didn't take anything from her hand.

June 23, 2006

Even hardened veteran subway riders well used to avoiding eye contact with all the crowd workers can at times feel some hostility toward even the most pleasant among them. As riders hurry toward the platform, lost within their mental surround, or *Umwelt*, they may resent the purposive intrusions of even the most well meaning whose imploring glances they have to ignore. And they may feel particular resentment of the daily reminders from those who wish to adjust their moral or spiritual compasses. Only the musicians and performers in the station are likely to lift their spirits and gain their momentary attention. The lower mezzanine is an official spot for the Music Under New York (MUNY) program. South American bands often play there for a couple of hours each day and provide entertainment enjoyed by a significant fraction of the population.[31] A dancer of unusually short stature who often uses the space to tango with a puppet to the sound of a speaker also attracts the attention of intrigued riders.

After 2008, some of the concessions in the stations were finally rented to a variety of stores, a flower shop (lovely but not profitable), a music shop, and no doubt others as this is being written. Their presence may eventually further enliven the mezzanine space and offer particular services to individual riders, just as the vendors at street level do.

A Meeting Ground: Individuals Among Traffic

Despite being the preferred location of police and proselytizers, the station is regularly used by young immigrants as a meeting place. Teenagers waiting for their friends and parents waiting for their children regularly occupy the ground floor area immediately behind the turnstile (despite the lack of sitting spaces), as well as the benches on the lower and upper mezzanine. These spaces in the station let them wait without having to pay an extra fare before moving on to their final destination. This possibility is partly due to the commitment to universalism by the MTA workers, who will not single people out unless they impede traffic.

Logically, the same areas serve also as parting grounds, where friends spend a moment before going their own separate ways. This is common after school around 4:00 P.M., but also later at night when groups of young adults and teenagers come back from the movie theater or another event. In these cases, the police may even act as a benevolent host, as Margarita recalls:

> We used to play hide and seek. It was eleven at night and we were coming from watching movies in 31st Street, with a group of thirty people. It was a Friday or a Saturday, I don't remember. It [the station] was actually empty and we would make the person count on the other side, where the escalator goes up and he or she would come to find us. . . . Some of them went upstairs. But then the police came and this guy, the policeman, started playing with us and they would use their radio and he would say, "He's here, she's there . . ." . . . The policeman was Hispanic, or something like that. I never saw him again.

For these young riders, as we will see in a subsequent chapter, the subway is an environment free from the surveillance of home, school, and even the neighborhood, where they can experiment with an anonymous copresence within the protective bubble of group sociability. Even more so than the train, the station provides space to chat, sit, talk, run, and play in public.

The Station's Emerging "Fend for Yourself" Cosmopolitanism

In his careful observations of interracial and interethnic social life in American cities, Elijah Anderson calls our attention to places where he finds a particularly strong "cosmopolitan canopy."[32] By this he means that the interactions among the people in these places tend to produce comity, a relatively relaxed and impromptu sociability that crosses the normal boundaries of age, gender, class, race, and ethnicity. These tend to be beloved urban places that people choose as destinations in the city. Not surprisingly, they tend to be places where there are good things to eat and drink. Philadelphia's Reading Terminal Market is Anderson's primary example, but he finds many other such places in our cities. The variations among places marked by this cosmopolitan canopy, and the conditions of their continued existence, become part of his broader sociological inquiry into the production of urban community. Although it displays many of the criteria of the cosmopolitan canopy, the 74th Street station would not quite qualify as such a destination.

At the station, there is inevitably a tension between mass behavior and the demand for individual services. It can be said to be a cosmopolitan environment in that people of all descriptions come en masse to the station. Its draw is not as a trip destination but as an institution designed to foster transit transitions for trips to other end-destinations. Perhaps there are good things to eat and drink, but the station's ambience hardly promotes relaxed sociability. Nor do we, the riders, or they, the MTA officials, expect that it should. Although for some, like teenagers with almost nowhere else to congregate, it does serve this purpose. The station is better characterized as a particular institution within the subway system's situational community of transit. Much of what happens there daily is either routine or unintended. Indeed, the occurrence of real accidents and unusual situations in the system brings people together at the station, often for far longer than they wish. We have seen that the station is also a local institution of the Jackson Heights community.

The vendors who congregate outside the station provide services to people arriving from the different Jackson Heights neighborhoods. Many of these services encourage sociability, especially as customers and vendors get to know each other over time. Some of the same service, however, creates problems inside the station that MTA workers have to clean up in one way or another. Again, we see the tension between the universalistic mass transit environment and the particularism of the neighborhoods extending into and out from the station. But the most important changes we have documented in this chapter may be the ways the changing transit technology and efforts to cut MTA budgets have resulted in what might be called a "fend for yourself" cosmopolitanism.

In the face of rather drastic MTA cuts in human services inside the station, subway riders are increasingly left to cope with problems and unusual occurrences themselves. Although the station has been well renovated, it has also become more automated. Machines—including MVMs, turnstiles with MetroCard readers, escalators, elevators, and announcement systems—all eliminate the need for labor and increase the speed and efficiency of service. But this is in theory, not necessarily in practice. In the face of their frustrations with the machines, riders increasingly must fend for themselves. Part of that fending requires that they help one another when they can, even if only to be able to move forward themselves. They help women with strollers down the stairs because there is no one to regulate traffic on the elevators (if they are working) or because the escalator is broken. They may help the elderly when they have difficulties with the card readers. The examples abound of an emerging cosmopolitanism in such assistance: the people who tend to do it are more sophisticated and competent subway users. They are often the ones to whom lost visitors to the city can turn, after a few tries perhaps, regarding directions inside the station or about which trains to take to the airports. Although the 74th Street station is a major transit hub for the city, there are no maps anywhere. Again, people are left to fend for themselves.

It is the more savvy subway rider who often comes to their aid and, in so doing, increases his or her sense of being a New York cosmopolitan with the relevant local knowledge. None of this is what we may wish for, but it does call our attention to the city's increasing reliance on the skills and competencies of its riders as they negotiate their way through the ever-changing subway environment.

5   Trust in the Subway

Exploring the Situational Community in Transit

The presence of urbanity, tolerance, civility, cosmopolitanism in oneself is linked to distance in the relationship between self and the relevant other or others. That is, the different other is tolerable, perhaps even worthy of appreciation only if, psychically or physically (that is, symbolically or spatially), he or she is sufficiently distant to pose no threat.

Lyn Lofland, *The Public Realm*

After the second tower fell on the morning of September 11, 2001, thousands of us began trying to get off Manhattan Island. People from out of town searched in vain for hotel rooms. The streets were filled with people wandering from one corner to the next, looking for a bus or a cop to speak to, or hoofing it toward the East River bridges. In midtown, there was yet no smoke or dust, but lower Manhattan no longer seemed to exist. Sirens were going off everywhere. Near the Empire State Building, squad cars with sirens blaring appeared and closed the block. I fell in with a stream of walkers from all the office buildings who were hurrying toward Penn Station and the subways.

At the subway and Port Authority Trans Hudson (PATH) train entrance at 34th Street, a crowd had gathered. Everyone was calm but visibly shaken. We exchanged facts and rumors. A uniformed representative of the Metropolitan Transportation Authority (MTA) appeared at the subway entrance to announce that no subway or PATH trains were running at this time. Although he was extremely professional, his face was ashen. A squadron of combat jets roared over the buildings above us. As we turned away, I saw that many people, myself included, were weeping.

At Penn Station, the crowd was huge, but miraculously the Long Island Rail Road was running trains to Jamaica and beyond. We held our breaths until the train came out of the East River tunnel into Queens.

Later in the afternoon on September 11, 2001, despite the chaos in lower Manhattan, the city's subway and mass transit system carried commuters off the island as it does every workday. Thousands rode safely across the rivers for their homes in the boroughs. Yet the destruction of the Chambers Street–World Trade Center station was a wound to the system from which it is still recovering. After the suicide bombings of September 11, the subways of other Western metropolises also became targets of terrorists. Devastating attacks on the Madrid and London subway systems in 2004 and 2005 pointed again to the insecurity of urbanites in the face of terrorists. Likewise, these wounded subway systems quickly recovered so that the circulation vital to metropolitan life could resume. Indeed, under normal conditions in New York, the subway runs with enough regularity—especially when viewed in its entirety—that we almost come to take it for granted, though we do so at our peril.

In 2012, when subway tunnels were flooded with seawater after Hurricane Sandy, New Yorkers were confronted with the new environmental realities of a coastal metropolis. Along with the possibility of terrorist attacks, they were forced to reckon with the vulnerabilities of the mass transit infrastructure in the Anthropocene, the era of global climate change, rising seas, and new demands on our technological infrastructures.

On December 27, 2012, New Yorkers were forced to deal with another shocking attack on their sense of security and their trust in one another underground. This deadly affront occurred within the subway itself. On a Thursday evening, on the platform of the 40th Street station in Queens, an unknown assailant pushed a forty-six-year-old immigrant from India, Sunando Sen, to his death under the 7 train as he was standing on the platform. His gruesome death made sensational news. A "random attack" by a mad person—in this case on a personal crusade against Muslims and Hindus, according to the police—is a crime that causes particular subway nightmares. We are painfully reminded how dependent we are on one another and on our shared understandings of the social order in the subway.[1]

There were forty-nine deaths in the New York subway system in 2014, only one of which was a "random" attack.[2] Nonetheless, every death in the underground results in frustrating delays, as do severe illnesses on the platforms or the cars. Veteran riders who have seen ill passengers cared for by the police and medical personnel shrug off these stoppages, knowing that they could be next. New Yorkers depend so fundamentally on the subway system that neither acts of terrorism nor a deranged attacker influences subway ridership once the system is restored and fully operating. Regular patrons are aware of the low probability of attack and can take precautions by standing farther from the edge of the platform.

Social order and trust among subway riders is so vital to what makes the system work that it deserves special attention. This subject has received some fortunate, if inadequate, attention in the research literature, and so we need to consider theories of order and trust in public space more generally. In this chapter, therefore, we explore the origins of trust underground with reference to past research and theory as well as our own observational data and the commentary in the subway's community of bloggers and online reporters. The voices of subway commentators on the Internet reveal much about the inaudible thoughts of thousands of riders who make up, at any given moment in the city, what we have termed "the situational community in transit." Our feelings as we ride in the subway cars or wait on the platforms, our ability to disregard the subway system entirely while we lose ourselves in thought or music, all are aspects of a special, if transitory, sense of community among subway riders.

But can something so fleeting as a gathering of riders in a subway car be thought of as a community? What could be the benefit of describing as a community what often seems to be an anonymous collection of commuters, tourists, shoppers in family groups, and subway sleepers? As soon as we begin to speak of the subway as having a social order and requiring interpersonal trust, we have begun to cite some of the necessary aspects of human communities. In earlier chapters, we showed that subway riders do prepare themselves in various mental and physical ways to enter a specific social environment of mass transit. In this chapter, we further explore the community in transit that emerges from the situations subway riders regularly encounter. We look for the formal and informal norms on which this transit community's social order depends. We examine the behaviors and ambiguities associated with the roles that subway riders perform in different environments of the subway system, as well as the riders' own accounts of their behaviors in different situations underground.

Communities are social environments in which we carry out significant life functions. Accordingly, commuting is a routine but significant time in our lives, during which we accomplish some very important purposes: transit, mobility, encounters, discovery of the city. Although the strangers whom we see everyday on the train can feel familiar as anonymous neighbors,[3] the situational community in transit is, almost paradoxically, based on a set of norms that usually insist on maintaining anonymity and civil inattention. But there are many exceptions to anonymity and many mishaps in the unfolding of civil inattention, all indicative of varying degrees of individual experience and competence in this underground community.

We have learned from the careful observation of riders' behavior on the 7 train that the smooth functioning of the system depends on their skills acquired over years of daily commuting. In earlier chapters, we saw two specific competences that subway riders put into practice when walking to the subway: context reading and code switching. In this chapter, as we explore the norms underlying the social order of the subway, its dos and don'ts and the skills they require, we signal the importance of a third subway competence: the ability to read or interpret situations that arise underground and to give accounts of them to ourselves and others. This and the other rider competences and role performances we examine all contribute to the building of trust in the subway's community of transit.

For some observers of urban life, the subway environment would seem to represent the impersonal urban world of anonymous relations controlled and supervised by a technical machine and a bureaucratic administration. But the official rules of rider conduct established by the MTA, and its ability to enforce them, are limited. Much depends on the behavior of riders in the different situations that may occur during their transits.

Rules and the Establishment of Trust

An advanced urbanized society demands that its members increasingly entrust their bodies to highly technological systems that may appear quite abstract and remote from our sphere of competence.[4] The subways of any large city—along with the nuclear industry, modern medicine, the computer industry, and virtual networks—are complex systems that require very specialized and advanced expertise. Users are mostly left in the dark as to the workings of these systems and thus must place a great deal of trust in the hands of specialists. As a veteran New York City subway engineer told us, maintaining the subway system was "like a doctor operating on a patient while he is busy at his workplace."

Inured to frequent delays and schedule changes, veteran riders may know a lot about the likely consequences of underground events that cause delays or service changes, but they also recognize the limits of their knowledge.[5] For newer riders—more recent arrivals to the city, out-of-town visitors, tourists, or infrequent subway travelers in general—trust in the trains and in other passengers may be more tenuous. The blunders of less experienced riders and the evidence of anxiety or fear they often exhibit is quite easy to detect and calls attention to the many "taken-for-granted" aspects of daily life underground.

According to Anthony Giddens, our trust in modern technological systems is often built and maintained via a series of "access points" at which experts come into contact with users. Experts usually hide the back stage of their workplace and construct a front stage without defects and contradictions. In the front stage, this encounter can take place, offering a decor, costumes, and an overall performance that conform to the reliability that users seek. Doctors' offices, professional conventions, and press conferences are the most common examples of this staging of trust.

Unfortunately, in the subway, these "access points" have always been problematic, as we saw in chapter 4 on the 74th Street/Roosevelt Avenue subway station and as anyone who ever bent down to ask a question through the hole in the old token booth windows knows. Ridership continues to mount, and passengers regularly experience delays and congestion. Clerks usually are busy when one needs reassurance, and then one also realizes that the police are absent.

An outstanding characteristic of the subway is that riders are crammed together in a closed environment with limited options for escape (much like a boat or an elevator but with many more people). In a serious emergency, escape will not be possible without genuine collective effort. Under these conditions, it is essential not only that riders trust the technological system of the subway but also that they trust one another to maintain order and adhere to the tacit and explicit norms of life underground, and, above all, that they keep moving whenever possible.

The "rules" that subway riders follow do exist, although they are ambiguous under some conditions and subject to much improvising under others. Nor are the unwritten rules of getting and going along shared equally among riders so as to be fully effective. In addition to a well-tried set of informal norms that specify how riders should behave toward one another, there is an underlying social-spatial order of the subway that is automatically generated in that it arises out of the specific social, material, and physical conditions of the subway as a means of mass mobility and an interconnected network of public spaces. The underlying social order of the subway can be best described as a "working consensus,"[6] in order to emphasize the common need to move through its spaces without undue delay and thus to assume that everybody will behave accordingly. It basically means taking the social order for granted and trusting it, just as riders take the trains and the tracks for granted. Such implicit trust often requires that we behave as self-enclosed person-vehicles rather than as outgoing personalities with bodies. The nuances and implications of these observations will become clearer when we consider the contributions and limitations of the subway's formal order as codified in the MTA's rules and regulations.

Institutional Order: The Gray Areas
of Subway Official Rules

"There are thousands of rules, but nobody to enforce them anymore," observed a retired transit officer.[7]

The managers of the MTA and the New York City Transit Authority (NYCTA) are certainly aware (as are most mass transit organizations in cities around the world) of the challenges caused by collective behavior in the subway. Indeed, since the subway's inception, they have been trying to influence riders' actions through both coercive and persuasive measures. Injunctions like "Stand clear of the closing doors!" or "Let them off! Let them off!" repeated at every stop by train conductors, or instructions like "If you see something, say something!" attempt to shape riders' behavior so as to prevent accidents and crime, smooth out the flow of traffic, and save money. A subway employee told us,

> If riders could be disciplined enough to save 30 seconds while getting on and getting off at each station, we could save enough time to remove one train per line without reducing the headways [time between two trains]. This represents a potential savings of $20 million.

At some stations, yellow lines have been painted on the platforms indicating where the doors open and how passengers waiting to board should stand to the side. We know of no evaluations so far by the MTA of this experiment.

The NYCTA official "rules of conduct" are publicly available on the Internet,[8] but they are not posted prominently throughout the system. The rules are nine pages long and are written in a legal style more opaque than informative for riders. So it is up to the Transit Bureau police and NYCTA subway staff to enforce the regulations, whether or not riders are aware of them. In fact, a number of them, like the rule about not leaning on doors, are routinely broken without consequence, whereas others, such as paying the fare, are quite strictly enforced at the turnstile by the police and the NYCTA workers and can incur heavy penalties.[9]

To examine the limitations and ambiguities of the subway's official rules is not to deny how important they are. The official, written, rules of subway conduct—against smoking, spitting, or playing the radio out loud, for example—are largely obeyed. Rules against interfering with the train's operation, to cite another category of subway rules, may seem obvious, but they have to be made clear at all times, given the possible consequences (for example, of pushing an emergency button). Even so, the MTA's written rules inevitably contain strictures that cannot be well enforced, often because they are subject to so many different interpretations.

Which written rules are most often broken? We do not have systematic data on rule infractions, other than our own years of subway observations, but clearly the rules with regard to commercial activity are among the most selectively enforced.

Section 1050.6(b) stipulates:

No person, unless duly authorized by the Authority, shall engage in any commercial activity upon any facility or conveyance. Commercial activities include (1) the advertising, display, sale, lease, offer for sale or lease, or distribution of food, goods, services or entertainment (including the free distribution of promotional goods or materials); and (2) the solicitation of money or payment for food, goods, services or entertainment. No person shall panhandle or beg upon any facility or conveyance.

Occasionally, police in the main stations like Times Square attempt to remove peddlers of various sorts on the basis that they are conducting a commercial activity (see the case of Scientology in chapter 4). On the trains, however, vendors and performers of all kinds are working, unopposed by the task force. Why? There is no question that the rules are far wider in scope and ambition than are the abilities of those charged with their enforcement, especially rules pertaining to what riders bring and leave on the trains.

Section 1050.6(f) stipulates:

> No person shall bring or carry onto a conveyance any liquid in an open container.

This rule must be among those most broken in the entire system. How many New Yorkers sip coffee on the morning subway? How many cans of soda or bottles of Snapple are found rolling with the swerving of the train, ignored by riders except for an aimless kick this way or that?

Section 1050.7(c, e, and j) also specifies that passengers must not

> sleep or doze where such activity may be hazardous to such person or to others or may interfere with the operation of the Authority's transit system or the comfort of its passengers;

> create any sound through the use of any sound production device, except as specifically authorized by 1050.6(c) of these rules. Use of radios and other devices listened to solely by headphones or earphones and inaudible to others is permitted;

> (1) occupy more than one seat on a station, platform or conveyance when to do so would interfere or tend to interfere with the operation of the Authority's transit system or the comfort of other passengers; (2) place his or her foot on a seat on a station, platform or conveyance; (3) lie on the floor, platform, stairway, landing or conveyance; or (4) block free movement on a station, stairway, platform or conveyance[.]

Even though these rules are routinely broken, they are staunchly defended by MTA officials, as they must be. Some of them have become part of the conductors' onboard announcements, as well as the endless rants and blogs from journalists and riders about "subway incivility," which echo the formal MTA rules. But many of the rules are ambiguous in their wording and leave their interpretation to the enforcers' discretion and zeal. At one point, for example, is one obstructing passage? How does one know if the sound leaking from an earphone really is inaudible? How can a listener wearing earphones know whether the music is audible when it is intended to cover the ambient noise of the train? The same questions arise with sleeping, placing a foot on the facing seat—a newly added rule[10]—spreading legs, or "manspreading" (for more about this, see chapter 6, on gender relations) . . . When does it really "interfere with the comfort of other passengers"? Who is to decide? "Try figuring that one out without interviewing the rest of the train or bus" explains a writer in a *New York Times* column:

> Not that any of these bans seem to be taken seriously. Right now, on the 9 train, I count exactly 10 seats obstructed by bags and books as well as the splayed limbs of men sitting cross-legged or wide-legged, while there are more than 20 people who could presumably use them. Oh, yes, and here come, from opposite directions, a Vietnam vet asking for money and a woman selling batteries. All the doors, meanwhile, are being leaned on, so you can't see a single 'Don't lean on the doors' sign.[11]

Many of these rules obviously demand the active consent and participation of subway riders themselves. Two examples of new rules recently proposed by the NYCTA, one successfully and the other unsuccessfully, are good examples of the ambiguity and enforcement difficulties the subway's formal order often exhibits.

Movement Between Cars

Section 1050.9(d) details the constraints regarding the riders' movements between cars:

> No person may ride on the roof, platform between subway cars or on any other area outside any subway car or bus or other conveyance operated by the Authority. No person may use the end doors of a subway car to pass from one subway car to another except in an emergency or when directed to do so by an Authority conductor or a New York City police officer.

Despite an unclear motive, this rule was introduced in 2004 without resistance from riders' groups. In informal talks with MTA workers, we learned that it was an attempt to crack down on the presence of dangerous criminals and would-be offenders. According to the NYCTA, out of the 3,600 people arrested for riding between cars in 2006 (up from 700 in 2005), 126 had outstanding warrants, 4 were carrying loaded guns, and 45 were carrying illegal knives, including switchblades.[12] Clearly, people arrested for riding between cars (or for jumping the turnstile [see chapter 4]) are part of a preemptive strategy, based on the broken-window theory and zero-tolerance policy introduced in New York in the 1990s and again in the 2000s. We might also view this measure as an attempt to make mobile vending and performances more difficult, a rule that, as we have seen, is not enforced in the cars. In the past, teenagers have taken to standing between the train cars and playing in what is a dangerous moving space, but at other times it was helpful for passengers to be able to move between cars in search of more space or to avoid unwanted interaction. This suggests that some rules promulgated by the institution are designed to address demands that are not easily compatible with the actual social and spatial organization of the train. Although this rule is now generally obeyed on the trains, it remains confusing to many passengers.

The Photo Ban: "A Gray Area"

Rule 1050.9(c) of the state code says:

> Photography, filming or video recording in any facility or conveyance is permitted except that ancillary equipment such as lights, reflectors or tripods may not be used.

For years, the MTA has tried intermittently to ban photography throughout the system.

The MTA and the city's efforts to ban photography by individuals without formal permits was opposed by a wide coalition, ranging from journalists and subway buffs to civil rights advocates.[13] The MTA argues that its proposed ban is designed to prevent terrorists from gathering sensitive data on the subway's vulnerable infrastructure. Indeed, September 11, 2001, in New York, the Madrid train bombing of 2004, and the London subway bombing of 2005 made subway administrators everywhere look again at their rule books. In any event, this ban immediately raised the ire of civil libertarians, and it also violated a long-standing tradition of documentary photography on and in the subway.[14] Mutual visibility, we will see, which photography illustrates, is a defining, organizing principle of the social order of the subway, and weakening it may in fact raise, rather than lower, the riders' perception of vulnerability.

Photographers and curators argue that their photographs of the subway serve to document a certain state of the city at a given time. For example, Walker Evans's famous pictures of subway riders during the Great Depression[15] and Bruce Davidson's series of transit photographs in the early 1980s testify to the ways New Yorkers and the city coped with difficult economic times, according to Sewell Chan:

> "It's just a place where you see humanity exposed, in a way that doesn't often present itself. It is a special situation within New York, a leveling out of people socially, on the subway. It's almost a playground for photographers," says Bob Shamis, curator of prints and photographs at the Museum of the City of New York.[16]

The curator also added: "People let their guard down, in terms of how they are seen on the subway, their demeanor and their stance."

Photographers' most common explanation of their work is their exceptional proximity to the exposed and diverse masses of workers that make up New York City. Suddenly, pure actuality becomes visible. Not only are people stuck together in close proximity, but they also seem to display an abandonment that colors pictures with an air of authenticity elsewhere protected by hard layers of reserve. Travis Ruse, cited in 2005 for producing the "best photoblog of the year" by a coalition of professionals, assembled an astonishing collection of portraits of commuters.[17] Unlike Walker Evans, he did not hide his camera but simply clicked away at riders, who did not seem to mind. "I felt by photographing not just the subway, but specifically during the commuter hours, I could relay a picture of the working masses of New York City," he told a reporter.[18]

That the keen observer finds an exposed authentic self in what otherwise is among the most public and exposed places in the city is another paradox of the subway that we explore further here. In any case, even though the attempt to ban photography failed, photographers often are stopped by Transit Bureau police officers who pretend—which is against the law—that it is prohibited. The following personal episode at the 74th Street/Roosevelt Avenue station is typical:

I [Stéphane] am taking pictures from the upper level when I notice that two uniformed policemen, who were standing at the top of the first landing, watching the turnstiles, have disappeared. I immediately have the feeling that they are coming after me. Five seconds later, they emerge on the balcony and head straight to me. I have had the time to put my camera away in my bag. One officer is a white woman, short, middle aged. Her black hair is pulled back in a ponytail. The other is a tall African American man in his thirties.

They approach and tell me that I am not supposed to take pictures in the subway. I reply a little testily, but with a smile, that I believe it is authorized. The male officer says it is not. He asks me if I have an authorization. I answer that I don't because I do not use a tripod. The lady is a little tenser than the man and she asks if I have an ID with me. She steps back, waving for me to stay where I am. For a couple of minutes, they look at my card and roll through their papers. "What do you do?" they finally ask. "I am a professor at the CUNY College of Staten Island and I study the subway." The man shows me a paper in his thick notebook of rules. It lists suspicious activities. He points at one item: "Unauthorized picture taking or filming of MTA property." He tells me that it carries a $20 ticket. When I see that, I decide not to contradict them. I say that I didn't know, that the NYCTA people that I work with told me it was OK. The man explains that it is because of terrorism, sort of apologizing. I apologize, too, which seems to calm the woman who accepts my excuses with a "it's OK, but next time . . ." After they are gone, I wonder how the book of rules they are carrying can contradict the public rules posted by the MTA. Later that day, I ask the 7 train line manager if it is forbidden to take pictures. He tells me that it isn't. I tell him about what happened and he says: "It's a gray zone."

Journal excerpt, 74th Street/Roosevelt Avenue, August 5, 2008, 4:30 P.M.
on the upper mezzanine above the main space of the station

In this case, the MTA agrees that taking photos in the subway is generally not illegal but that under suspicious circumstances, it can be prohibited and punished. Gray areas in the enforcement of laws that seek to regulate human behavior in public are hardly limited to the subway. The judgment of suspicion, as we know from such modern classics as Michael Lipsky's *Street-Level Bureaucracy*,[19] is subject to ambiguity, discretion, social profiling, and simple differences in how agents understand and play their occupational roles (to say nothing of racism, boredom, or indigestion). But the uncertainty over subway photographers is not merely the result of bureaucratic discretion. Actual conflicts of value are at play among riders, which make it difficult to know whose rights are to be protected and whose slighted. The act of taking photos on the subway itself may be regarded by others as an invasion of privacy, even if the subway is generally understood as a public place. In all public places, strangers taking photos are regarded differently by individuals and groups. Much depends on the specific circumstances of the riders and the enforcing agent.

To make the constabulary duties even more complicated, conflicting aims within the MTA produce ambiguities of their own. For example, new rules about the consumption of food and drink are continuously proposed as additions to the existing regulations. To cut down on track litter, rats, and fires, the MTA is experimenting with bans on carrying food onto platforms or in cars, all the while issuing concession licenses to food vendors at every station. These contradictions create their own enforcement ambiguities and, for passengers, an entanglement of rules that creates even more ambiguity as to what is actually allowed or forbidden on the trains. So while they form an essential moral structure for the subway system, the official rules are not what New Yorkers refer to when they speak about "subway rules."

The Common Sense "Code of the Subway": Muddled and Contradictory

As the *New York Times* Forum tells us, "You Know You're a New Yorker When . . . you're standing nose-to-nose with someone on the subway & yet you're not looking at each other" (2012). All the high school students with whom we worked agreed that "no staring" is one of the cardinal but unwritten rules of subway comportment. But their diaries are full of examples in which staring and eye games are the most exciting, threatening, or romantic experiences of their daily subway ride. Both the informal rules and the art and games of their transgression become part of the subway's quotidian culture. As we outline the basic "code of the subway" as an idealtypical normative culture, we will also consider the frequency and subtlety of deviance from the same code. Moreover, accounts of the subway's normative culture from veteran riders and the extensive subway diaries of our students yield only a fuzzy notion of these unwritten rules.

Fortunately, there is considerably more scientific literature on "behavior in public places," especially in the indispensable generalizations of psychologists and sociologists of the micro-order of interaction.[20] Their work can help us go beyond the folk sociology of regular subway travelers. We apply the findings from studies of public space to our observations of subway behavior in order to identify what seem to be the underlying principles of the subway's social order as it is produced through the interactions of riders and subway personnel.

Riders as " Vehicular Units": The Social-Ethological Perspective

Concerned with the apparent disaffection for the subway among New Yorkers in the late 1960s and throughout the 1970s, social scientists in New York and a few other subway cities sought causes in the subway experience itself (for a historical overview of ridership trends, see chapter 8). Was crowding, for example, a possible cause of declining ridership? Much of this research followed an ethological research model in which behavior is closely observed under different conditions but motives and emotions are not directly measured. Matthew Fried and Victor DeFazio, in one of the outstanding studies of the era, showed that as crowding increases and personal space becomes limited, individuals are forced to give up the modicum of physical distance they once were able to preserve and to accept physical contact.[21] Fried and DeFazio's observations show, perhaps counterintuitively, that rather than looking for a seat, riders often look for a spot that allows them the most defendable territory, one that minimizes contact. This behavior demonstrates, according to the authors, natural human territoriality. In low- and medium-density situations, riders defend their territory through personal distancing. Thus the end seats of the long bench (they studied the IRT 9 and 7) are preferred, while the middle seats remain empty at middle-density level when a substantial number of riders are standing. More recent ethological work on congestion on the PATH train also confirmed this tendency.[22]

In the highest-density situations, when the last desperate riders are cramming themselves into an impossible human crevice at the doorway, there is no more space. When they are unable to preserve a physical distance, riders resort to withdrawing ("decathecting") parts of their body (arms, shoulders) to form a sort of body sheath. This led Fried and DeFazio to write that in high-density situations, riders shift from a physical territory to a psychological territory. The latter is controlled more through behavior than through physical distance. It requires nonverbal communication, an avoidance of eye contact, and specific body positions. Thus, faced with a lack of space, riders resort to those behaviors, especially the studious avoidance of eye contact, that produce mental distancing.

From the perspective that subway riders have an innate desire to protect their territories, crowding in the cars is understood as highly negative. Fried and DeFazio considered the constriction of passenger overload not only as negative and contrary to natural inclinations but also as increasing risks of situational perversity, such as unwanted sexual contacts. Unless something was done to ease subway crowding and protect riders' personal territory, they predicted, fewer New Yorkers would choose the subway as their main mode of commuting. They were mistaken.

Subway ridership in New York City, and especially on the 7 train, began to increase steadily in the 1990s, even though the train cars have not become any more amenable to distancing behaviors. Perhaps New Yorkers are simply ready to forgo the relative comfort of their personal space in favor of more calculated, practical objectives?

A study from the same period by environmental psychologists Gary Winkel and D. Geoffrey Hayward contradicts the ethological interpretation of people's territorial behavior and points in the direction of riders' decision making and the competences that come with experience.[23] In their study, "Some Major Causes of Congestion in Subway Stations," the authors show that subway riders have a clear tendency to produce crowding as they cluster around entrance points on subway platforms. This phenomenon causes congestion during rush hour, both on the platform and even more on the trains. "Why is it that people do not consciously alleviate congestion by walking to the rear of a bus, by walking to the farthest cars to look for a seat, or by moving along a subway platform away from the entrance?" the authors ask (and many riders wonder that, too).

Our own fieldwork confirms that most riders position themselves on the platform so as to minimize unnecessary walking by remaining close to the platform exit, or by "pre-walking," as subway reporter Randy Kennedy termed it:

> Pre-walking involves walking to the correct place on your departure platform so that when you get off the train at your destination platform you are at the correct place to zip right through the turnstile or exit you want, allowing you to avoid the crowd and to lead the charge back up into daylight. (In other words, no more trudging behind the living dead who take half an hour to climb a set of stairs.)[24]

As we explained earlier, morning commuters on the 7 train make bets on which train to wait for on the crowded platform at the Flushing–Main Street station. Clearly, personal optimization of the trip appears to be an important factor guiding riders' behaviors. Many riders prefer to get there quickly rather than to walk or wait, while others, less numerous, prefer to increase their personal space and comfort at the cost of a speedy ride. On the 7 train, this can result in extra walking to increase the odds of getting a seat. Knowing that the crowd forms something of a normal curve with proximity to the platform entrance and exit, one can walk to the very end of the platform to maximize the odds of obtaining a seat, an attractive subway bet for anyone with serious homework, for example. Often, however, there is no time to walk very far because riders always board the first available train.

The ethological stance remains separate from messy subjective explanations and riders' own accounts of their thinking. Such a stance also soon yields to a behaviorist, rational choice analysis of which values—especially time versus comfort—different riders wish to maximize. These and related studies do point to some important aspects of commuter behavior during rush hours. Yet their emphasis on the individual rider under changing physical conditions tends toward a view of riders as a mass of vehicular units moving through the system like autos on the interstate. Missing in the flow analysis are the innumerable interactions, however fleeting, among the different types of riders. These include those moving in groups, especially exuberant, if not irrational, groups of teenagers; families with children; a mother with a stroller and a toddler in her charge; people carrying large packages or small vending carts; as well as lovers or partygoers.

Momentary personal interactions continually break the ongoing flow of human vehicular units. At the doorways and turnstiles, one hears innumerable utterances like "Excuse me," or "Sorry," "Me desculpe," "Can I help you . . . ," "Lo siento mucho," as well as the occasional "Goddamit watch where the f—k you're going!"

A Situational Individualism: The Symbolic Interactionist Perspective

That the rate of cooperative gestures and utterances far outweighs that of adverse ones does not alter the fact that the hostile ones are those we remember longest. They stick in our craw as we think about city life and invite us to make invidious distinctions among different groups. Nonetheless, the orderly flow of so many individual lives is always impressive. It challenges social scientists to seek the set of underlying norms that would best describe the unspoken rules of a given social order. From the work of George Herbert Meade to that of Alfred Schutz, Erving Goffman, Howard Becker, Isaac Joseph, Lyn Lofland, and others associated with the symbolic interactionist perspective, we learn that social orders are forever being created and re-created through the interactions of society's members. They may be interacting in subways, classrooms, ships, or space stations; it does not matter. In every human milieu, we receive and respond to micro-cues in the form of glances, shrugs, and bodily gestures, as well as to utterances, overt gestures, and so much more that we read in one another's motions, dress, and overall presentation of self in a given social situation. These readings and responses construct the social order we experience at any given moment. In *The Public Realm*, her landmark analysis of how interaction creates the social order of urban public space,[25] Lyn Lofland summarizes the normative "principles" or unstated "shoulds" that urbanites obey, consciously or unconsciously, as they navigate the city streets and pedestrian areas:

1. *Cooperative mobility*.[26] Urbanites should navigate the streets of the city without bumping into one another. It contributes to an overall smoothness of urban flow that some equate to an "urban choreography." Go with the flow.

2. *Civil inattention*. Inattention guarantees everybody in public spaces a certain amount of protection against unwelcome attention. Mind your own business, but keep an eye out. Goffman explains:

One gives to another enough visual notice to demonstrate that one appreci-
ates that the other is present (and that one admits openly to having seen him),
while at the next moment withdrawing one's attention from him so as to express that he does not constitute a target of special curiosity or design.[27]

3. *Audience role prominence.* Inhabitants of the public realm should act
primarily as an audience to the activities that surround them. The small
child who starts to wander into the "show" being performed by teenage
break-dancers has not yet learned that our default mode in public space is
that of spectator. Hang back and watch; don't get in the act.

4. *Restrained helpfulness.* Specifically targeted and clearly limited requests
for mundane assistance should evoke a helpful response that does not engage
one beyond the immediate and local interaction. Be ready to help? Maybe.

5. *Civility toward diversity.* Persons in public spaces should practice
evenhandedness and universality in their treatment of others, but demonstrations of friendliness or fellow feeling toward strangers can be perceived
as inappropriate and should be avoided. Be fair, but not forward.

Does it matter that in daily practice, all these norms are constantly
ignored, flaunted, trimmed, or juggled by riders involved in endless situations of micro-morality? As with the formal rules established by the
MTA, the informal—that is, unwritten—norms of interaction in public
spaces identified by researchers in the symbolic interactionist tradition are
basic to the subway's social order. But in practice, such norms are also subject to many subtle interpretations and situationally selfish deviations.
Breaches of norms, however, often prove their overall importance to maintaining social order, if not their power. Consider even the most basic of
these norms—turn taking and cooperative mobility.

Cooperative Mobility: "First Come, First Served"

8:15 P.M. on the elevated subway platform at 74th and Roosevelt Avenue, in the
glow of the city's lights against the dark western sky, waiting for the east-
bound 7.

The platform is crowded with people who are making the change from
the IND trains to the 7 local. Some, like me, have only one or two stops to

go, while those who live beyond nearby Corona are more anxious to find seats or desirable standing room. They crowd the platform where they believe train doors will open for them. These human clumps along the platform expand in size as we wait for the next train.

The local arrives. The doors open. A fan-shaped crowd of twenty or more people from all over the world forms a ragged corridor to let people just like them exit. Before the last exiting passengers find their way to the subway doors, the ragged corridor on the platform has become more like a gauntlet. The human friction increases. Incoming passengers in first position near the open door push their way toward available seats or space. There are a few rude bumps and cross looks at this point, but there is no time for prolonged dispute. The larger platform crowd moves forward; passengers angle their bodies as they squeeze toward the open door. First come first served, measured in inches and angles and split seconds, is the prevailing rule.

Field notes, 2012

Cooperative mobility, as observed in this excerpt from our field notes, relies on basic turn taking and moving with the crowd. It is largely a taken-for-granted behavior essential to the many urban situations in which riders or pedestrians or drivers merge and converge. Much of urban life depends on the principle of turn taking, the practice of "first come, first served," and the shared desire to keep making forward progress. But in their desire for a bit of advantage, for a seat, a good place to stand, or a quick exit, to mention some familiar examples, riders constantly violate the informal rules, including that of first come, first served and cooperative mobility. Although many of these deviations are "close calls" or unintentional acts, some have major consequences for the entire system, particularly people who violate the norm of cooperative mobility by holding the subway car doors open and thus delay the train at the platforms.

Door Holding: A Very Frequent No-No

In 2009, the MTA developed an ad campaign to decrease the frequency of delays caused by riders holding doors open at the stations.[28] The MTA graphic (figure 5.1) and a *New York Times* article about the ad immediately prompted a blitz of online contributions to the *City Room* blog, to which this exchange is particularly relevant:

Gregory A. Butler: September 7, 2009, 8:19 P.M. The people who do the MTA's ad campaigns are obviously not from New York City. Holding the door is a tradition here—the MTA would be better off adapting their subway service to that tradition rather than trying to reeducate New Yorkers to not hold the doors—after all, this is NEW YORK, not Toronto or Duluth!

Edward: September 7, 2009, 9:19 P.M., #42. It was that kind of thinking that made NYC such a rat hole in the '70s and '80s. You get mugged at 1 A.M. in the East Village? What were you doing there at that time of night? Or if your car got stolen, you were advised that "it's New York, what do you expect, cars get stolen all the time?"

It's not asking a lot to expect people to be considerate of others, no matter what city they live in. Many of us have managed to ride the subway for years without holding a door open. And how exactly is the MTA supposed to assist NYers in holding the doors open? Provide crowbars with each MetroCard? Ugh, such nonsense![29]

From our own observations, it would appear the highest frequency of delays by holding open the subway doors is caused by groups of teenagers returning to their home neighborhoods from school. Since they often travel in groups, it is not uncommon for some of them to hold doors for friends who lag behind. But it also is true that door holding is a frequent and more annoying occurrence during rush hours, when it would seem to be an "equal opportunity infraction." Indeed, almost all of us seem to reserve the

Keep The Doors Clear So Others Can Board

Bottom line:
Blocking doors blocks traffic, and slows service for everyone. You get the picture.

Figure 5.1   Official Metropolitan Transportation Authority campaign poster in the trains, 2015.

occasion when for some reason of the moment, it seems absolutely impera-
tive to hold the door so that we can squeeze into the train or a family member
will not be left on the platform. In the aggregate, a consequence of these
self-serving rationalizations of what we all know are the informal (and in
this case formal) rules of ridership are the delays that cost the riders precious
time over a year of commuting and contribute significantly to frustration
with the system.

Civil Inattention: Alone Together

According to Janey Levine, Ann Vinson, and Deborah Wood,

> When seated [in subway cars], people usually assume inconspicuous behav-
> ior—sitting squarely, at first turning neither left nor right, and maintaining
> expressionless faces. People without books or papers . . . may begin to stare
> at fellow passengers, alternating fleeting or blank stares with an innocent
> staring off into space. These stares and glances at fellow passengers are quite
> restricted and concealed and are made so because they are not to be inter-
> preted as invitations to others to begin an encounter; they are the behavioral
> components of what Goffman has termed "civil inattention."[30]

For her evidential support, Lofland relied on this comprehensive and
rather rare empirical study of subway behavior from the 1970s in which the
researchers made many observations about the subway's social order, such
as the one earlier about civil inattention. Again, as for any informal social
norm, the instances of deviance are important behavioral aspects of the
norm's strengths and limitations. With the adoption of new technologies
for being present and yet having one's attention focused elsewhere, in some
instances—far too many for some riders—insistence on the norm of civil
attention becomes a form of self-assertion: "I have the right to blab on out
loud in a high voice on my cell phone about my personal business and you
are damn well supposed to pretend that you don't hear me."

Levine, Vinson, and Wood found that the vulnerability perceived by
riders produced a general avoidance marked by blank stares and a wide
range of auto-involvements. Contemporary riders increasingly reinforce
their appearance of unavailability. Those with earphones may be listening
to music or the radio, but they also are signaling their unavailability for

involvement. Those who seem to be absorbed in their smartphones or reading tablets are almost equally "hidden" behind their technologies. A distinct but still significant minority of riders read tabloid newspapers, local and foreign. (That older person leaning against the subway doors, his body obscuring the "Do Not Lean on the Doors" sign, may be folding his *Times* in New York style, but from the younger riders' perspective, he might as well be doing origami with a bed sheet.)

To some critics of city life, the practice of civil inattention in spaces of mass transportation transmits a feeling of loneliness. Riders work at being alone in the crowd. This "alone-together" paradox is a recurring themes for sociologists who write about the double effect of freedom and alienation in cities.[31] The subway thus often stands for the most anonymous public space one can find, a "stereotyped symbol of urban alienation."[32] Anyone who has experienced a lifetime of public transit use, however, will likely reject the notion of the subway masses as alienated monads, citing episodes of helpfulness and fellow feeling to counter the myth of urban alienation. In regard to the behavior of teenagers on the trains, analyzed in the following chapters, we will see that games of attention seeking and personal display break the boredom of daily trips back and forth to school. Breaches of civil inattention and games of glances make life on the subway far more interesting than it would be otherwise, although at times such breaches can also become stressful and challenging. Now that so many riders are visibly engaged "elsewhere," however—texting and tweeting to colleagues, loved ones, or would-be lovers—the outward appearance of the subway masses is even more that of intentional socializing at a distance rather than alienation.

How available or unavailable is the seemingly inattentive New York subway rider to social interaction and the needs of others? The most revealing social experiment to examine this question came from the edgy and always revealing research of Stanley Milgram, our late colleague at the Graduate Center of the City University. In the 1970s, he and his graduate students performed an experiment in subway norm breaching. The students, all relatively young and healthy, approached riders seated on the trains, chosen at random, and asked: "Excuse me, may I have your seat?"[33]

The results might seem counterintuitive to the stereotyped image of blasé, even gruff New Yorkers. But 68 percent of the riders approached gave up their seat, even though each sitting rider had presumably taken the seat on the first come, first served basis. In another experimental condition, when the demand was compromised by a weak explanation, such as when student experimenters gave a trivial justification ("I can't read my book standing up") or forewarned the seated riders (with the help of an overheard conversation, "Oh I wish I could sit down"), the results were much less positive (42% and 37%) but still significantly high. The Milgram experiment suggests that the norm—at least as it applies to seat retention—readily gives way to the norm of restrained helpfulness, if, that is, one makes a direct plea for help (and can get the seat occupant's attention).

Milgram's graduate students often reported experiencing high levels of stress both before and just after making their unusual requests for help from subway strangers. Although the norms may be frequently transgressed and exceptions made freely, their emotional weight is real and is not regarded lightly. Consequently, the norms of cooperative mobility, civil inattention, and spectator preference can contribute to what seems to be a social environment in which people are alienated from one another and reluctant to come to another's assistance unless prodded out of their personal spaces.

Audience Role Prominence: A Paradoxical Social Order

The empirical research we have reviewed does contribute to a perception that the subway is a public place where its users typically avoid attention and retreat into their own mental worlds. This interior turn can create a hyperindividuated, self-absorbed social environment. The same research, however, also suggests that the reality is far more complex. The norms of civil inattention and preference for the role of spectator help explain why responsibility for action is diffused and why, for example, riders infrequently step out of the audience to fetch the bottle rolling across the car floor or take personal responsibility for other collective annoyances in the subway system. Nevertheless, communication and altruism are not absent on the trains.

The possibility for altruism in the subway across the racial and ethnic backgrounds of riders was studied in a now-classic subway social experiment, "Good Samaritanism: An Underground Phenomenon?" by Irving Piliavin, Judith Rodin, and Jane Piliavin. They set up the following experimental "opportunity" for public altruism in the subway:

A "victim" collapses on the subway during a non-stop 7½-minute journey. The trains are not particularly crowded when the staged event occurs, between the hours of 11:00 A.M. and 3:00 P.M. on a weekday. Sometimes he is helped, either by another passenger who steps forward after a short while, or after a number of minutes by a man (known as the model) who is also part of the experiment. The "victim" is either a black man or a white man acting as if he is drunk in one condition, and as if he is sober, but unsteady on his feet, in another (he carries a black cane). Two female observers record what happens.[34]

The "victim" with a cane, regardless of his race, was helped more often and sooner than the drunk victim (sixty-two out of sixty-five trials for the cane victim, compared with nineteen out of thirty-eight trials for the drunk victim). Despite the differences in the time taken before help was offered, overall, subway riders were deemed "good Samaritans," contrary to the common reputation of New York subway passengers.[35]

None of these empirical studies or related journalistic accounts is entirely satisfactory. But they do describe a social order in which helping and staying back both occur, although with different probabilities. We learn from them that a given subway rider's behavior is extremely situational, subject to relative and only vaguely understood variables. The studies show that the situations best indicating that people will not retreat behind their own sense of vulnerability and threatened territory are those in which they feel they are visible to others, "on the spot," as well as how they actually interpret or categorize the situation.

The Subway Rider's Role Competences

New York subway riders can be good at repairing tears in the fabric of social order. An ability to interact with others in ways that conform to or reinstate the peaceful flow through the system is a competence that varies among all in the role of subway passenger. The mid-twentieth-century sociology of Robert Merton and others who developed and applied the language of role theory taught us to think critically about how we perform the roles we assume in society. Roles are sets of behaviors, orientations to action, skills, competences, and so on that we must learn as participants in a variety of social institutions, including, for urbanites, that of mass transportation. Some of the normative behaviors that Lofland and others described as crucial to the social order of urban public space, such as civil inattention, seem so natural that they almost appear as innate responses to strangers. But like all the other aspects of the rider's role, they are learned and, like most learned responses, are subject to individual variation.

To watch the socialization of civil inattention, for example, we need to observe mothers and infants on a crowded train car, as in this excerpt from our field notes:

> The car is not crowded as I enter and quickly find a seat next to a young mother and her infant. The mom is wearing earphones and engrossed in reading *Nowy dziennik*, the Polish *Daily News*. Seated in a folding stroller, the child appears to be about a year old, perhaps a bit more. She has blond curls, like her mother. She is alert and intently watching her mother and me from the stroller. When my glance meets that of the child, she cracks a broad smile and stares at me as if I were a familiar relative. I smile in return and, without thinking about it, wave my hand in a gesture of hello to the child. The mother catches my gesture from the corner of her eye, puts down the newspaper, and begins adjusting the stroller so that the child focuses attention only on her mother. I retreat into my own newspaper.
>
> March 19, 2012, 7 local at 74th Street/Roosevelt Avenue, Monday, 3:00 P.M.

By the time this child is three or four, she will have experienced many fleeting interactions with strangers and will be far more likely to turn away immediately from the stranger's glance. Seconds later, she may glance at the stranger again, very discreetly, practicing the skills of civil inattention. Of course, there will have been interactions like this one that turn out differently. The stranger might have been a friendly looking older woman, in which case the mother might have tolerated a more sustained interaction with her infant and even entered into a conversation about the child, her age, and her cute curls. The unspoken lesson for the child in that instance would have been that interaction with strangers is allowed in those cases when the attending adult is in full control of the situation.

Restrained Helpfulness: Accounts and Justifications

Being in control of the situation, as we understand it, is being aware of what we are doing, ready to justify or account for our behavior and feelings to ourselves (and at times to others). This is the third category of mass transit competence suggested by Isaac Joseph.[36] Accounts and justifications can be communicated in the form of shrugs, utterances, turns of the body and facial expressions,[37] or more complicated responses to requests for directions, assistance, and advice. The explanations we give ourselves for not behaving in various situations that arise are: "I thought he was not sick but drunk," "There were others who were closer to the situation and could see what was going on . . ." "She needed help carrying the stroller up the stairs and I had to jump in." Competent riders practice cooperative mobility by moving into the cars as far as they can to allow those behind to enter as well. They try to act in ways that confirm and reinstate the peace. And the skills they apply are the very same as those that symbolic interactionism considers as norms: cooperative mobility, civil inattention, restrained helpfulness, audience role prominence, and civility toward diversity. When we look at how riders play their roles based on their competences at utilizing the norms for their own benefit and that of the community in transit as a whole, we gain deeper insight into the very subtle work that so often animates the social order of the subway.

Cooperative Mobility as a Competence

An episode demonstrating the altruistic aspect of competence at cooperative mobility briefly became popular in 2012, when a video dubbed "Snack Man" went viral for the worldwide Internet audience.

> Charles Sonder, 24, said he boarded an uptown 6 train at Spring Street around 9 p.m. "Two or three Thursdays ago," heading from Home Sweet Home Bar on Chrystie Street to a bar in Midtown with his co-workers when a man and a woman began to kick and scream at each other. "That's when I stepped between them and just stood there," said Sonder, who was eating cheddar Pringles and a bag of Gummi bears at the time. "I didn't think of anything else to do." Sonder, a 6-foot-tall Rhode Island native [and former collegiate wrestling champion], said the fighters seemed to know each other. He continued to eat his snacks as if nothing was happening.[38]

Sonder, who lived in Fort Greene and had been in New York for two years, found out that a video posted on the Internet of the incident had gone viral when he received a text message Tuesday morning from his mother. "Hey,

Snackman," the shy superhero said she wrote. Indeed, the video had been seen by 550,000 people in a few days, and he had become "Snackman." "My Facebook was just blowing up this morning," he said.[39]

Snackman Sonder's special competence was demonstrated in the way he peacefully used his body to separate two potentially violent passengers involved in a domestic dispute. It helped that he was a former wrestler and that there were no weapons. More notable in this example is how the skills used to avoid trouble are shared among millions of subway riders who use them everyday to deal with uneasy situations of bodily copresence. The video illustrated a competent rider's special level of casual sangfroid, but it also affirmed what many New Yorkers already know: we are not interested in your dispute; we need to keep the peace to keep moving.

The competences we display in moving ahead on a first-turn basis show a remarkable indifference to the individual characteristics of class, race, or gender. Such neutrality is a reminder of the classical idea about cities that "Stadt Luft macht frei" (City air creates freedom). In "The Metropolis and Mental Life," Georg Simmel pointed out how revolutionary this freedom of passage in the streets was for the urban newcomer in earlier periods of urbanization.[40] But equality and fairness in circulation may also create their own forms of social structure in the community of transit, particularly in the lines and patterns of movement through crowds that develop and adjust in orderly ways. This is what the French urban sociologist Michèle Jolé, a colleague of Isaac Joseph, described as "the local construction of a social order, visible, foreseeable and understandable by all participants."[41] It can be physically constrained by spatial conditions, but it always reflects a normative organization. Participants use a principle of sparse economics to categorize people into a reduced number of the situation's contextual features, such as "head of the line" or "still exiting the car." These categories are usually not predetermined by the social traits of in individuals but instead describe the temporal order expressed in the line of an orderly crowd.

Forward motion is the first order of life on the subway, but even cooperative mobility, the seeming cardinal tenet of mass transit, is more a practical necessity than a rule. Bodily collisions are rather frequent, and human friction is common. If it is actually rude to bump into someone, it is also very unproductive as a way of getting places. Newcomers to the New York subway soon learn that a quick "excuse me" will most often diffuse ruffled feelings, especially since to stop and argue almost always draws the ire of other passengers, who must wait behind the disputants. Similarly, the elderly gentleman who hesitates in favor of others at the subway doors, in an instinctive but antiquated act of chivalry, will often be chided by those behind who are forced to wait an extra step or two.

Civil Inattention as a Competence: Scanning the Crowd

In practice, civil inattention actually involves a careful recognition of others. When a rider gets on a subway car, the first task to confirm trust is to perform a simultaneous double action: one is briefly to scan the car to assess the normality of appearances and locate a suitable seat or space, and the other is to present to the gathering the appearance of a normal regular rider. In this way, everybody in the car can assume that this newcomer is not going to disrupt the prevailing order. Much of the information available to evaluate the normality of the situation is located precisely in the unproblematic unfolding of the situation. We can thus see civil inattention as a skill used to maintain a social order that finds its strength in its constant reenactment. What exactly are normal appearances? What is a "regular" rider? Many assumptions load this expression, and they cannot become manifest except by asking every single individual in the train. Even then, the responses will probably be inconclusive. This is because, as Anthony Giddens explains, civil inattention requires a "polite estrangement." One does not want to know about the others. More generally, French scholars Louis Quéré and Dietrich Brezger refer to "standard appearances and behaviors" used to sustain civil inattention in public spaces:

> [The glance] shows an attention toward the other, even a recognition as a person, but because of its brevity, it also shows to the one being looked at that one is not trying to resolve her indeterminacy in any other way than a typifying determination of her person and activity, or that one is not attempting to participate in her actions, thoughts, or life. This implies that any identification is carried out only on the basis of standard appearances and behaviors.[42]

Once riders have perceived others according to relevant practical categories, they go on to assume that these persons will behave according to what they look like, typically as riders.[43] The more experienced riders become with the mass transit system, the better they develop their skill at reading situations and other people for normal versus abnormal appearances. From this perspective, we begin to understand how the social order of the subway constantly takes shape through interactions, which depend on actors' skills and particular situations or settings. Thus for a subway veteran, the decompensating schizophrenic ranting at one end of the car may evoke wariness and some distance, but it will not be grounds for exiting the car, as might well be the case for less experienced riders (at least once they realize that the person talking aloud is not speaking into a cell phone). Again, the differences in the way riders behave in apparently abnormal situations, as they understand it, can be attributed to many different personal qualities, especially what we are seeing as mass transit competence. Nor is competence reserved just for the good citizen. The chain or phone snatcher exploits the same subway codes, looking perfectly normal until the subway doors are about to close when he strikes and exits, leaving his victim on the moving train.

Civility Toward Diversity: Trust, Competences, and Social Diversity

There is no contradiction between the norm of "civility toward diversity" and the categorical determinations of status (such as race and gender) and the behavior of other riders. Indeed, the anonymity that guarantees a form of "polite estrangement" must be based on a form of ordering into categories that can, de facto, be considered "normal," because, according to Harvey Sacks, our perception is "concept bound."[44] We see, notice, or scan our environment according to a personal set of "classes," publicly available, without which it would be impossible to perceive. This means that we don't interpret a person's type according to a perception of some of her features but that we directly "see" a certain type of person. Of course, we have a large number of classes from which to choose.

Race and gender are two of the usual aspects analyzed in two articles by David Maines about the postures of riders seated on the long bench of the IRT (numbered lines, including the 7 train) and the L bench of the IND.[45] According to Maines, race and gender are classes of categories that people find useful in assessing the degree of normality of specific subway appearances and, from there, to decide on an appropriate course of action. If all the seated riders are of the same gender, they keep their elbows to the side, whereas they would draw them onto their lap when next to a person of the opposite sex. Maines observed the same phenomenon between black and white people. Maines's study showed that women had a definite prejudice against men and vice versa, and whites against blacks and vice versa.

Once riders have perceived others according to different practical categories, they assume that these persons will behave according to the stereotypes they hold for that social category.[46] Most frequently in public transit, riders' choices based on race, gender, or ethnicity determine whether or not to take an open seat next to that person. We know of no systematic measurements or observations that measure the rate of slights and micro-aggressions among people of different races on the New York subways.[47] But clearly the slights are not evenly distributed. Black males in public transit often mention how common it is for nonblack riders to purposely avoid sitting next to them. The particular racial demography of the 7 train, however, does not lend itself as well to the study of black–white racial interactions underground, as would research on trains serving Harlem and the Bronx. But there is no lack of racial diversity on any of the Queens lines, and as we have seen in earlier chapters, racial stereotypes are continually being invoked, challenged, and appropriately ignored, especially as a function of riders' competence.

As the city becomes even more diverse, subway riders must become increasingly competent at reading different situations for their possible threats. Individuals deal with the degree of uncertainty caused by a heterogeneous mass of riders by adopting microstrategies that allow them to build enough trust in the situation to remain regular subway riders. This is what Lyn Lofland summed up in her last principle of behaviors in public places: "civility toward diversity" or, more simply, "putting up with diversity." But the demands of coping with diversities of all kinds also help explain why a certain number of people do not feel up to the task of taking the subway: "If basic trust is not developed or its inherent ambivalence not contained, the outcome is persistent existential anxiety. In its most profound sense, the antithesis of trust is thus a state of mind, which could be best summed up as existential angst or dread."[48]

Apart from people with significant physical handicaps, some New Yorkers are unable to "put up" with life among so many strangers. Conversely, if so many more urbanites have switched to taking the subway, it is because they already feel confident enough in their ability to deal with the diversity made more visible on the train and trust that others will also be competent riders. All of this suggests that from a systemwide view, civil inattention, cooperative motility, and civility toward diversity may seem to be rules of an informal social order. From an individual perspective, however, they also are skills unevenly distributed among riders, even though every rider still needs to acquire them to some degree in order to navigate the subway and its social order.

The Social Order of the Subway as a "Working Consensus"

We can now sort the constraints put on behaviors into two sets: those imposed by the demands of interaction in the subway, predicated on maintaining trust, and those imposed by the demands of individual selves, based on their destination and their appearances. This great range of individuals varies enormously in their cultural and social class backgrounds. Such a situation, according to Anne Rawls, gives rise to what Erving Goffman described as a "working consensus" or an "interaction order sui generis":

> For Goffman contractual obligations are generated by the requirements of social interaction and the reproduction of the self through its relations to other selves in interaction.[49]
>
> "I will refer to this level of agreement as a working consensus."[50]

We have also seen that the actual demands of interaction originate in the modes of presentation of the different selves involved in the situation. Trust is indeed a demand that allows every participant to sustain an image of himself that is accepted at "face value" by all the others, and thus is dependent on social structure, class relations, or cultural values (such as ethnicity), thanks to a categorical mode of perception: "Within this view, we have a situation where persons ignorant of their future status in the interaction, enter into an agreement to accept at face value the 'front' of all participants, thus protecting all positions, which they might come to occupy in the future."[51]

For Rawls, therefore, the "needs of the social self-constitute the primary constraint on the interaction order." The challenge in the subway is to accommodate the need for trust within the scope of the trip with the multiple needs for individual projections of selves. This is achieved through a "moral commitment to the working consensus for its own sake [, which] is one of the 'ground rules' of interaction."[52] Thus a "contract is necessary because of the fragile nature of both the interaction and the social self. The constant threat of annihilation hangs over both: 'When an incident occurs and spontaneous involvement is threatened, then reality is threatened.' "[53]

The main rule of the subway is thus a commitment to trust the working consensus that everybody will behave as a rider and will not interfere with other riders' trips.

No Pants? Yes, but Pretend Not to Be Looking: Defending the Working Consensus

If New York subway riders trust one another, they can also be trusted to get on one another's nerves with some frequency. Establishing and maintaining trust among passengers depends on a universally imposed rider role, but that role is loosely scripted. The rider role requires, above all, that one not impede mobility and remain selectively inattentive to others. But the script is loose in that the rider role does not specify very much about what one can do while acting as if one were alone while on mass transit. Loud cell phone conversations, extensive makeup application, nail clipping, couples making out or arguing, singing along with the music in the earphones, and many other routinely annoying behaviors on the train occur without violating the basics of forward motion. While riders do complain to one another about annoyances, they even more frequently choose to remain silent rather than breach the anonymity barrier or threaten the overall social order within their car.

A good illustration of the strength of our determination to protect the subway's social order is the now annual "no pants subway ride," a form of urban "happening" that began in New York and has spread to numerous mass transit cities in the United States and Europe.[54] Alerted by cell phone text messages, on a given January morning hundreds of riders gather in subway stations in Manhattan and take the subways, individually or in small groups, without their pants (but wearing underwear). This event takes place in the winter, making the appearance of these riders even more incongruous. The instructions are to take the subway and pretend to be a rider—that is, to do as if one were properly dressed. Amazingly, no specific trouble has erupted from this horde of pantless riders.[55] As the pretend riders ride the trains, other riders obviously pretend not to take notice or, if they do, dismiss the observation and the behavior as an infringement on the "working consensus." In fact, the event itself can be understood as a collective test of the skills of New Yorkers' civil inattention. Pretend riders, with or without pants, are just taken at face value for what they claim to be. Despite exposed underwear, they remain riders and they are trusted to maintain the consensus, meaning the understanding that everybody is going to make it unharmed from point A to point B. Conversely, the pantless riders also show an amazing trust in the social order of the trains. Women in their underwear account for about half of the several hundred participants, who usually end up at a street party in Union Square later in the day. Of course, conversations about the unusual behavior frequently arise. Obviously, the working consensus allows for unexpected side involvements, provided they do not undermine the collective trust. And certain no-pants riders may have quite complex motives for their behavior, as in this example reported on by a participant in the 2012 event:

> One of the things I love about the scope of the No Pants Subway Ride these days is that we really take over the whole system. At 59th and Lex, three trains of pantless people arrived at the same time. Two groups were switching lines and one was just passing through. Anyway, the guy in the photo above wins the badass award.[56]

The "badass" rider the blogger refers to is a man who appears to be about the age of Iraq and Afghanistan war veterans. He is staring into his iPhone. Nearby are numerous passengers, none of whom is looking at him. He is wearing sneakers, a sweatshirt, and boxer shorts that reveal a prosthetic leg.

If the no-pants event can highlight the strength of the subway code, what constitutes a trust-threatening infraction? To undermine trust, one must actually disturb the activity of another rider. This would mean dropping the rider role by disturbing the intentional space of fellow riders who assumed that they could trust the social gathering. Another way to step out of role is to single out riders according to a category supposedly not pertinent to the situation. Following Harvey Sacks's concept of orders of relevancy, the usual categories of race, sex, gender, and age are brought up only through civil inattention and then are immediately dismissed as supposedly irrelevant to the rider role. Thus a cardinal rule in the working consensus is the "no lack of respect to riders' selves" by inappropriate attention to a person's gender, race, or other personal trait. (We examine these problems, especially with regard to sexual conduct and groping, in greater detail in chapter 6.)

The breach of trust is thus not measured against a violation of cooperative mobility and civil inattention as norms, but as a violation of the assumption of trust in the working consensus that these skills help maintain. This collective agreement to take the social order of the subway for granted is a key dimension of the working consensus.

In the face of a visible or sensory lack of respect, riders have a choice of either acknowledging the violation and undermining the consensus by making it public, or retreating even more into their own auto-involvement, a tactical and local reinforcement of the consensus in the face of risk. Auto-involvements, as we shall see shortly, are not only a possibility afforded by the rider role but also a reinforcement of the strength of the subway consensus. To some degree, they also represent a form of collective self-fulfilling prophecy that must be constantly reaffirmed but can also collapse. According to Isaac Joseph, it

> aims at keeping up, as long as possible, the ethical fiction of a social world able to auto-regulate itself without referring to judicial or repressive systems (complaints, police) and without major breach (vengeance, reparatory violence, etc.). It is thus an essential social function as it consists in rescuing social ties more than defending the face of the victim.[57]

Trust Permits Side Involvements, Which Produce More Trust

According to Randy Kennedy, "But New Yorkers also use the subway for another purpose that goes woefully underappreciated: as a reading room," and according to Edmund Love, "Subways are for sleeping."[58] The tightly enforced but loosely defined rider script contradiction underlies many of the apparent paradoxes presented in the subways. It helps us understand how so many riders can perform supremely intimate acts of self-absorption in the most exposed environment, as was well observed by a *New York Times* reporter, Ted Botha:

> Today, the conditions are good. No one is reading over my shoulder or coming too close (elbow-in-the-side close) or clipping their fingernails, a bathroom exploit that for some reason bothers me when done in public, whereas someone applying blusher between stops doesn't. Maybe it's the fear of being hit in the eye by an airborne cuticle.[59]

Once the requirements of trust demanded by the subway environment are met, every passenger in the subway should be able to enjoy a peaceful ride. Indeed, numerous reports, articles, and stories describe the many ways that subways are used for activities that have little to do with traveling. Reading, sleeping, listening to music, writing, daydreaming, putting on makeup, kissing, and becoming engrossed in a conversation, in total disregard of the rest of the car, are commonly observed daily on the trains. Despite the obvious constraints of space and crowding, many New Yorkers thus find the rides a productive time to reflect, create, and interact—that is, when they are not seized by angst about their immediate neighbor or the delay that will make them late for work (again!). One explanation for why the subway is such a good reading room (or other room) is that auto-involvements in fact constantly manifest the trust in the gathering by displaying civil inattention.

As we have seen, the subway rider role requires competences that are too easily taken for granted. This role demands a tight adherence to a script that if carefully followed produces remarkable levels of order despite vivid differences among riders. Many of us essentially disappear into a private world in which we assume we can simply "go about minding our own business." But what we observe proves that an entirely libertarian subway car would be a descent into hell. Inevitably, some of the private business that we carry out as a way of maximizing self-interest may rub against the larger needs of the community in transit, sometimes with sparks.

Side involvements, however, while they do reinforce the working consensus, also include a range of possible interactions with others that go beyond the rider role. And on many occasions, their outcomes are unexpected. The essentially nonverbal forms of communication that such interactions allow often lead to contradictory interpretations, as in this incident from the subway diary of Margarita, one of the high school students with whom we worked (see chapter 6):

> I took the E train in the first wagon, going to Manhattan. It was very crowded and I almost hit a lady with my two bags. Then later on I noticed this man that was in front of me of about 30–35 year old. He had bruises on his arm and it was because he did drugs. I noticed because of his eyes. At Ely stop, an American man of 20–23 year old was standing in front of the drug addict just in front of the door, the middle door in the first wagon to be exact. I was listening to music and there was this Asian lady with her baby boy of about 3–4 year old, an old lady from the same place, and another lady from the same place with her daughter of about the same age as the boy. The women with the baby boy had a baby carriage. They were standing and moving back and forth, pushing me, but no one would stand up and try to help out and give them a seat. However, while this was happening, the drug addict was robbing the white man and he was not noticing. He would not pay attention to the signs I was giving him. When we got to Lexington, I told the man and he couldn't believe it. However, he did not get off. He was in shock and did not react to it. I was very mad because I could not do anything about it by the time I got to work it was 11:30 A.M. and everything seemed so wrong because of it. I am still mad when I remember.
>
> Diary, June 19, 2006

When we asked Margarita what kinds of signs she used to try to warn the victim, she explained that she tried to communicate by looking at him and bringing the thief to his attention through her telling glances. She thinks that it didn't work because the man thought that she was hitting on him. In any case, he didn't get the hint. If what Margarita thinks is true, he must have been clearly dumbfounded to realize that what he was taking as a flirt (flattering for his public self) was in fact a sign that he was being conned (a demeaning image).

Margarita's failure to communicate danger troubled her. As a young woman of immigrant background, she had taken the risk, however modest, of stepping out from the subway's anonymity to be a good citizen. She was left with questions about her behavior and about the subway's moral environment. Yet her own doubts about her ability to deal with a local breach of trust gave her some ideas about what she might do in a similar situation in the future. This kind of self-reflection can promise increased subway competence in at least one New York commuter.

Competence and the Situational Community in Transit

The working consensus of the subway system is increasingly strained by crowding, delays, service cuts, and less experienced riders, especially tourists. The competences of system users become ever more frequently challenged. The folk ethnography that riders utilize—sifting normal from abnormal appearance, instantly weighing potential responses to breaches of the subway order—becomes even more sophisticated, at least in the practice of veteran riders. The three sets of competences that we have outlined so far—context reading, code switching, and account giving (including cooperative mobility and civil inattention)—all testify to specific values that characterize the subway's working consensus. This consensus promises that every genuine rider has an auto-enforced right to safe travel throughout the whole city of New York, whatever his or her social characteristics (age, gender, race, ethnicity, class, and so on).

Mastering the competences of the subway rider's role opens access to a situational community of riders in transit, a community providing a context for the urban newcomer's desire to assimilate as a New Yorker. Since one cannot simply assert this as an unproven thesis, we will continue, in the remainder of this volume, to examine a variety of evidence regarding this and related processes.

This chapter has outlined some of the fundamental aspects of the subway's social and spatial order based on our own data and as it has been explored by social scientists and journalists over the past few decades. Many of the classic subway studies that we cited have little contemporary relevance, since they have not, for the most part, been replicated. In their defense, the basic conditions of the subway's social order do not seem to have changed substantially, even as ridership has risen along with the diversity of subway patrons and as new technology comes to the trains. The notable lack of replication and continuity in the subway research is also the result of moral concerns raised in later decades. The studies by Milgram,

Piliavin, Levine, and others that we cited were especially revealing because they purposely put real subway patrons into situations that demanded immediate and sometimes difficult choices. Once they had acted, for better or worse, these involuntary "subjects" were left to deal alone with the subjective and moral implications of their actions. Contemporary standards of research ethics, as monitored by institutional review boards at all universities and research institutes, no longer support the systematic duping of unsuspecting research participants. It is also true that the moral quandaries and negative self-evaluations that such research can engender in those who fail to act altruistically attest to the personal consequences of our public behavior and to our powerful, if often unexamined, feelings about the conduct of urban life.

The classic subway studies also dwell heavily on accounts and behaviors of the single passenger—who becomes idealized as the "rider" or, at times, "the other"—to dominate the analysis. In the following chapters, therefore, we will pay more attention to group situations and to interactions that cross the boundaries of gender, race, and social class.

Trust underground, as we have shown in this chapter, is a defining aspect of the situational community in transit. Its existence relies on the written and unwritten rules of behavior we have discussed. These rules, however, are essential but not completely sufficient to explain the actual workings of the subway community in transit. The nuances and fragilities of trust and social order underground require a more critical comprehension of rider behavior. We have shown that different reactions to common and atypical situations on the trains and platforms can indicate riders' relative competences as subway citizens. Competence enacts the values of cooperative mobility and how skillfully riders maintain the subway consensus that the train always moves forward. Yet there are moments and situations in which the most competent riders prove themselves willing to act against, or in spite of, the progressive motion.

The most dangerous situations underground occur not from the random criminal, but in situations—such as a suddenly blocked stairwell—in which the crowd's desire to advance can lead to disaster. People who read the situation quickly and try to prevent panic, who immediately start communicating clearly with those around them, are displaying competences in a potentially deadly situation. Fortunately, we have not witnessed such potential disasters in the course of our observations. But we have seen, in many less dire conditions, as when crowded trains are delayed for anxious minutes, that alert riders can alleviate extreme tensions. They may take it upon themselves to communicate their knowledge ("Don't bother going down to the platform, the train is not running") and thus act as invaluable members of the subway's situational community.

In the next two chapters, we further pursue the subject of rider competences with questions about how they are acquired and exercised in situations in which gender and age are issues engaged in the community in transit. Thanks to its peculiar ecology and social order, the subway has become an echo chamber of the issues that New Yorkers bring with them as they encounter one another underground. Certainly that was the case in a racially tense New York of the 1980s when Bernhard Goetz, the so-called subway vigilante, shot four young black men whom he believed were threatening him on the subway. That grim, tragic episode, at the nadir of the subway's reputation for trust and racial tolerance, echoed the fears and moral crises that were occurring in the city aboveground. Racial tensions still exist, and confrontations can erupt at any moment above- or below ground. However, in our research on the subways and on the 7 train in particular, we find that as ridership steadily increases, specific issues of gender and age become especially indicative of contemporary strains and competences underground, as we will show in the following chapters.

6 Gender Relations on the Subway

In the same way that a life for which no categories of recognition exist is not a livable life, so a life for which those categories constitute unlivable constraint is not an acceptable option.

Judith Butler, *Undoing Gender*

A mong the thousands of trips taken on the New York subway each day, a few result in serious breaches of gender inattention (civil inattention applied to gender). One of the recurring complaints about the subway—in addition to cost, delays, and overcrowding—is lewd behavior by males toward females on the trains. The communication norms of the subway, like those of society at large, make it difficult for women to speak up and complain about such offenses, of which groping is the most common and emotionally painful. An unknown number of violations of women's personal space goes unreported every day. With millions of rides taken on the subway each week, however, even a small proportion of such incidents can constitute a large absolute number of justifiable complaints. The many testimonials to unwanted touching that appear regularly in the blogosphere, as well as in our own research (notably the diaries kept by high school and community college students), suggest that the incidence is high enough to warrant very careful attention.

In this connection, it is helpful to remember that along with the population diversity in which New York takes pride come wide variations in cultural values and attitudes toward the appropriate roles and demeanor for men and women. Part of becoming a New Yorker on the subway involves accepting the egalitarian assumptions inherent in the social order of New York's subway system. This can be challenging for some newcomers.

Throughout the city's history, gender relations in public spaces have been a contested and sometimes dangerous aspect of city life.

Attempts to separate riders by gender have been numerous in subways around the world. Subways in Mexico City, Tokyo, Tehran, and other cities reserve some train cars for women. In each case, the reasons cited are slightly different, with or without religious overtones, but the rationalization always refers to the image of vulnerable women easily victimized in urban public spaces. Although the gender asymmetry imposed by patriarchal norms is not always contested, it is clearly at the root of most conflicts.[1] Likewise, in most of these cases, the separation is never quite successful or practical, but it clearly points to a problem in many cities around the world.[2]

During the twentieth century in New York, as in most European cities with subway systems, as women asserted their right to be free from harassment in public places and conveyances, men gradually came to understand that they were expected to respect this right. Yet complications and misunderstandings abound. Even in one of the world's most sophisticated and cosmopolitan cities, being a woman on the subway entails a greater risk of unwanted interaction or abuse than does one's race, ethnicity, or social class (although there are a few stretches on the subway system where racial or ethnic tensions may outweigh those of gender).

Nonetheless, women crowd the 7 train, and indeed the entire subway system, during rush hours and are well represented throughout most of the day and evening. As noted in chapter 2, more men than women commute to the city by automobile. Women also are overrepresented in the lower echelons of the city's domestic and commercial labor force and hence are more likely to have to ride the subway. In addition, many of the thousands of student riders are girls and young women. In this chapter, we explore the special strategies that women have developed to deal with issues involving gender relations on the trains. As we will see, these competences are a subcategory of the urban skills known as "street smarts," and the situations that require them are not always so clear-cut. It also is not always obvious how a woman should act to avoid embarrassment, humiliation, and even injury. Our research offers some guidance in this regard, based on our analysis of how gender relations underground are representative of larger gender issues in the society above ground and on our observations of the competences that women subway riders have learned in order to deal with groping and its emotional consequences.

Consider the experience of Connie, a seventeen-year-old Latina high school student, petite and attractive, who wrote in her subway diary that during one trip on the 7 subway, she encountered "a pile of people waiting for the train," which forced her to stand among a group of male riders where she felt vulnerable. Sure enough, her fears were realized. "I don't know who is touching my leg," Connie writes, "and I get angry":

> I start to talk loud and tell the people to stop . . . not to abuse the situation, and some guy started laughing and asked me if I was OK. I didn't like the way he was asking me if I was OK, so I tell him that it is none of his business and I try to stare him and then because they didn't stop and the train was full, I threaten them telling: I am going to tell the police.
>
> Another woman was screaming and saying a lot of bad words because they were touching her rear. The girl was really angry, but I couldn't see who it was because people are obstructing my way. I just listen to what she is saying. Then I went to take the E train (at 74th Street/Roosevelt) but I [was so upset that] I took the wrong train. . . .

Connie, subway diary, June 2006, 7 train

A veteran subway rider even as a teenager, Connie is displaying a number of competences in dealing with subway groping that we will explore further throughout this chapter. But her diary entry also shows how profoundly upsetting the experience is for her, so much so that she ends up taking the wrong train at the 74th Street/Roosevelt Avenue transit hub.

Women on the Subway: Historical Background

There is no reason to believe that the 7 train is any more difficult for women to negotiate than other subway lines are. In fact, since its opening in 1917, the 7 train, like many other subway lines linking Manhattan to the outer boroughs, has afforded women a powerful means for achieving spatial and social mobility. Since its opening in 1904, the subway has offered women opportunities to travel beyond their immediate neighborhood and gain better access to paid employment, education, shopping, and leisure. But because women accounted for only about one-quarter of rush-hour passengers, the subway started as a male-dominated space, and women were frequent victims of various forms of harassment.[3] In addition, the media portrayed the subway as a space where the rocking of bodies to the rhythm of the train led to a promiscuous atmosphere encouraging romantic encounters. Popular songs such as "Down in the Subway" (1904), "The Subway Express" (1907), and "I Lost Her in the Subway" (1907) explicitly evoked the temptations and benefits of such "subway crushes."[4]

At the beginning of the twentieth century, newspapers published articles expressing outrage at the insults that young women, especially middle-class women, riding on the subway had to endure at the hands of men, whom they assumed to be mostly working class. In 1909, following a suggestion by a leader of the Women's Municipal League, the Hudson and Manhattan Railroad opened a rush-hour women-only car on its line linking Jersey City to Manhattan but discontinued it three months later, apparently for economic reasons. During this experiment, other feminist groups, such as the Equality League of Self Supported Women, argued against such gender separation, which in their view threatened the already limited rights of women in public spaces.[5] Although sexual harassment in the subway was a problem, it was not considered severe enough to counter the benefits afforded by this new mode of transportation—chiefly the right to be in the subway at all and to travel independently through the city. Women's rights regarding voting and financial independence were considered more pressing than sexual harassment in public places. Besides, harassment was pervasive everywhere, from the domestic sphere to the workplace.

Nevertheless, the police hired women to act as decoys and thus deflect the behavior of "men who made it their business to insult and annoy women and girls."[6] According to one recent history of the issue, "interest in women's safety in public transit waned after the 1920s, at least in part in conjunction with the return of middle class women to their home."[7] Another factor, beginning in 1924, was the drastic reduction in the flow of immigrants to New York City. The issue of women's safety then largely disappeared from the public spotlight for about fifty years, during which time the proportion of women in public places gradually increased. Even though women had gained greater access to jobs outside the home during and after World War II, subway ridership diminished dramatically as large numbers of people acquired cars and moved to the suburbs. In the 1970s, the city's financial crisis and the resulting lack of investment in infrastructure made the situation worse, and subway ridership plummeted to an all-time low in 1981 and 1982.

During that period, the issue of women's security resurfaced in the media. It went well beyond harassment, extending to violent crimes in general, including rape. Such crimes took place in deserted alleys and on empty subway trains and platforms. Even though women's vulnerability was not limited to the subway, in the public mind conditions on the subway came to symbolize the general state of exposure and abandonment prevailing in the city as a whole.[8]

The situation improved in the 1990s. Thanks to investments made during the previous decade, the subway was running better. Subway cars were cleaned of graffiti; safe waiting areas were designated near manned token booths; and emergency phones were installed. In 1989, the Metropolitan Transportation Authority (MTA) appointed William Bratton as chief of the Transit Police Department. Bratton implemented a "zero tolerance" policy in the subway. By cracking down on offenses and misdemeanor crimes, the police strove to remove more serious criminals from the system. Then when Mayor Rudolph Giuliani appointed Bratton to the position of city commissioner of police, Bratton applied his zero-tolerance approach to policing throughout the city. According to the police, cracking down on fare evasion and other minor crimes had helped them make the subway safer before greater safety was achieved in the rest of the city.[9]

Another important event occurred in 1998, when the MetroCard was introduced. By permitting free transfers from the bus to the subway, it halved the cost of commuting for many New Yorkers in the outer boroughs. Ridership increased dramatically and has remained high ever since. As a result, crowded trains have once again become a problem, and groping has resurfaced as a public issue. In 2009, when James T. Hall, chief of the New York Police Department's Transit Bureau (part of the police department since 1995), testified before the City Council, he declared groping to be the "number one quality of life offense in the subways."[10]

The subway and its riders are different today from a hundred years ago when gender first became a public issue on the subway. The 2006 American Community Survey (ACS) found that in Queens, a larger proportion of women (54.6%) than men take the subway to go to work. Our own observations during the peak time between 8:00 and 9:00 A.M. show that more women than men enter the Flushing–Main Street (55.2%) and 74th Street/Roosevelt Avenue (54.5%) stations. In short, the subway is no longer a male-dominated space, at least in numbers of riders. Moreover, rates of violent crime have receded, and sexual harassment in the workplace is no longer ignored or tolerated. Accordingly, groping and other forms of gender discriminations in the subway can now take center stage in the ongoing struggle for gender equality in the city.

Does Gender Matter in Public Space?

As women have gained greater access to the city's public spaces, in large part thanks to the subway, gender has become less pertinent to the norms of behavior in public. Evidence of this trend is the gradual disappearance of chivalry—which, while paying respect to women through such behaviors as holding a door open to allow them to pass through first or automatically giving up one's seat to them, also views women as more vulnerable than men and hence in need of their protection. Today, holding a door for someone else is apparently determined more by the fact that the preceding person held the door for you than by the gender of the person following you.[11] Perhaps the only situation in which gender is still relevant is the entry of a pregnant woman into a train or bus, in which case nonpregnant women and men usually give their seat to her. Indeed, the treatment of pregnant women is frequently discussed in popular newspapers and blogs. Some believe that New Yorkers are more chivalrous than they are reputed to be, an opinion explored in two articles by journalist Peter Donohue in the *Daily News*, in which he asked a pregnant woman to keep track of how long it took for someone to offer her a seat on the subway or bus:[12]

Each quest ended successfully with an unsolicited offer of a seat, usually in a matter of seconds—except for the No. 7 line, where our volunteer had to wait three long minutes. "It's fantastic," said Ted Donohue, 35, a part-time actress and full-time wife of this reporter. "It renews my faith in New York and the kindness of New Yorkers." But for every rider who graciously offered their personal perch, several others sat idle, some clearly pretending not to notice the plight of the pregnant. . . . "Overall, New Yorkers are polite . . . if you catch their eye. But you have to make sure you are seen."[13]

Pregnancy tends to put women in the more general and sex-indifferent category of vulnerable people, including the elderly and the disabled.

Following Candace West and Don Zimmerman, we could say that today there is no excuse for "doing gender" on the subway. In other words, gender is not a relevant category for the task of riding the subway.[14] When riding on the subway, one should not need to act like a woman or a man, and one should not need to know whether the person standing next to you is a woman or a man.

As David Francis and Stephen Hester have shown, however, gender is a naturally observable identity feature of copresence in daily life that is always available to its participants.[15] This means that even if gender is irrelevant to the task of taking the subway, riders still "see"[16] one another as men and women. But seeing is not doing, and riders usually do not summon these gender identities during their ride.

Erving Goffman long ago observed the diminishing pertinence of gender identity in public spaces, despite its omni-availability. Accordingly, we have used his theory of interactional relations to explain the social order of the subway in terms of "civil inattention" and riders' expectation that others will maintain the gender-indifferent role of rider while on the train. But Carol Gardner, a student of Goffman, showed that this expectation cannot be taken for granted and that many women are in fact wary of men's presence in public, mostly out of fear of being harassed or worse.[17] In this case, the gender of subway riders becomes more relevant, as it can be used to assess the situation and take appropriate measures, such as not standing with one's back to a male passenger or avoiding crowded trains altogether. Even when fear is not a factor, gender-oriented behaviors have been observed by both riders and researchers. For example, a popular Internet blog called *Men Taking Up Too Much Space on the Train* displays hundreds of pictures of men spreading their legs apart while sitting next to women pressing their legs together,[18] and in 2014, the MTA added a poster against "manspreading" in the trains. These men are tacitly accused of "doing gender" in a situation in which they should not do so.

In an ethological study conducted in 1977, David Maines showed that women and men sitting on the long bench of an IRT subway car generally put their elbows at the sides of their bodies when seated next to a person of the same gender but that they more often brought them forward onto their laps when seated next to a rider of the opposite gender (the same observation was true of white and black subway riders).[19] In these situations, gender is not irrelevant, but neither is it decisively relevant. Moving one's hands from side to lap reduces actual body contact with another rider, which for women becomes more problematic when that rider is male. Women who are concerned about harassment generally try to avoid situations in which their visible gender identity could suddenly become a reason for contact. This means that should anything suspicious or unexpected happen, the male and female category will always be readily available as a vehicle for judging a person's actions and motives. In other words, "a person engaged in virtually any activity may be held accountable for performance of that activity as a woman or man, and their incumbency in one or the other sex category can be used to legitimate or discredit their other activities."[20] In sum, on the subway, gender should ideally be only secondarily relevant. It can become primarily relevant when riders are anxious about harassment or when an action that is not related to the task of taking the subway develops along gender lines.

Arrangements Between the Sexes in the Subway

One reason, if not the only reason, why gender is still relevant in public settings as anonymous as the subway, is tied, if only secondarily, to the structure of courtship, at least in its traditional form implying distinct roles for men and women. As Goffman pointed out in 1977, courtship as traditionally understood demands that women protect their territories of self (from their conversation to their body) and grant access only to suitors they fancy. Men, in contrast, must probe these barriers in search of signs of rebuttal or encouragement. Thus "breaching of existing distance, partly on speculation, is, then, a standard part of the male's contribution to cross-sex dealings, at least as far as the male is concerned."[21] Since initiating any form of courtship implies a violation of distance, it consists of moving sex from a secondary order of relevance to the primary order. In other words, public places such as the subway are perfectly adapted to courtship. As Goffman put it:

> It follows, then, that females are somewhat vulnerable in a chronic way to being "hassled"; for what a male can improperly press upon them by way of drawing them into talk or by way of improperly extending talk already initiated stands to gain him (and indeed her) a lot, namely, a relationship, and if not this, then at least confirmation of gender identity.[22]

Of course, norms have changed since 1977, but since encounters in the subway take place between people unknown to each other, it seems only logical to assume that riders will generally believe that people around them, more often than not, abide by variations of the dominant principles of courtship, for lack of a better alternative.

If this is the case, the infinite number of situations of copresence in the subway should make it a premium terrain for encounters both consensual and not. The difficulty in the subway, however, is to manage to establish contact in an environment generally guided by nonverbal behavior. Both a consensual encounter and sexual harassment in public space start as a violation of the moral order of the gender category's relevancy. But these violations are not the same. Consensual relations usually start with a gaze and a few words, but never with a wandering hand. Whereas the violation is positively sanctioned in the first case, it is negatively evaluated in the second. In the rest of this chapter, we compare the unfolding of these encounters.

We found that both romantic encounters and harassment are common on the subway. In addition, as we saw in chapter 5, since verbal communication is usually minimal, interpretations are relatively free of constraints, making the subway a site for side involvements such as mental reveries. Many of these auto-involvements are about fantasized encounters. Although most riders are thus not doing gender in the subway, it turns out that gender and sex are an ever-present concern, in either a potentially threatening way or a possibly romanticized way.

Romantic Encounters on the Subway

One day, I was on the train with my friend Stephanie and I was looking at this guy. I told my friend that I was sure that I knew him but I couldn't remember from where. We continued our conversation but he was sitting in front of me and when he looked at me I automatically started looking at him too. I was dressed very cute. He had jean pants, a blue and white shirt, a pair of black pumas and a black cap. He was so quiet and serious. However, the guy came to me and asks me if I remember him. I tell him no but his face seems familiar and he tells me that he was the guy from the Internet on the Myspace website. Then I remember and he gave me his telephone number and that he wants me to call him to talk and go to clubs or some place to know each other. The next day, I call him and that day I went out with him.

Connie, June 2006

Of the twelve high school students who kept diaries about their travels on the 7 train, two reported romantic encounters. This is, of course, not a representative number, but it illustrates the possibility of such encounters as well as a pattern of encounter consistent with the theory of the moral orders of relevance. In the first case, Connie, the seventeen-year-old student who earlier was in a situation of harassment, the encounter built from a previous online chat that made the copresence in the train a lucky happenstance, unplanned by the young man. He could then approach her while making gender relevant to an interaction that went beyond the space and time of the subway.

Juan, a shy seventeen-year-old student from Colombia, met a young woman as he was writing in his diary. She asked him what he was writing about, and they had a short conversation in English before realizing that they both were from Colombia. A few days later, he ran into her at the Jamaica Mall, and this chance encounter led them to exchange phone numbers and begin dating.

In this incident, the young woman pulled aside the invisible curtain of gender neutrality with an "act of recognition" that might make a modern feminist proud. However, as Juan admitted later, he did not sit next to her by chance. Several other empty seats were available, but he had noticed her and decided to sit near her. Although he did not know how to proceed further, he succeeded in improving his chances of contact without actually initiating it. The young woman may have noticed that he had passed up other open seats and, after her own evaluation, decided to respond to his awkward overture.

This example of a romantic connection underground calls attention to the many initial encounters that never progress but about which riders routinely imagine and fantasize. A good snapshot of this phenomenon can be found on Craigslist under the heading "Missed Encounters." By typing in the keyword "train," we found 199 messages posted in a single week in December 2013 (December 1 to December 8), all talking about a missed encounter on the subway.[23] One-half of the messages were posted by "a man for a woman"; one-third by "a man for another man"; and only one-fifth by "a woman for a man." (Only one post was by "a woman for another woman.") By this measure, fantasies about such encounters seem to loom a lot larger in men's imaginations than in women's. The general structure of a post is fairly constant. For example:

> Eyes met on the 7 train and beyond—m4w—41 (Flushing)
>
> I know this has virtually no chance of finding you, but our eyes met several times on the 7 train heading into Flushing around 9:00 A.M. We even ending up next to each other on the escalator and you smiled—I should have spoken. You, a beautiful Chinese Woman, dark eyes and beautiful hands. You wore all black. Me, tall dark-haired guy wearing a black jacket. Email me . . .

The title usually contains information about the time of the encounter and the subway line. It also lists the category of encounter (in this case "m4w," a man for a woman). The post then goes on to describe the situation, the person to whom the post is addressed, and the person posting it. Finally, it invokes the possibility of a future encounter.

The writer of this post resembles Juan in that he also did not allow the gendered encounter to take precedence over the trip itself and continued on his way. In other words, gender remained secondarily relevant. Because no gesture is generally made that would bring gender into play, most of these "missed encounters" do not go beyond a fleeting exchange of glances or a few inconsequential words. Nonetheless, the missed encounter is clearly gendered in nature, as the title "man for woman" announces. Although 200 posts in one week is not a large number, they certainly represent a much larger phenomenon, one that is largely invisible but often present on the subway. In a study of missed encounters on the Paris metro, Frank Beau discovered that half the numerous messages on a dedicated website were posted by women and most of the writers claimed to be between the ages of eighteen and twenty-five.[24] As in New York, however, those messages underline the fact that riders may fantasize about one another but rarely attempt an actual encounter. Beau also found that in most cases, the glances and verbal exchanges were initiated through a "transitional object," such as a book or headphone, or a small incident, such as a bump or something happening near the protagonists. This is a common encounter mechanism in public spaces that William H. Whyte called a "triangulation":

an interaction initiated between two unknown strangers via the mutual perception of a remarkable person, object, or event providing an acceptable subject of conversation.[25]

Despite regular articles about subway romance and fantasy,[26] the media have not made the subway a likely place for romantic encounters. To the contrary, most articles about gender and the subway deal with harassment.

Sexual Harassment on the Subway: Groping as an "Indigenous" Crime

The first report on sex crimes in New York City, released in 1980, tied them to the social and physical setting of the subway:

> It is clear from comparison with New York Police Department crime statistics that there are indeed significantly more nonfelonious sex crimes on the subways (adjusted for daily population) than there are on a proportional basis above ground. In 1977, for example, Transit Police Department statistics accounted for roughly 75% of New York City's total sexual abuse [groping] and public lewdness [exhibitionism] arrests, with figures for the first five months of 1978 following a similar pattern. Figures for 1976 are also comparable. It is therefore our strong impression that sex crimes on the subway constitute a virtually indigenous and perhaps unique problem of urban underground "ecology" and one for which indigenous solutions may prove to be advisable.[27]

If this is the case, it means that sexual harassment arises from the spatial and social order of the subway within which it has found a niche; that is, it is "indigenous" to the subway. Under what circumstances does sexual harassment occur, and are there any "indigenous" solutions to the problem?

In exploring this question, we had to rely on a limited body of research on subway crime. Most of these studies are interested in felony crimes, such as assault and rape, which must be considered separately from lewdness and groping. In fact, crime studies differentiate between two sets of occurrences in the subway. In a review of this subject, Martha Smith and Ronald Clarke distinguished "crimes facilitated by lack of supervision" from "crimes linked to overcrowding."[28] Felonies are recorded mostly during off-peak times, largely biasing criminal representations of the subway during the night hours, as petty crimes generally are not reported. In addition, violent crimes do not seem to be more prevalent in the subway than on the streets or in the domestic sphere. But robberies, such as pickpocketing and purse snatching, and sexual abuse (that is, groping) do happen during peak times. According to Anne Beller, Sanford Garelik, and Sydney Cooper, "Sexual abuse offenders prefer the crowded rush-hour trains and platforms, probably because crowding maximizes the possibility of physical contact and can even provide a more or less credible cover story for the less obvious forms of it that this kind of offense classically entails."[29]

Although these are sound reasons, they do not really explore the ecology of crowding that such offenses require. Moreover, these offenses remain relatively invisible because they usually are not reported. As a consequence, some recommendations rely on a strategy of spacing, assuming that crowded conditions inevitably promote undesirable behaviors. For example:

> Lopez (1996) has recommended maximum passenger densities for subways in order to limit overcrowding. He recommends that densities should not exceed two persons per square meter in stations, that passenger flows in passageways should not exceed 66 people per meter per minute, and that in trains, no more than 40–75 percent of seats should be occupied.[30]

These numbers look decidedly defeatist. How can peak-hour traffic be transformed into midday traffic? And since exhibitionism and violent crimes take place when fewer riders are present, wouldn't such a policy merely trade one type of crime for another?

Clearly, a preferable strategy would be based on a better understanding of the spatial and social conditions in which groping occurs. To that end, we need to turn to less scientific accounts of such occurrences, attempting to identify clues not to the external factors involved but to those inherent in the crowd itself. The following reflections, while not pretending to generalize, attempt to identify some of the social mechanisms underlying groping.

How Prevalent Is Groping on the Subway?

Common knowledge and popular articles suggest that groping is prevalent on the subway.[31] In 2007, an inquiry by the office of Manhattan Borough

President Scott Stringer attempted to get a better picture of this problem. Several organizations asked their members and contacts to participate in an Internet survey. Apart from the Straphangers Campaign, a rider advocacy group, all these organizations were already involved in gender politics and defense of women's rights. The most obvious caution regarding these data is that the incidence of harassment is difficult to assess. Nevertheless, this inquiry is part of an ongoing campaign to raise awareness of such issues, showing how, with more crowding on the trains, the problem of groping has become more prominent in recent years. The inquiry was supported by an organization called Hollaback! which published it on its blog, where it also collects reports of harassment.[32]

The report, "Hidden in Plain Sight," was based on 1,790 questionnaires collected online over a period of one month: July 2007.[33] Sixty-seven percent of the respondents were female. The main findings were as follows:

- Sixty-three percent of respondents reported having been sexually harassed in the New York City subway system.
- Ninety-six percent of respondents who indicated that they had been sexually harassed did not contact the police or the transit authority to file a report or seek assistance.
- Sixty-nine percent of harassment and 51 percent of assaults took place during the morning and evening rush hours.

The first number, which indicates that about two out of three riders have experienced sexual harassment, should be viewed with caution, as the sample consisted of voluntary, nonrandom respondents and was not controlled for gender. Still, in absolute numbers, it may represent a very large and significant proportion of subway riders. The second number seems more reliable and suggests the difficulty faced by victims in reporting their plight to the police. Finally, the third finding raises interesting questions regarding the relation between crowding and sexual harassment.

Who Are Gropers and Exhibitionists?

The 1980 study, referred to earlier, by Anne Beller, Sanford Garelik, and Sydney Cooper, is the only available scientific analysis of perpetrators of sexual crimes in the New York City subway system. Even though it was conducted more than thirty years ago, its findings remain relevant. In the eighteen-month period between January 1977 and June 1978, the Transit Police recorded a total of 2,529 complaints and arrests for sex crimes. Of these, 1,151 concerned sexual abuse, or groping; another 1,283 concerned public lewdness, or exhibitionism; and 95 were reports of rape. During the same period, 265 men were arrested for sexual abuse and 307 for lewdness. All the arrests took place in Manhattan.

Two interesting findings of the study are that more than half the offenders were married and more than half were neatly dressed. A larger proportion of exhibitionists (42.4%) than of gropers (28.1%) were "dirty" or "sloppy." These data suggest that groping is more often carried out by people who do not stand out from most other subway riders than by people who seem marginal or crazy. Does the anonymous cover of the crowd push them to do things they would not do elsewhere? As riders are pressed together during rush hour, we have to wonder whether the potential for deviance is located as much in the people as in the place.[34]

From this perspective, the fact that groping is once again receiving prominent media coverage shows that the subway has become a new front in the struggle for gender equality. Women's reactions to groping, along with the efforts of nonprofit organizations, politicians, and the MTA itself, indicate that sexual harassment can be conceptualized and acted on in different ways.

Who Are the Victims of Groping and Lewdness?

According to the 1980 report on sex crimes in the New York City subway system, half the women who had experienced sexual harassment in the subway were between the ages of twenty and twenty-nine, with the two other major segments aged ten to nineteen years old and thirty to thirty-nine years old. The victims were predominantly white, with the nonwhites divided almost equally between Hispanics and blacks. Just as we must be cautious about racial profiling regarding the offenders, we also must avoid profiling when the victim is white, and even more so when the alleged offender is a person of color. This class and racial bias was evident in newspaper articles published in the first half of the twentieth century, whose authors seemed to consider the harassment of white middle-class women a greater threat than the harassment of working-class and black or Latina women.[35] Although police crime statistics are probably more reliable today, we have not been able to obtain them.

A last suggestive finding of the 1980 study is the fact that physical injuries following a groping or a flashing incident "usually result from the victim's decision to defend herself, verbally or physically, against the offender."[36] This is a question that we will discuss more fully later in the chapter.

Finally, if the 2007 poll conducted by the Manhattan borough president is accurate and if the proportion of women who complain about sexual harassment in the subway has not changed very much since the late 1970s (big ifs!), the number of complaints that women logged with the police in 1977 should represent about 4 percent of the actual episodes of harassment occurring at that time. Since we know that 1,370 complaints were logged in the nine-month period from October 1977 to June 1978, we can estimate that each year approximately 45,000 women were victims of exhibitionism or groping. The latest public data are a declaration by the chief of the New York Police Department's Transit Bureau that there had been 587 reports of sex offenses in the subway from January 1 to November 15, 2009, and 412 arrests.[37] The number is lower than that in the late 1970s, but it is difficult to assess the trend. What has been done since then to solve this problem?

A Contemporary Feminist Struggle

The battle against sexual harassment in the subway in New York City began in the media in August 2005. A man had exposed himself and masturbated in front of a young woman in an empty R train. The victim, Thao Nguyen, a twenty-two-year-old website developer, took a photo of the offender with her cell phone. When the police refused to accept the picture, she posted it on two popular websites, Flickr and Craigslist, where it quickly attracted more than 45,000 views and many reactions. The *Daily News* ran a brief article and printed the picture on its front page.[38] Dan Hoyt, a forty-three-year-old white man who was a co-owner of two successful Manhattan restaurants, was quickly identified by other victims and co-workers and was arrested and later sentenced to two years' probation. Many newspapers and websites published this story. Hoyt showed no remorse. In an interview with *New York* magazine, he insisted that if he and Nguyen had met under different circumstances, she might have really liked him. "You know, she'd go, 'That guy's pretty cool. He's got this restaurant, and he's fun,'" he said. "She'd probably want to go out with me."[39]

This reaction outraged Nguyen and other victims. Among them was Emily May, the director of Hollaback!, a nonprofit organization aimed at fighting sexual harassment in public places. When asked how she became an activist, May recalled a conversation that she and three other women had had with a group of three male friends in 2005. They told the men many stories of harassment and informed them that "it happens all the time." This made the men exclaim, "You live in a different city than we do!"

With the help of her friends, May opened an online forum where victims of harassment could post pictures of offenders. Their slogan was "When hollered at, holla back!" Since 2005, the website has collected hundreds of posts narrating episodes of harassment.[40] It has also expanded into a multicity endeavor, with sites in other cities not just in the United States but in other countries as well. Interestingly, the New York City subway, where the first high-profile incident took place, is a recurring location in reports of two types of harassment: exhibitionism and groping. Catcalling is also a common experience for women entering or exiting the subway, indicating that the zone of encounter between the subway and the neighborhood is an ambiguous public space (as we pointed out in chapter 4). It is interesting that race is not mentioned in posts describing groping incidents. (The site managers remove or edit all the posts containing what they consider discriminatory words.)[41]

Emotional Resolution: Fear, Shame, and Anger

Few blog posts include a picture of the alleged harasser, and when photos do appear, they tend to be unclear. Indeed, the main purpose of the forum seems to be not so much to arrest the criminals as to offer emotional support to victims. For example:

Saturday, June 24, 2006
  This guy made me WANT to get off the train at 42nd street . . .
  I hopped on the downtown 6 train tonight at about 7:30. It was a very crowded car, and so of course everybody was bumping up against each other. There was an arm against my rear—or so I thought—so I moved up a couple of inches. Then, there it was again. And again. And again. Eventually I realized that it wasn't an arm at all—it was a hand that was getting friendlier and friendlier as the train moved from 51st to 42nd. I kept turn-

ing around to give him dirty looks, but I think he took that as an invitation! The more I glared, the more the hand stayed put. When we arrived at the next stop, I moved to the far end of the car and snapped these shots. Faces of the innocent have been blurred, of course.

In practice, the efficacy of this method is due less to the power of the Internet than to the emotional satisfaction that this form of nonverbal communication offers to the offended woman. "If you can't slap them, snap them!" announces the blog. In this regard, posting written comments and photos of an aggressor may be compared with the three steps of emotional expression and resolution described by Jack Katz, in which drivers categorize their offender and constitute themselves as a victim of this or that type of driver (such as contemptuous executive, dumb blonde).[42]

1. First, moral meaning is given to the social situation, as the driver takes the posture of a victim.
2. Second, the meaning of the immediate social situation is generalized, using all sorts of stereotyping.
3. Finally, the driver can perform as a ritual actor before the general audience whose presence he or she has invoked.

Indeed, many comments on Hollaback! strive to establish for violated women the status of victim, which shows how difficult that labeling is to acquire on the spot, as well as in society regarding sexual offenses.

Monday, June 30, 2008
I have to start by applauding this website. I heard about this site on the CW11 evening news. I hope it lets women know that it is NOT their fault. I only wish I had someone to tell me that when this incident happened to me.

In the Hollaback! forum, victimized women can express themselves in a way that does not call for on-the-spot attention or rely on some form of immediate public justice. Hollaback! is essentially self-rendered justice backed by a taken-for-granted majority opinion. Whereas speaking up on the spot can lead to a form of instant minitrial in which both the aggressor and the victim make their claims, posting on the Internet is more like a conviction without the possibility of appeal or cross-examination.

Hollaback! provides a vehicle for emotional conflict resolution and encourages victimized women to resume riding on the subway by mitigating the emotional damage they have experienced.

Separate or Ignore: When Gender Meets Politics

Whereas other subway systems have resorted to separating men and women, this option has not been considered in New York City since its short-lived experience in 1909. The staff at Hollaback!, spearheading the campaign to stop sexual harassment, thinks that separation is only a "band aid solution" that may be necessary in some places but is not suitable for New York City. Instead, Hollaback! advocates for cultural change through awareness campaigns, leadership building, and the production of better data on harassment. Unfortunately, despite its remarkable dedication, progress has been slow.

After the survey by the Manhattan borough president in 2007, the MTA had to be coerced to agree to put up posters in subway cars. Unlike other transporters in Philadelphia, Boston, and Ottawa, the MTA supposedly was afraid that the posters would merely lead to more lewd behaviors.[43] Those finally posted in 2008 read: "Sexual Harassment is a Crime in the subway, too—A crowded train is no excuse for an improper touch. Don't stand for it or feel ashamed, or be afraid to speak up. Report it to an M.T.A. employee or police officer."[44] Unfortunately, too few posters were displayed to have an impact. Although they may reappear once in a while, they are easy not to notice. They also were not translated in other languages such as Mandarin and Spanish, which would have found more readers on trains like the 7.

The MTA's reluctance to collaborate with outside organizations is mirrored by the New York Police Department. Despite intense lobbying and actual discussion at the City Council, the Transit Bureau does not release data on crime in the subway. Instead, the police prefer to crack down on sexual abuse covertly. Activists and researchers thus have to rely on spotty reports or produce their own data. In 2010, Hollaback! partnered with a team of web developers and released a mobile application that can send a geolocalized post to their website and at the same time send a message to members of the City Council. Finally, Hollaback! is very active in communicating about street harassment in schools, universities, and unions, and it is trying to educate employers and elected officials about the problem.

Typical Reactions to Groping

Another type of response to sexual harassment is often overlooked, even though it may be the most significant of those we have considered: the reactions of women (and, rarely, men) to harassment in the subway. One of the explicit goals of Hollaback! is to empower women by making them realize that what is happening to them is not unique. This is intended to remove the feeling of embarrassment that often keeps women from reacting overtly rather than suffering in silence. But is it working? How do women actually react, and how can those reactions contribute to better conditions for women riding the subway? Using the Hollaback! website and online reactions to two articles published in the *New York Times*, we were able to gather ninety-seven written descriptions of women's responses to groping or flashing on the subway. These accounts suggest the gamut of possible reactions as well as, more interestingly, the emotions attached to them.

The article that drew the most reactions was on the *New York Times*'s opinion page, entitled "I Was Groped on the Subway," written by a twenty-nine-year-old woman named Kimberly Matus. She recalls boarding a crowded train at 72nd Street on a Friday morning. Just before the doors closed, a man hopped on and pressed behind her:

> I tried to evade him but couldn't move an inch in any direction. I looked over my shoulder thinking the buckle of his bag must have been digging into me but there was no bag. Only his navy sweat pants. *Is that what I think it is? It can't be.*
>
> I shifted my hip to the right and then the left, but his body shifted with me. My eyes darted to each of the commuters around me, mutely asking for help. When none of their eyes met mine, I wanted to say something but no words came out. I held my breath until we got to the next stop.
>
> When we arrived at Times Square, I pushed passed him with the force of the other riders behind me. I said nothing as I glanced down to see the bulge below his waist.[45]

Matus goes on to describe how undercover police officers, who had witnessed the scene, approached her as she got off the train and asked her if she would provide a written statement and identify the harasser they had just arrested. The article brought 596 reactions in five months, including 51 testimonies of groping. One of the reasons for its success probably lies in the almost stereotypical way in which the event unfolded. First, the mode of the harasser's operation seems to be a common one: waiting until the last second before boarding and pressing himself against the back of a woman. It is difficult for the victim to escape from the situation, and other passengers are unlikely to be aware of what's happening. Second, and more important, remaining silent is by far the most common reaction described in the testimonies (fifty-three out of ninety-seven).

In a study of women's reactions to harassment on buses in several U.S. cities, Robert Emerson and Carol Gardner divided the responses into two categories: (1) maintaining a "nothing unusual is happening" stance and (2) adopting a "something unusual is happening" stance."[46] Based on our data, we have subdivided these reactions into four types: (1) silent and passive, (2) silent and active, (3) direct confrontation, and (4) talking out loud. The first two types maintain the appearance of normality by pretending that nothing unusual is happening, whereas the latter two imply the participation of witnesses.

Nothing Unusual Is Happening: Silent and Passive

Women in the subway face several impediments to speaking up against groping. One of these is the ambiguity of touch. Is it voluntary or involuntary? If it is involuntary, women seem to fear that if they speak up, they will be publicly blaming an innocent man, which not only is unethical but also threatens their own status. What if the man responds and the woman is shamed in front of all the other riders? What if he becomes violent? And even if the woman's assessment is correct, won't the people in the car judge her as guilty as her offender for provoking the incident? In this case, she would share the blame in a classic case of victim and offender bound together as accomplices in crime.

To restate the problem: Is it worth the risk of sharing the shame of groping in public rather than enduring being groped anonymously? A woman might conclude that it is not in her best interest to speak up because she cannot be absolutely certain that she is being violated; that is, the man may be pressed against her involuntarily owing to crowding. But even in cases in which the groping is unequivocal, speaking up remains a significant barrier, as in the following example:

Everyone is on your side

I took the subway back and forth to high school for all four years. The ride each way was a little over an hour. I always found comfort in the anonymity of the subway and slept all the time during the ride. On the F train back home one day, I was holding on to one of the poles above. It was extremely crowded and I could feel someone touch my butt. I saw his reflection on the window, against the black of the walls as the subway flew through the dark tunnels. I couldn't believe what was happening. I always thought that I would turn around and yell at the pervert if I ever found myself in that situation. I imagined myself slapping him in the face or kicking him in the balls. But what I ended up doing was feel extremely embarrassed. Questioning whether this was actually happening. What if this was a mistake? I would be so embarrassed if I called him out when he didn't do anything. I was so shocked. I just wanted to get to my stop and leave. I felt so dirty on the inside and out.

After it happened, it was hard at first to grasp the reality of it. I always kick myself for not standing up for myself. I regret it even more when I heard the same thing happen to my younger sister when she started going to the same high school.

My advice to all of you? Talk it out if it ever happened to you. If you do find yourself in that situation, remember that everyone is on your side. There is no doubt that what he is doing is unlawful. Kick him in the balls and let everyone know in the car who the pervert is so this won't happen to someone else you care about.

Diana, Hollaback! forum, July 31, 2007[47]

Most of those writing testimonies begin by questioning the actuality and intentionality of the contact and then go on to wonder how they should react. Most of the time, this reasoning leads to inaction and the pretense that nothing is happening, as if somehow the victim could detach herself from her own body:

I was running late to work and jumped onto a 6 train at 86th Street just before the doors were closing. A tall guy jumps in right behind me. The car was extremely crowded, almost no room to move whatsoever, but I was able to move a little further in to give the guy behind me some room. So we're riding and I feel something graze my butt, but as quickly as it happened it went away. I'm thinking to myself, that better not be his hand and I try and look down and see some form of a briefcase in his hand. The subway lurches and I feel something on my butt again, and this time it lasts a little longer so I move forward as much as I can, but there is a girl in front of me, a girl to the left of me, and a pole to the right of me, so there's really nowhere to go. The guy lets go but then puts his hand back on me (at this point I've figured out that it's not his briefcase, he is grabbing my butt instead of grabbing the pole right next to him). He mutters to me "excuse me" and takes his hand off. I am thinking to myself: "Can this really be happening to me right now? What do I do? Do I scream at him? Do I wait it out? Do I shove him off of me?" We kept going like that until 51st Street where I got off, thoroughly disgusted, him grabbing me and saying excuse me and me trying to pretend I wasn't in my body. I wish so much that I had said something to him or done something to end it, but I was paralyzed with fear. I know it sounds kind of stupid to just stand there and let it happen, but I was so scared of what he might do to me if I embarrassed him or said something. Since that happened, I've told myself I will never let myself be a victim of subway groping again. I only wish I had known to take a picture of him! Fucking creep.

Molly, Hollaback! forum, October 10, 2006, 1:22[48]

Invariably, the emotions linked to such episodes are fear, anger, and disgust, which can take a toll on the victim's willingness to continue taking the subway at rush hour. They can also persist for a very long time, as several of the comments on the *New York Times* website recall events that happened twenty or thirty years earlier. For these victims, posting their testimony may indeed help them attain some kind of closure, a finding that was confirmed by a research team at the Georgia Institute of Technology. The researchers interviewed thirteen women who had posted testimonies on the Hollaback! website. They found that posting their story helped the women shed some of the emotional burden associated with the event and might also help them mobilize to address the issue.[49]

Nothing Unusual Is Happening: Silent and Active

Whereas more than half the testimonies in our sample record situations in which women remained silent and helpless, nine women describe how they maintained the appearance of normality while taking covert action to stop the harassment. In earlier times a popular reaction, described by Michael Brooks, was to use a hatpin to deter wandering hands and bodies.[50] A similar covert action is described in a response to Kimberly Matus's article posted on the *New York Times* website:

> When I began taking the trains to high school at age 13, my mother recounted a story to me of being groped when she was a teenager, a cautionary tale to make me aware of perverts such as the fellow in the author's story.
>
> In those days of the 30's and 40's women still wore hats. After the first incident she kept a hatpin in the sleeve of her coat. On one occasion she used it on a groper. She still had it and gave it to me. It was stuck in the sleeve of my winter coat as I traveled to school.
>
> Groped once in warmer weather and not wearing my coat, I aimed my foot for the feet behind me and stepped as hard as I could on the assailant's foot and lifted my other foot off the floor with my full weight on the groper's trapped foot. He stared right into my eyes and could say nothing as we made a long express ride past many local stations. At the first opportunity he moved out the door. Triumph!!

Stepping on the harasser's feet and elbowing him are frequently mentioned covert actions. In the case just described, the response was effective and the resulting emotion one of triumph. In other cases, however, this type of covert action does not work. Such a situation is illustrated in the following response to a *New York Times* article by Karen Zraick, "A Personal Story of Sexual Harassment,"[51] which elicited seventy-four comments, including seventeen testimonies:

> 25. November 11, 2010
>
> A few years ago, when I was seventeen, I was riding the 4 train uptown at rush hour. There was a Yankees/Red Sox game and the train was packed. At some point on my ride, I felt something brushing against my inner thigh. I assumed it was a briefcase but, it kept moving, up under my skirt and into my panties, and then I realized it was someone's hand. I tried to squirm away but the train was too crowded. I stomped on his foot but he didn't stop. I elbowed him in the stomach but the car was too crowded for me to wind

up properly. He didn't stop. When the train finally got to the station, I sprinted onto the platform and ran, sobbing to a pair of police officers. I told them what happened. They refused to take my report saying there was no chance they would ever catch the guy.

In retrospect, I should have screamed and made a scene on the train. And, I should have taken the cops' badge numbers and lodged a formal complaint, not that anything would have come of it. But, I shouldn't have had to. This should not be something women have to tolerate on a daily basis. Groping and honking [when driving] both send the message that women's bodies are not their own, that they are the property of anyone who happens to pass by and take an interest. Holla Back is a great way to take back a certain degree of agency.

In the instances in which covert action was unsuccessful, the emotions described are similar to those expressed by victims who remained passive: fear of the harasser and anger at oneself and others for not being more proactive.

Direct Confrontation

Many women who remained silent while being groped express regret at not having confronted the harasser, and they exhort other victims to speak up. Interestingly, direct confrontation appears less frequently in the testimonies posted on the *New York Times* website (thirty-eight victims remained silent, and ten confronted the harasser) than on the Hollaback! site (fourteen and fifteen, respectively). This difference probably stems from the fact that these media have different audiences. On the activist Hollaback! website, confrontation of the harasser is encouraged, and comments criticizing a victim's action are systematically rejected. Thus Hollaback! offers a more supportive online environment and encourages victims of sexual harassment to take action.

The reported outcomes found considerable variation among the twenty-four reactions describing the victim's direct confrontation of the harasser. In nine cases, the harasser either submitted or fled. But in six cases, the harasser pretended innocence, and in eight other cases the harasser did not see any wrong or even verbally retaliated. Physical violence against a woman is described in only one case, which occurred at the subway exit leading to the street. The variation in harassers' responses to direct confrontation can be explained in two different ways, both suggested by Erving Goffman:

1. The harasser may have a conventional view of gender roles and expect the woman to react passively or silently, if at all. As we have seen, these types of reactions are described in the majority of the testimonies. A harasser with such expectations would likely be surprised by a confrontational reaction. He would have to improvise an answer, as his stereotypical image of women would not be of any help. This lack of guidance would explain the unpredictability of these harassers' reactions, which range from passive submission to verbal or physical retaliation.

2. The harasser may feel that his cover has been destroyed by the accusation and that, having been exposed, he does not have much more to lose by retaliating.

In most instances of harassment and abuse, the victim experiences a range of emotional injury. Fear and horror are common in situations in which the harasser retaliates verbally, guilt and embarrassment in situations in which the harasser pretends innocence, and disgust in situations in which the harasser flees. Only two cases, in which the harasser was finally arrested, produced a positive emotion: a feeling of being "right" and "glad."

The following example, a reaction to Matus's article in the *New York Times*, illustrates the embarrassment (or guilt) that results when both the harasser and the other riders ignore the victim's accusation:

May 13, 2013, 10:16 P.M.

Some creep many years ago put his hand up my skirt when I was on the subway with two friends—a woman and an older man. I cursed the fondler out and he moved quickly away, but then I saw my friends looking at me as if I was nuts, and other passengers—all male, as I remember—looking very annoyed. No one knew what I was cursing about—they thought I was being too demanding in a crowded car. The transgressor to them was me, not the fondler.[52]

In such cases, it is possible that witnesses to the incident have difficulty figuring out what has actually happened and whom to believe. This problem has the effect of casting doubt on both the victim's and the harasser's versions of the incident. The result is a classic binding of aggressor and victim in a shared experience of disapproval. When men don't visibly act like perverts, women often risk being dismissed as hysterical.

Talking Out Loud

Finally, eight testimonies describe situations in which the victim did not yell at the harasser but instead described the situation and asked for its immediate termination. For example:

> When this incident happened to me in a packed subway, I put the pervert in his place. In a loud voice, I said, "Excuse me mister, I realize this is a packed train, but I think your private area is way too close to my butt to the point of you having a hard on!!" Almost everybody looked towards where we were. You should have seen the look on his face. He was fortunate that the door opened; he exited in a flash. The pervert found someone who was not going to tolerate such behavior. I say, be proactive, speak up!!
>
> Comment on Matus's article, May 14, 2013

In this case, the woman not only talked to the harasser but also exposed the situation to nearby riders, making all of them witnesses to the abuse. In all the testimonies, the effect of the victim's action was immediate: the harassment stopped. Only two emotions were described: feeling dirty (probably shared by most victims) and embarrassment at talking out loud to no one in particular:

> When I was in my 20's, in the late 60's and 70's, I used to get groped regularly riding NYC subways during rush hour. It happens when you're standing, body pressed to body and it's so packed you can't tell whom the hand fondling your bottom or breasts belongs to. Furthermore, the men show no facial signs while committing this crime. I finally wised up and spoke loudly into the crowd, "Will you take your hands off of me!" The groper stopped

but I felt like a loony talking out loud to no one in particular and no one other than the groper acknowledging my plea.

Comment on Matus's article, May 13, 2013

In these testimonies, the offender was not directly accused of harassment and the other riders were not asked to take sides. Rather, they were asked to watch for any wrongdoing by men standing nearby.

The four types of reactions to harassment described here are significant for what they can tell us about gender relations and the subway. Direct confrontations (usually involving screaming) and talking out loud are reactions that appeal to other riders to take note of the offense and to support the victim, if not physically, at least through verbal and nonverbal communication. However, the unfolding of the situation is much more open-ended in the case of direct confrontation than in the case of a spoken denunciation. How can we account for this difference?

The Unpredictable Dynamics of Scandal

Screaming at the harasser can be understood as an attempt to rally public support and shame him by making him a subject of scandal. In the anthropological literature, scandal has long been viewed as an efficient mechanism for reinforcing or contesting social norms that are largely shared in a given community.[53] The function of a scandal is to identify deviant behavior in a way that calls for immediate sanction of the culprit. Often, the norms are so strong that the sanction is applied by the culprit himself. Conversely, a scandal can fizzle, a result that indicates that the norm invoked is no longer, or is not yet, as strong as the person making the accusation thought it was. Thus, creating a scandal is a risky endeavor, one that can turn against the person attempting it.

The unpredictability of the public's reaction to a woman screaming that a man is a pervert probably explains why so many victims choose to remain silent, either suffering passively or taking covert action. The fear experienced by the victim thus may have two components: fear that the harasser could become violent and fear that no one will come to her aid. And indeed, women who denounce their offender often face a resistant audience that refuses to take sides:

It is currently 94 degrees in New York City. Like every other woman in this city, I was wearing a sun dress. As the train pulled up to the platform, I walked towards it and felt a hand on my ass. I turned and a guy apologized for "bumping into me."

I yelled that he hadn't bumped into me, he had groped me. He turned and walked away so I yelled after him "did you think that you could grab someone's ass and nobody would care?" A few guys started looking at him and me, so I pointed and continued to yell that he had groped me. We got onto different subway cars and the train pulled away.

Three stops later I realized that I didn't feel like going out after all so I switched trains and headed home. Even though I yelled back, I still feel awful and ashamed. I don't ever want to wear this dress again. I keep telling myself that it wasn't my fault for dressing provocatively but I still feel like it was. I wish I had thought to take his picture, as I can see his face perfectly in my mind.

Debra, Hollaback! forum, June 8, 2008[54]

In this account, the victim tried to elicit some form of public support but received no response. She started feeling guilty, as if the harassment were somehow her fault.

In all the cases of direct denunciation, the scandal revolves around the idea that men should not sexually abuse women. When this technique works, the harasser flees in shame or is even arrested or molested by other riders. Gender norms are thus slowly reworked to contest men's assumed right to violate women's barriers. But this outcome is not very common. Instead, it is more common for the harasser to act either innocent or offended, a response that casts doubt on the reality of the abuse. We can conclude that norms about gender behavior cannot always be invoked in the subway environment. In addition, some individuals may not consider groping a deviant behavior. Such an attitude is especially likely to be found among men who have a traditional view of gender roles and for whom any situation may present an opportunity for sexual approach or harassment. Such attitudes are illustrated in Connie's testimony, quoted at the beginning of the chapter, in which, while riding on the 7 train, she hears a woman cursing at men while she herself is also trying to fend off gropers. In these cases, trying to create a scandal may actually have counterproductive effects; in fact, they may reinforce traditional gender norms, including that of male domination of women. In all these cases, gender roles are hotly contested and either confirmed or reworked, but they always remain present. Gender thus becomes a source of continual conflict.

Scandal fits the agenda of the activist organization Hollaback!, which would like to see norms regarding gender relations reworked so that women can more effectively create a scandal whenever harassment occurs. But because of the lack of reliable data on the scope of the phenomenon and, more important, its different forms and limits, Hollaback!'s approach has not yet caught on to any significant extent.[55] In particular, it has not managed to attract different segments of the population (with the exception of LGBT activists). The scandal thus remains contained in a relatively narrow circle. This prevents it from developing into an "affair," with different sides discussing the problem and possible measures taken by political institutions.[56]

Reworking Gender Norms by Undoing Them

Talking out loud, as opposed to directly confronting the harasser, is not an attempt to create a scandal by invoking gender norms. Rather, it is an attempt to set aside gender as a relevant category while relying instead on the basic norms governing behavior in public space. In the testimony referred to earlier, Connie reacted to illicit touching by asking her fellow riders not to abuse the situation and by telling a man who takes a seemingly protective stance toward her that "it is none if his business." She doesn't denounce anyone in particular, but she reminds everyone on the train that this is not an appropriate place for touching, even though bodies are squeezed together. When the groping does not stop, she threatens to call the police, and this threat seems to be effective. In the end, however, she is so distraught that she catches the wrong train at her transfer stop, 74th Street/Roosevelt Avenue, but she does not feel guilty for dressing as a woman or angry at herself for not taking action. Throughout the incident, Connie's reaction does not invoke gender norms. Instead, she asserts that despite the congestion on the train, the men around her still should behave as riders only and owe her the civil inattention that she is accustomed to in less crowded places (see chapter 5). Her choice is all the more telling, since gender norms among the mostly immigrant Latino population on the 7 train in the Corona area are less likely to support her plea.

Women who talk out loud in order to fend off sexual abuse in the subway are attempting to enforce the general norms governing access to public space. In so doing, they are also decreasing the pertinence of gender identities in public space. But this does not mean that gender and sex become totally irrelevant. As Connie showed in her diary when describing a romantic encounter in the same train in which she was harassed, the gender category remains available in both positive and negative ways. It is how the norms of behavior in a public space are defined and applied that determines the encounter's outcome. Talking out loud and asking for respect of one's privacy in public spaces is a way of "undoing gender," to borrow an expression popularized by Judith Butler.[57] Rather than erasing gender categories, it keeps them in the background while allowing riders to go from point A to point B unharmed.

Gender Identities and Gendered Encounters

The subway is, paradoxically, a space where gender identities are exposed in close proximity but must remain ignored. While this is usually unproblematic, it can nourish silent fantasies expressed in songs or personal adds. It also often leads to gendered encounters that are either consensual or experienced as harassment. By pressing bodies together, the recent and regular congestion of the New York City subway has made groping a public problem discussed by grassroots organizations such as Hollaback!, the City Council, and the MTA. Even though statistics and data are not available, we have identified four types of reactions to groping by women riders. Remaining silent and passive is the most common reaction and causes some women great emotional trauma. Covert action, such as stepping on the offender's foot, allows women to fend off harassers while keeping the experience private. Direct confrontation, in contrast, tries to announce a scandal that will unite the public against the offender. But its effects are unpredictable and can even go against the victim. Finally, talking out loud about the event is the most effective strategy to stop the harassment and shame the offender. This reaction builds on the normative order of the subway, which grants civil inattention to all riders and makes the use of gender identity ("doing gender") an automatic discrimination. It is consistent with social dynamics at work on the train and contributes to keeping gender in the background as only secondarily relevant to the rider role.

Realizing that gender is a category always available in interactions may help both women and men decide when it should or not be relevant to the situation at hand. The ability to make such decisions would serve to enhance the value of gender equality in public spaces. Reactions showing that gender can remain relevant but must not be abused not only indicate competence in using the subway; they also may advance the cause of women by limiting the social disorders often associated with ideas of gender asymmetry. Clearly, awareness of gender issues has come a long way since the opening of the New York City subway. Public spaces like the subway still have a role to play in improving equality of access to the city while also playing a role in the romantic imagination of New Yorkers.

7 Teenagers on the 7 Train

I like riding the subway together cause it's fun. When I ride alone, I feel bored and tired. There's no one to talk to, which is why I wait for them and they wait for me.

Aysha, sixteen years old, 7 train diary

As I nod my head listening to my iPod, this white lady in front of me smiled at me. I am still trying to figure out why she smiled at me, but people in New York do weird stuff.

Hélène, seventeen years old, 7 train diary

Every weekday from about 2:00 to 4:00 P.M., more than 500,000 teenage boys and girls burst onto the city's subway cars from almost every station in the system. The students use special free or half-fare MetroCards distributed by the city's Department of Education, which in 2006 and 2007 issued about 600,000 such passes to students enrolled in grades 7 to 12.[1] In Queens, about 150,000 students get a free or discount fare to the bus and or the subway.

Rambunctious Kids or Discreet Riders

On their way to neighborhoods and homes, teenagers typically arrive on the station platforms in small, exuberant groups, ready to release pent-up energies and to perform acts of adolescent bravado. Veteran New York subway riders are inured to their shouts, jibes, and singing, as groups of schoolmates jostle one another in the cars and on the station platforms and create adolescent scandals large and small. Their antics may alarm tourists and others who are unfamiliar with the daily rituals of release from teachers' rules and school constraints. Occasionally, though, the teenagers do create serious incidents or contribute to the more stressful aspects of subway ridership. A search on the Internet for teenagers on the New York subways offered these representative entries:

Group of about 20 teenage girls attack a NYC subway rider . . .[2]

Teen seriously hurt, loses eye subway surfing[3]

Subway kills teen on Upper West Side[4]

When I rode the subways at the age of 13 . . . my butt got pinched a lot . . . maybe I had suburban girl written all over me[5]

But headlines like these misrepresent the actual risks to the teenagers themselves and others during their daily invasion of the subway system. Out of the millions of rides they take weekly, these sensational stories account for an infinitesimal proportion of rides. In fact, the city's subways and buses offer its students and their families wide-ranging access to schools and cultural institutions throughout the entire city. And while some students may spend an hour or more traveling to and from home and school, many report that their subway ride is where they get part of their homework done after school. But this private work usually is done once the groups of students have dispersed and the youngsters become lone riders, strangers among other commuting urbanites, with homework to think about.

Teenagers in public places represent a specific type of stranger, particularly on the subway. Gill Valentine noted the ambivalence in the way adults perceive teenagers.[6] On the one hand, teenagers are often perpetrators of disruptive acts. Colin Symes showed how youths who commute by train form "microcommunities" in which they defy adults' glares and act out their youthful identities without concern for other riders.[7] Other researchers have documented the teenagers' perspective toward adult supervisors in public spaces, such as those of skateboarders in shopping malls and town squares, who often complain about those adults and authority figures who either deny or restrict their right to occupy public space.[8] On the other hand, teenagers are also seen by adults, and particularly by parents, as potential victims. Scholars have traced the relationship between the consequent increase in efforts to control their children in public places like the subway system and the disinvestment in public spaces, such as parks and school playgrounds, in cities since the late 1970s.[9] As a result, teenagers "often have nowhere to go except public spaces, where they often come into conflict with other groups."[10] In other words, along with being seen as rambunctious, teenagers are also thought of as a vulnerable group that needs to be protected, especially in urban public spaces.

Subway Diaries

In our fieldwork we observed many occasions when teenagers gathered in groups both inside and outside subway stations. In addition, in their diaries our students frequently told us that it was best for them to meet their friends at the subway before and after school because they often lived in different neighborhoods and the subway stations were where their daily itineraries converged (for more on this, see "Subway Diaries" in the appendix). In these situations, teenagers are highly visible and often, as we shall see in this chapter, make themselves "a target of special curiosity" for other riders.[11] When they ride alone, however, teenagers seek the opposite effect, to be as invisible as possible. They ride as others ride and try not to attract attention. Thus teenagers as a population group on the subways are unique in that the additional attention they attract while in groups usually vanishes when they ride alone.

Like many immigrant youths in cities, all of the twelve high school students who kept subway diaries for us socialized primarily with people from their own ethnic group when they were in their home communities. Because the subway is one of those places in the city where they are expected to know and observe the unspoken norms of behavior in public, their subway diary entries often show how they are learning to become more cosmopolitan and tolerant of others. Yet their writing also indicates wide variations in the students' urban competences and their tolerance for cultural and personal differences.[12]

Although they are young and relatively new to the city, our students have learned the social skills required to ride the subway. Hélène, eighteen years old and from Haiti, expressed in a journal entry a feeling shared by all the students about becoming used to the stress of riding on the subway:

Getting on the train in the morning is very hostile. You have people pushing you all over the place and you can barely get a place to stand. What's really weird about this whole thing is that for me, it is starting to be a normal
matter comparing to when I first started to take the train. I tell [you,] I used
to be so scared that I thought I was going to push out of the train one day.

Each student diary entry offered findings and questions that we could
apply to the next case, until we achieved "saturation," or the point that the
cases ceased to provide new information.[13] With the journal entries as our
unit of analysis, we expanded our sample. Our twelve students described a
total of 245 trips in their journals, an average of 20 trips per student.

The students revealed many of the aspects of being a rider on the subway that people ordinarily take for granted—specifically, observing others.
For instance, in an entry in her journal, Ana, sixteen years old and from
Argentina, wrote about adults on the train staring at a young couple who
are kissing:

For me that is just something normal and if I wouldn't be doing this [keep-
ing a journal] I wouldn't even have noticed them.

Although all riders make observations and have interactions and encounters similar—and often identical—to those that the students documented, describing them in a diary illuminates their meanings and hidden
interpretations (for more on the diary method, see "Subway Diaries" in the
appendix).

We used three research methods to supplement the diaries. First, we divided the students into four small groups for a researcher to lead them on a
one-time "walking interview."[14] Like the diary method, walking interviews
provide the researcher with rich contextual data from the participants. We
used this method to observe the students, to listen to them discuss their
surroundings, and to learn their thoughts about the subway *in situ* but in
the context of a visible group. Most important, the walking interviews allowed us to see how the students behaved as a group of riders, as opposed
to their traveling alone. A researcher went on the train with them from
school to their home neighborhood and audio recorded the conversations.
During the walking interview, we asked the students specific questions
about the trips and everyday encounters that they described in their journals

and had them clarify their subway experiences. With one exception (Bangla), we paired each group with a researcher fluent in the native language of the group's students (Chinese, Spanish, or French). This strategy allowed the students to converse with us about the people and surroundings of the subway without too much concern that the people they were depicting and who may have been listening would understand. We were especially interested in pairing languages because in their journals the students indicated that they often talked in their native tongues about other riders when they were traveling with their friends.

Second, we singled out six of the students (four girls, two boys) for more in-depth "go-alongs" that went beyond the regular interviews we conducted.[15] We chose these particular students because they transferred to the 7 train at the two stations—74th Street/Roosevelt Avenue and Flushing–Main Street—on which our larger project focused. We video-recorded the one-on-one go-alongs and focused our questions on the students' experiences in the public spaces of their neighborhood as well as on the subway and their attitudes toward other racial and ethnic groups in their neighborhood.

Finally, toward the end of the project, we gave the students disposable cameras and asked them to take pictures of significant sites on their regular trips. For our final meeting with them, we sat together as a group and discussed their pictures as well as some other aspects of the project. With a fresh perspective from behind the lens, we wanted the students to look at the places, people, and situations that they saw along their trips that they may have taken for granted after a month of writing about them. We then had them look at these pictures and describe or narrate what they saw in order to learn more about what they understood about being on the subway.[16] Given the difference in our ages, the photos were another way for the students to communicate to us how they experienced the subway.[17]

Subway Manners

All the students demonstrated in their writing that they had learned and agreed with the basic subway norm of balancing engagement and avoidance. They had accepted the subway's social order as a collaborative endeavor in which strangers strive to perform well as riders do, by respecting other strangers and maintaining civil inattention (see chapter 5). Ting, sixteen years old, reflected this universal attitude at the end of his diary,

Rule #1: you don't step on my turf, I don't step on your turf.

Since they see themselves as expert riders, students feel embarrassed when they unintentionally violate a norm, but in so doing, they acknowledge the norm's existence and their own mistake in crossing the line. One afternoon, Anais, sixteen, was riding on the train with two friends when the following incident took place:

Throughout the conversation I look at a publicity board of LaGuardia College, which is behind two sitting Asians (boyfriend and girlfriend—kissing). They apparently think I'm looking at them because they give me one of those annoyed looks. For a mere moment, they just look at me and I understand immediately why they're doing so. So I turn to my friends and ignore them (the Asians) throughout the whole trip.

June 7, 2006, 4:40 P.M., Flushing-bound 7 train

Here, Anais illustrates that she knows the general rule that it is acceptable to look on the subway but not to stare. Staring represents a rupture in the subway's social order of civility and an impingement on another person's social boundaries. Even though she did not intend to stare at the couple, she interpreted their reaction to her as they thought she did. When we asked Anais about this incident while reading her journal with her, she explained,

I never stare at people directly. I didn't mean to stare at them, but that's what they thought. I think they were annoyed because they were kissing.

After getting caught unwittingly violating this norm, she reacted to her embarrassment and tried to repair her standing as a good rider by consciously avoiding the couple for the rest of her trip. Her comment to us indicated that even though they imagined that she was staring at them, the supposed violation might not have been specified had the couple not been flirting with violating a norm themselves (that is, a public display of affection), which demonstrated her understanding of the social order as negotiated.

A Diversity of Experiences

Riding Alone and Together

All the teenagers understood that as strangers among other strangers, they had to respect others' personal space if they expected others to respect theirs. We also found significant variations in how they experienced being a rider and how they reacted to breakdowns in its social order. For example, students who ride with their friends experience the subway very differently from when they ride alone. For some of our student writers, when they rode alone, the subway became a setting for reflection or homework, their own amusement, or chance encounters. But others riding alone regarded it as a boring routine. Instead, they preferred to limit the chance of being made an object of attention or of making others the object of attention by retreating into their chosen media, into "auto-involvements" that made it easy for them to feel secure and alone in the crowd.[18] For them, being a rider was a disengaged role with a rather detached experience. Finally, some students found themselves as targets of attention because of their own social identity, or they interpreted the norm violations of other riders on the basis of their social identity. For them, being a rider was often a stressful, precarious role. All the students when riding alone invoked forms of "categoric knowing"[19] and used their own "folk theories"[20] in their observations and interactions with other riders. However, the role that their folk theories played in their experiences varied depending on how they experienced being a rider.

When they are in groups of friends, teenagers experience the subway and being a rider as a far more social experience. As members of a peer group, who usually share an ethnic background and language, they are aware that on the subway they cannot help but represent their culture and its particularities. Intuitively, they also understand that as New Yorkers on the train, they can also exercise the right to be different and not remain silent about their difference. Particularly for those who are more insecure about themselves and their identities and experience being a rider as a precarious role, the group offers them enough protection to engage with other riders, ignore norm violations, and understand the norms that they otherwise regarded as strict rules as being more flexible and negotiable. We will see later in this chapter that students from immigrant backgrounds also may act out and violate subway norms, just as groups of nonimmigrant teenagers often do, but with differences and meanings that often relate to their own ethnic identities and their broader claims to equality as teenaged New Yorkers.

Riding Alone but Not Apart

Nadine is a sixteen-year-old student from China, now a resident of New York. She usually takes the bus from the stop 100 yards from her family home to the Flushing–Main Street station, where she transfers to the 7 train. Her morning ride ends at 33rd Street in Long Island City (Queens), where she attends high school. In group discussions, she is discreet to a fault, but in her writing, as in this passage from a single 7 trip, she reveals her more socially imaginative self:

> This woman, probably in her 20s, keeps looking at me. I try to pretend she is not, but I catch her glances when she looked at me. I don't know what she was looking at. She might be looking at my shirt. (I personally think it's cute. It's red, and it has Disney characters.)
>
> This guy, about late 20s, was reading a newspaper (*Newsday* I believe). He opened up the newspaper in front of his face. Hmm . . . he is looking at the woman sitting across from him. But he is still pretending he is reading his newspaper. I wonder what he is looking at. I found it funny because sometimes people look at you, but pretending they are not. They are looking at you, and you catch them but still don't ask what are you looking at. I think it's the subway['s] unspoken manners.
>
> June 15, 2006, 11:57 A.M., 7 train

Nadine understands and agrees that staring at other people on the train is a norm violation, but one that usually has to be forgiven or rationalized (it was that nice shirt). She catches a heterosexual attention subterfuge and gives herself credit for being a subway citizen who knows the system's "unspoken manners." Even when alone, Nadine and the other students who wrote for us often experienced encounters on the subway as enjoyable, and they sometimes amused themselves by acting in the role of rider. Their subway interactions also provide insight into how daily subway ridership becomes a significant part of their assimilation into the city.

Yue is fifteen, petite, outgoing, and friendly. Her writing, as in this episode, displays a lively social intelligence at work:

When I got in the train [at 33rd Street], I saw three Chinese girls were talking to each other, and my sixth sense told me that one of the girls is from my homeland, Wenzhou. So I decided to stand near to them, so I could hear what they talking about.

I heard them complaining about the society and their parents were forcing them to find a job in the summer time. I knew that they were new immigrants after I heard their conversation and I was so into it because I think it's funny.

One of the girls who I think is from the same place as me, I heard she spoke Wenzhounese on her cell phone, and she told the other two girls that she disliked one of the girls in her class, because her name is the same as the girl who took away her ex-boyfriend. She used Wenzhounese when she saying this happened to her. She might have thought I can't understand Wenzhounese, however, I know what she's talking. So I really felt funny when this happened. I felt funny and exciting because I know her secret (which I believe).

Then, one of my Wenzhounese friends called me, so I pick up the phone and talk to her in Wenzhounese on purpose, so the three could know that I knew what they talking about. They got out of the train at 111th Street, then I got off the train in Main Street Flushing. Then I walked home instead of taking the bus. So I got lots of fun in this trip!!!! I felt sorry for them.

June 16, 2006, 4:00 P.M., Flushing-bound 7 train

What made this experience so much fun for Yue? Moving near the three girls who are speaking her native dialect to eavesdrop violated a norm ("I really felt funny"), but learning another's secret was "exciting." Instead of risking getting "caught" or perhaps edging away, she was confident enough to talk on her phone in the same language. Although she said nothing about the other girls' reactions, what she did was telling enough. If they all had continued on to Main Street, perhaps they might have started talking, but the three exited in Corona and Yue was going to the more distant and more affluent neighborhoods of Flushing, beyond Main Street ("I walked home instead of taking the bus"). She ended by admitting to feeling "sorry for them" and no doubt a bit superior herself, more sophisticated perhaps, more like a young women who knows her way around and not a "new immigrant."

Not all our student diary writers enjoyed their experiences on the subway, but those who did were especially likely to call on a precocious sociological detachment and to apply received wisdom or folk theories about other ethnic and racial groups. Ting, the sixteen-year-old from China, is a very bright student and wrote expressively in his diary about people on the subway. He paid close attention to who was around him, what they looked like (for example, "high status," "dressed working-class") and what they were doing, and he often provided his own thoughts and feelings about the situations he encountered, as in the following episode from a morning at his local station:

> There are good things happening in Flushing [station]. This morning a dark, short Native American was playing a musical instrument made of bamboo tubes, from the shortest and increased in length in order. . . . His hair is dark and long, very typical of a Native American. He had two speakers set up, large traveling bag open before his feet, and he stood and played that beautiful melody with his flute near the microphone. There was some change in the large open bag before him. There were also some CDs.
>
> His mellifluous melody is the closest thing I ever heard to nature. The music has a pristine quality of innocence. This morning was not his first performance. The first time I saw him play about two days ago I had the strong impulse of buying his CD (but I was broke, plus I was hurrying into the station).
>
> If I'm at the entrance to the station the tendency is not just to simply go in, but hurry in no matter how early you are. It is one of the habits of New Yorkers. When you are in the habit of hurrying, somewhere along the line you'll forget why you are hurrying.
>
> June 14, 2006, 11:00 A.M., Flushing Station

Here Ting expresses an interest in a different culture that he classifies as "authentically" representative of Native American music. For him, the public space of the subway becomes a stage where he joins with others who have also stopped to take in a cultural performance.[21] He can now relax his tendency to avoid others and engage more with the Native American musician and perhaps even elevate the encounter into a focused interaction by buying a CD and having a conversation (or he could simply walk away and go back to avoidance, with no consequences). In contrast, other students in our research group found the daily ride annoying and chose to withdraw and to allow the media to take them elsewhere.

Alone and Self-Absorbed

Juan exemplifies the students in our group who avoided social contact and preferred to hold firmly to the norms of being a stranger. A normally friendly seventeen-year-old student from Mexico, Juan wrote in his journal,

> I hate the usual kids who always get on the train and start screaming, yapping, and behave like animals, so I sort of wrap myself in a bubble so that I do not have to interact with this noise.
>
> I got to the 85th Street Station, run up the stairs and I am listening to PUNK, "The Casualties," their album "En la linea del frente." When I'm sad, I like to listen to punk because it makes me feel with power to control my emotions and therefore feel happy.
>
> I got into the train and just walk to the opposite door and stared out the window. When I am sad, I feel lonely and looking out the window separates me from the people around me because I do not have to make eye contact with them. If there is any noise, I have to increase the volume, not to hear the noise around me.
>
> When I take the E [train], I am thinking about how my high school career went by so fast, just like the train pulls up to a station and leaves it.
>
> June 14, 2006, 11 A.M., J train

Encased in his earphones, Juan does not pay much attention to other riders and enjoys how the freedom of being a stranger on the subway allows him to dwell on other aspects of his life (his future in this country, his upcoming graduation). He has established a routine performance as a rider that enables him to be detached from the setting, although some of his diary entries show that complete withdrawal from the complexities of subway interactions is not always possible:

My ride from Sutphin to Roosevelt is generally smooth, quiet, and because it is the longest, is the one where I do most of my reading. Right now I am reading an autobiography of a man who was enslaved and brought to America in the 1800s and it has many illustrations and drawings of the period.

As I was reading my book (always standing against the door) a black man approached me, begging some coins. He took a look at my book and saw a picture of a slave man being whipped. The man looked into my eyes and gave an expression of disgust as I told him I did not have any money. It is funny how fast people can draw conclusions and beliefs based on the most unimaginable details.

June 7, 2006, 8:00 A.M., Queens-bound J train

What "conclusions and beliefs" and which personal "details" did Juan believe provoked the subway panhandler? Reading while standing in his usual spot (another common behavior for these students), he recognized that the man was upset with him and assumed it was that although Juan was reading a book about African American slavery, he did not choose to give money to this particular African American man. Juan found it "funny" that the man would jump to this conclusion about him. Again, we see that all-purpose use of "funny" that adolescents and many adults often resort to as a surrogate for more thorough exploration of feelings. In time, when Juan enters college and becomes more aware of his dual identity—Mexican and American—he may more fully understand the layers of irony in this racially and ethnically tinged interaction and how, as sociologist Elijah Anderson would suggest, both men had just experienced a minor "nigger moment,"[22] with its jab of disrespect.

Alone Against the Others

Finally, some of our student subway diary keepers found riding alone to be a precarious and, at times, a stressful experience. Typically, these students reacted strongly to norm violations in the subway system, even though they occurred all the time.

Mehedi, a seventeen-year-old from Bangladesh, usually takes the bus from his home in Jackson Heights to the 74th Street/Roosevelt Avenue subway station, where he transfers to the 7 train and exits at 33rd Street. He is a shy but very responsive and smiling student who rides the train alone in the mornings and most evenings. Mehedi's journal regularly featured discussions of discomfort, as well as an interpretation of the subway's social norms as rigid rules. In the following, he reacts to a violation of the "no pushing" rule:

> I always stand in front of the doors, because I feel good. If I go in the middle of the train it is hard for me to breathe. So I always like to stand in front of the doors of the train. That day, the train was crowded; people were pushing each other to get in. However, there was some problem with two mopes in the train. One was a black guy, the other was an Asian guy. So they start to get a big problem about pushing each other, the black guy telling the Asian guy "why did you push me?" The Asian guy was like "I didn't push you." So after 5 minutes later they stop this fighting.
>
> I felt so unhappy that day. People were pushing me and I got so much pissed off. I couldn't talk [at] that time. I felt I wanted to kill everyone. I couldn't wait to get out of the train.
>
> June 7, 2006, 8:18 A.M., 7 train

Like Juan and many other of these students, Mehedi likes to stay close to the train door. But even in this spot, the nearby argument between "mopes" threatens his own comfort as he links their behavior to a general violation of rules (constant pushing) that directly affects him. This episode reveals how little margin for error Mehedi allows in regard to norm violations. He understands the subway as an environment where riders can easily damage the social order. He feels helpless ("I couldn't talk [at] that time") and lets what is going on around him affect him personally (he is unhappy and "pissed off"). Students uncomfortable with subway norms often invoke negative folk theories about other groups to explain why some people violate norms.

Both Anita and Connie are seventeen-year-olds from Colombia who live in Jackson Heights and often ride the train together. They experience the subway much as Mehedi does. Although their complaints go beyond being upset over overcrowding and breaches of norms, Anita and Connie regularly complain about the subway's smell, which they claim originates with the South Asians on the train. "The smell was really nasty," says Anita in an entry.

It was like food. To be specific the smell was like Hindu food with garlic. It was horrible and because of the humidity the smell was intense. I couldn't continue my way on that train.

And Connie recounted the following episode:

When we enter the train next to us was seated two women who were Hindu because they had dresses that women Hindus wear. One woman was wearing a yellow dress. Her skin color was brown, her hair was black and very long. The other woman had a pink color dress. They were sitting next to me and they were talking in their language. When Anita and me were next to them and they smelled bad, bad like onions. The smell came from their bodies. So we had to move because the smell was very bad and all people were moving and did facial expressions. When we got out in the station we breathed the good air because the train smelled disagreeable.

June 21, 2007, 8:30 A.M., Manhattan-bound E train

For Connie and Anita, smell violates a norm by not respecting the boundaries of others (an "obtrusion," according to Erving Goffman).[23] But Connie does not regard what she perceives as a bad smell as a consequence of crowds in tight spaces. Instead, she ethnicizes smell and understands it to be a physical trait of South Asian people. The smell intrudes on the social order of the subway and threatens her already fragile comfort level.

Our student subway riders rarely broke the norm of civil inattention to engage with others directly. Out of the hundreds of diary entries about their lives on the subway, only one of our students, Anita, introduced earlier, described a confrontation with riders whom she perceived were breaking the subway's rules by not respecting her privacy:

Curiously, I was looking at the advertisement posters when I see a young girl looking at me with attitude and I didn't know why. She was with her friend and I could see how both girls look at me and talk. Really, I was getting mad, because I don't even know them so she don't have the right to look at me like that. So what I did was both girls got off at 74th Street and I did something because I was taking the E train. It was 8:40 A.M. and both girls take the same direction as me. When we was waiting for the train I tell them why both was looking at me and if one of them knows me because I want to know what is the problem. The girls got nervous and tell me that they admired my skirt and I start laughing and I leave.

June 15, 2006, 8:40 A.M., 7 train

Anita interprets the two young girls' staring personally and gets mad because riders "don't have the right" to stare at her. She is upset enough here to violate the "rule" of civil inattention and say something to the young girls directly about their transgression. She makes them "nervous" because such confrontations are unexpected. Perhaps if the girls were not young and did not get off with her at the same station as she did and wait on the same platform for the same train, Anita would not have confronted them. The key is that the only incidence we have of such a confrontation came from a student who generally experiences riding alone as stressful, and who reacts strongly to norm violations against her.

Riding in Groups, Experimenting with Subway Norms

Except for four students who always ride the subway by themselves for various reasons (for example, they do not live near school friends; they go to work right after school), all the others preferred riding in groups because it makes the ride "less boring" and changes an otherwise dull moment into a more social or "fun" occasion. Indeed, even those students who regard riding on the subway as stressful and believe that the subway's social order is precarious, when they are riding with friends they often describe enjoyable underground experiences with their peer groups. They thus are relating to a subway social order that seems more congenial and relaxed.

Anita, who dislikes subway smells and betrays an aversion to South Asians, illustrated this change in perspective as she rode home from school with a friend:

Today I'm going to take the 7 train in Queens Plaza because I decided to walk with my friend, because the day looks beautiful. I'm still waiting for the 7 local train. During that time I'm playing with a little ball with my friend [and more teenagers begin] to play with us. The police man is around here and he looks like he doesn't like what we are doing. . . . Finally the train is coming we [are] all going to take because we don't want to get in trouble. We are three girls and four guys. We start playing in the wagon. Actually, we think the people located on the seats up are bothered by us but we didn't pay attention. . . . Also a little kid came where we are and started to play with us. His mother called him. We all started laughing because he tried to be like us.

June 12, 2006, 3:17 P.M., 7 train

As she describes the beautiful day, Anita's entry starts off on a much more positive note than do her descriptions of her solo ventures. She is just as aware that other riders are staring at her as she is when she rides alone. But now she neither takes their stares personally nor racializes the offenses. Instead, she uses the group to help her not "pay attention." The fun that she and her friend create even attracts other teenagers to join them. Unlike the girls whom she confronted for staring when she was alone, in the company of peers she enjoys this impromptu engagement with strangers in her age group and notices that the adult riders say nothing to her about their behavior. In fact, part of her enjoyment from this activity derives from her observation of other riders' reactions. Whereas she reacted strongly to the norm violations of others in the earlier example, here she plays with them herself. Unlike when she rides with her friend Connie, who shares her feelings about crowds and South Asians (whether they are alone or together), Anita does not see fellow passengers as problems. She also identifies and avoids the policeman, a rare authority figure who is a potential threat to the fun they are having. His presence causes them to board the train, where Anita does not mind being the target of others' attention.

Asserting Their Rights to Be Different, New York Style

For students from immigrant groups that stand out in the subway crowds because of dress or racial features, the comfort of the ethnic peer group does not always ensure increased confidence or even subway fun. Feeling the open stares of others can create its own forms of public theater and reactive assertions of the right to be seen and respected in public.

Aysha is a fifteen-year-old student from Bangladesh. She is a darkskinned Muslim and wears a hijab, sometimes with Western clothing such as jeans and a blouse, and sometimes with a more traditional outfit, an "Indian dress." Aysha writes that she is often the target of staring while on the train, which causes her great stress despite her auto-involvements. As she says early on in her journal,

> Everywhere I look, I see them looking at me, and not only one, all of them! Either sitting down, standing, or talking to someone. . . . How annoying is that? I'm sure no one wants to be stared at.

Throughout her journal, Aysha mentions people who stare at her and how much subway riding bothers her. But she experiences the subway much differently when she is with her friends.

On June 26 at 8:30 P.M., Aysha, her sister, and her friend Shirin are coming home from the graduation ceremony of two of their friends. They all are wearing traditional Indian dress for the occasion. After the ceremony, they get on the 7 train together, but it is late and past the time that their parents allow them to be out alone. While on the platform, Shirin remembers that her station comes after that of the sisters, so she must ride the train a bit longer and alone after they get off. She asks,

> How am I going to go alone all the way to 82nd St. by myself? Why don't you guys drop me please to at least 61st St. please!!

Aysha and her sister look at each other, and Aysha replies,

> Hmmm, Shirin, I really would, but you know I'm already late, and after going home now I'm going to get a big lecture, and I'm really tired of those big lectures!

Although she recognizes her friends' curfew, Shirin is persistent and asks them a few more times to ride with her. Meanwhile, Aysha notices people staring at them:

> We got people's attention probably because we were all dressed and wearing Indian dresses, but I didn't really care. That happens all the time and because after the entrance everybody was looking normal and never paid attention to us because today was a very hot and exhausted day for everybody.

As we saw, Aysha recognizes that other riders look at her because of her uncommon appearance. Unlike when she travels alone, when traveling with her friends who are wearing similar clothes she does not mind the gaze of other riders because she is used to it and receives only "normal" looks. She does not take it personally and absolves others from their ethnic-based norm violation (it was a "hot and exhausted day for everybody").

As the train nears Aysha and her sister's station, however, Shirin holds onto their hands to keep them from getting off. As Aysha writes,

> "[All in Bangla] Please, Shirin, we are already late, please can we leave, let us go" but she wouldn't listen. She nodded her head back and forth and said "Come on guys, look I'm going to ride alone, and I am wearing this dress, and those perv idiot guys are gonna stare at me, please drop me in 61st Street, then you guys can leave." Since she wasn't letting go of our hands and the door was already closed we decided to drop her off at 61st Street.

This excerpt illustrates the effect of the alone/together switch on the perception of others by these young riders. Whereas the looks are described as "normal" when riding in a group, they can become perverse at the thought of riding alone.

Aysha describes a scene that she and her friends created on the 7 train one day. Her friend Shirin—the same Shirin who could not ride alone to her stop—"was trying to find a spot to hold on and stand next to us," and two men were staring at them:

> Labonya said [all in Bangla], "I dare you to sit on the floor in the middle of us," and Shirin immediately looked at Labonya and really sat down.
>
> I was looking at us in shocked embarrassment. I was like, "Oh my God. Come on, get up!" Hasan was looking at my expression and looking at Shirin too. He didn't know what to say, rather than keep repeating, "You don't have to sit there, get up!" She just sat there.
>
> A guy probably 50 or more years old, wearing a brownish shirt, black hair, and holding a paper, looking at us with an evil eye and his eyebrows squeezed, as my eye caught his eye looking at us, he put his face down and just nodded back and forth. As I looked at him, his expression says "Lord, help these kids."

We were like the center of attention now, because Hasan and Labonya were laughing at Shirin and telling her sorry and so I was laughing a little bit, but not a lot because I hate annoying people. When I saw the guy looking at me and doing that I shut my mouth and were staring at people as if I were lost. I looked at Shirin, then Hasan the same way and told them to lower their voice, I was hoping my stop would be here any minute!! As usual Labonya never stopped being too hyper and I never stopped getting embarrassed in public.

June 15, 2006, 4:30 P.M., 7 train

They were being playful despite the public glare. In their South Asian party clothes, they must have attracted attention in the subway car. But they were being a bit bad and giggling or blushing about it, making a teenage scene on the 7 train just as any other group of New York teenagers would.

Learning Civil Inattention as a Skill

As these immigrant teenagers ride the 7 train to go back and forth to school everyday, they switch between two specific experiences: riding alone and riding in peer groups. For the students who do not feel at ease on the train when alone, this alternation offers them occasions to see the norms of subway behavior in a different light. While the violation of norms such as no staring and no touching bothers them when they are alone, this appears to be more a result of riders' skills at negotiating copresence when riding in groups. Notably, civil inattention is a skill consisting of giving accounts of one's presence and intentions that these young riders must learn to assess and utilize. Riding in a group or alone helps them realize that they do not have to give up their identity in order to disappear into the crowd of riders. They can be New Yorkers and Muslim, New Yorkers and Hispanic, and so on as long as they are competent at riding the trains.

8 Subway City

The 7 Train as an Engine of Urbanism

The history of transit spaces usually becomes a study of incidents, building on sources, often opportune and surprising, that reveal the mechanisms that have forged the collective imagination and the ever-changing practices and bodily languages of urban travelers.

Carol Saturno, "La Gare de l'est et les guides de Paris,
un siècle de modes d'emploi"

The expansion of the New York City subway system in the early decades of the twentieth century brought along its path almost everything sociologists understand by the term "urbanism." Perhaps first and foremost, the subway has literally become the engine of the city's "growth machine" of builders, financiers, government agencies, and speculators.[1] As we shall see in this chapter, the extension of the subway also expanded the New York urban way of life beyond the narrow borders of the East River.

Congestion City: Urban Density Before the Subway Suburbs

By 1910, the consensus in New York City was that the only solution to Manhattan's growing pains was to reduce the island's housing density. This meant sending workers to live in the outer boroughs, though close enough so they could commute to work. For years, reformers had denounced the living conditions of the poor in downtown Manhattan.[2] In 1879, the "old tenement law" imposed a window in each room, an indoor toilet for every twenty residents, and an air shaft for ventilation. But crowding got worse as more immigrants moved in. Journalist and photographer Jacob Riis made these conditions public in 1890, and a mobilization helped pass a "new tenement law" in 1901.[3] It set the land coverage to no more than 70 percent of the lot and increased the size of air shafts to courtyard proportions.[4] Although the law improved housing conditions in newly built areas, its effect was minimal in already congested areas. The Lower East Side was the worst, with more than 248,000 people per square mile, the highest density in the world.[5]

When new electrical technologies made the subway possible by allowing the trains to run underground, many people accordingly saw it as a means of mitigating the effects of the city's exponential growth without losing the benefits of a nearby and able labor force. When the first subway line was opened under Broadway in 1904, linking downtown Manhattan to the Upper West Side, Harlem, and the Bronx, these northern Manhattan neighborhoods rapidly became built up with "new tenement" buildings for a lower-middle-class and working-class population. The train soon was at capacity and reformers "began to warn that the overcrowded conditions in the old tenement districts were being repeated."[6]

In 1908, the Committee on Congestion of Population of New York organized an exhibition at the American Museum of Natural History. The "congestion show," as it was called, documented living conditions in the tenement buildings and advocated for new mass transportation. The proposed solution was to build multiple subway lines that would open many new lands to construction at the same time. To avoid repeating the congestion in the new settlements, planners pushed lower-density housing.

The dual subway contracts, signed in 1914 between the city and the IRT (Interborough Rapid Transit) and the BRT (Brooklyn Rapid Transit, later renamed the BMT [Brooklyn–Manhattan Transit]) companies led to the opening of many new lines between 1915 and 1920. The length of the city's rapid transit network doubled from 296 to 619 miles, and the frequency of trains more than doubled on the already existing elevated lines in and out of Manhattan.[7]

The 7 train, built between 1917 and 1928, from Times Square in midtown Manhattan to Flushing in northeastern Queens, was one of the lines that contributed to the city's population spread into the outer boroughs. It also helped New York grow into an international economic and cultural center. In this chapter, we discuss the role of the 7 line, built in the middle of fields and meadows, in shaping the city by stimulating the growth of a string of communities toward the North Shore of Long Island.

The 7 train today continues to move generations of newer New Yorkers—now many Chinese, Korean, Latino, and East Asian families among them—eastward from the older communities of the central city toward the golden shores of Long Island, one of America's most celebrated trajectories of assimilation and upward mobility. In Flushing, where the 7 train ends, the Long Island Rail Road and the Long Island Expressway service a suburban ecology of single-family homes and commercial sprawl. The bedroom communities of Nassau and Suffolk Counties tend to increase in affluence along what urban historian Kenneth Jackson named the "crabgrass frontier,"[8] ever advancing from the outer-borough communities of Bayside and Douglaston, to Great Neck and Port Washington, to Northport and Stony Brook, and out to the horse and wine country of the exurban North Fork. Any distinctions between the urban and the suburban ways of life hinge first on the use of mass transit versus the private automobile. We also find a clear contrast between living in the denser parts of the city, where apartment buildings predominate, and living in a single-family home alongside many similar homes. For a more comprehensive theory of how mass transit influences these choices and how it shapes the broader meanings of what we mean by urbanism, we turn to a consideration of the theoretical background for these concepts.

Sociological Perspectives on Mass Transit and Urbanism

The most famous definition of the city—which attempts to be a general one rather than those based on historical antecedents of urban growth (for example, the city grows around a fort, a cathedral, a market, or all of these)—was offered by Louis Wirth, a student of Robert Park, Ernest Burgess, and other early Chicago school sociologists. The city, Wirth argued, is a "relatively large, dense, and permanent settlement of socially heterogeneous individuals."[9] Given that definition, he speculated, there should be observable consequences of these defining urban traits for the social organization of the city and for its inhabitants' way of life, which he called "urbanism." These traits made the city an object of sociological study, with its own social organization and its own effects on individual personalities, distinct from those of the countryside or of other patterns of territorial settlement.

Wirth drew heavily on Georg Simmel's article "The Metropolis and Mental Life" (1903), largely inspired by the then exponential population growth of Berlin. Simmel explained that from having to cope with innumerable interactions with strangers, urbanites developed a more reserved, or blasé, personality that made them less sensitive to the perception of differences but also pushed them to develop their own eccentricity in order to stand out. Thus in addition to traditional values, which urbanites could cultivate in the diverse enclaves where they made their homes (which the Chicago school called the "natural areas"), they also had to learn the basic sociability of anonymous copresence among strangers and to develop specific tastes and skills useful in the larger urban environment and on the job market. Different "moral regions" emerged in the rapidly growing cities, organized around specific interests, including the financial center, Tin Pan Alley, the theater district, and the bohemian Greenwich Village. These areas of the city had formed their own subcultures with specific norms and social institutions, as well as specific criteria for inclusion. In the city's public spaces, however, density and heterogeneity had a leveling influence that leaned toward a basic equality among urbanites. That is, an urban "citizen" could expect to be treated like others on the streets and sidewalks, in a first come, first served fashion.[10] At the same time, the city's marketplaces and commercial areas fostered secondary relationships between buyers and sellers, for example, not based on kinship or even on any interpersonal acquaintance. But these more impersonal relationships also could be subverted by endlessly clever city dwellers to become economic and cultural niches where personal relationships could again be exercised (for example, in the selection of employees from the same social networks). At the level of urban politics, only organized interest groups, most of which were formed in neighborhoods or moral regions, could give voice to their members' concerns. In essence, the urban way of life imposed on city people by the effects of size, density, and heterogeneity itself affected the city's social and economic organization. The city was thus a milieu whose spatial ecology could be described as a whole, even if it maintained relations with its hinterland and with other cities and was affected by national and international trends.

Wirth and the Chicago sociologists who were his mentors were especially concerned with questions about how cities grow and the effects of increasing or changing size, density, and heterogeneity over time. On the one hand were urban plans and all the many intentional—or seemingly intentional—aspects of how people with power left their mark on the city's physical and social structures. On the other hand, city people always seemed to create neighborhoods or places that did not exactly follow the plans or overt intentions of the rich and powerful city leaders. Changing technologies, as well, had effects that altered the urban landscape in substantial ways. Robert Park and his students believed that two technological innovations greatly accelerated urbanization in the late nineteenth century: transportation and communication.[11] In essence, the commercial metropolis was the product of railroads (and harbors), newspapers, and telegraphic communication. These means of distributing people, goods, and information created great centrality around hard-built axes of circulation and places of production. Newspapers were the locus of exchanging ideas among strangers. New spaces of mass transportation or mass gatherings, as in parks and beaches, were marked by anonymous copresence, the togetherness of strangers so characteristic of the large city.

But even though they were efficient in speeding production and circulation, the urban institutions of communications and transportation could also create congestion. They drew migrants in large numbers to the center, where they lived and worked close to the markets and docks and factories. Thus, as we noted earlier, at the turn of the twentieth century, New York City's streets were choked with traffic, the shop floors were cramped, and housing was in such high demand that families had to double up in the dingy tenements.

American urban sociologists in the first half of the twentieth century were hardly alone in observing the results of planned and unplanned city growth. Indeed, growth could make the city good for business, but not for living conditions. And in time, as conditions deteriorated for the nearby immigrant working populations—who were thought to produce a miasma of toxic vapors—the environment could also worsen for business and property values. If financial loss and toxic miasma were not enough, the combined effects of density and heterogeneity were thought to contribute to stripping recently arrived immigrants of their ability to maintain their traditional cultures and institutions, thus causing their troubled children to become estranged and turn to the streets. There the younger immigrants as firstborn hyphenated Americans were vulnerable to the solicitations of the underground, illegal economy, and marginal social beliefs and practices.[12]

Riots, revolts, and radicalism were other urban dangers often evoked by politicians and reformers in the twentieth century's early decades.

Mass urban transportation was often hailed as a solution to the ills of the crowded city, and Charles Cooley was one of the first American sociologists to include mass transportation in his analysis of urban growth and change. A pioneer American sociologist, Cooley is known for his social psychological conception of the "looking-glass self,"[13] the idea that individuals form their personal identity through experiencing how others see them. Cooley's works were widely read and influenced contemporary thinking about the city. "The extreme concentration of population at centers has," he stated, "deplorable effects upon the health, intelligence and morals of persons who have to live in such places." Modern transportation, however, could help solve these problems by dispersing urban populations into the sunlight:

> Transportation having rendered extreme concentration possible now turns around and by means of street railways and other forms of urban travel endeavors to mitigate its evils. Humanity demands that men have sunlight, fresh air, grass and trees....
>
> On the other hand, industrial conditions require concentration. It is the office of urban transportation to reconcile these conflicting requirements; in so far as it is efficient it enables men to work in aggregates and yet to live in decent isolation.[14]

Likewise, in his well-known but understudied essay "The Growth of the City," Ernest Burgess also promoted the effects of dispersion and streetcars.[15] He observed that once migrants had spent time in the center of Chicago, in the communities and areas of first settlement, and once they had gained an economic foothold in the city, losing along the way some of their traditional values, they could then move to a more mainstream American way of life in the nearby suburbs. As they moved to more comfortable outer zones of the city, they did so very markedly along the roads and train tracks that radiated from the Loop or the downtown business district. The urban mass transit system, whether elevated, as in Chicago, or partially buried underground, as in New York, was hailed almost unanimously as the democratic solution to a better urban future in a large city.

The "Subway Suburbs": The Subway Makes the City

When the New York City subway was built, it did exactly what reformers had hoped.[16] The city expanded and gained inhabitants from many different origins, and the subway distributed them over all the boroughs:

> Even though the total population of New York City increased 56% between 1910 and 1940, the number of people who lived in Manhattan fell 19 percent during this period, from 2,331,542 to 1,889,924. As the population of Manhattan began to drop in 1910, the outer boroughs reported dramatic gains. Between 1910 and 1940 the population of the Bronx shot up 309%, that of Queens jumped 218%, and that of Brooklyn increased 165%. The subway's importance as a catalyst of decentralization is revealed by the fact that 91% of all city residents lived within a half mile of a rapid transit railway in 1925.... Clearly, people were moving out along the paths of the IRT and BRT lines.[17]

New York became the economic and cultural engine of the nation, the curve of subway ridership up to 1946 tending to confirm Louis Wirth's ecological hypothesis. As the city became larger, denser, and more heterogeneous, social contacts among urbanites fostered competition and innovation and produced a social environment more innovative and productive than the simple sum of its individuals. As a means of supporting secondary relations beyond the "natural areas" of the city, subway ridership is an indicator of this cultural and economic activity.

In figure 8.1, the parallel growth of the city's population and of the subway ridership begins on the left in a pattern consistent with Wirth's theory. As more inhabitants moved to the city, the subway stimulated the development of new community areas that quickly became defined by new institutions, churches, schools, and political clubs, spanning new neighborhoods in this period of sustained urban growth. During these decades, the port was still an active part of the city, even as the airports were expanding, and, we must remember, thousands of workers were still employed in Manhattan's garment district or in its printing trades, not to mention the more middle-class and upper-middle-class occupations in the financial services. From 1900 to 1946, the city's population rose from 3.5 million to

Figure 8.1 Subway ridership per year and New York City's population per year, 1900–2012.

almost 8 million, and ridership grew to a record 2 billion rides per year (an average of 260 trips per person per year, but ridership then was predominantly composed of adult men [see chapter 6]).

Most of this growth took place in rural areas of the Bronx, Queens, and Brooklyn, opened to development by the subway between 1915 and 1928. The lines were built by the IRT and the BRT (later the BMT) companies under the terms of the "dual contracts" signed with the city in 1914. Clifton Hood, one of the few historians of the New York City subway, calls them the "subway suburbs." Unlike in older European cities such as Paris, the subway grew ahead of the city. In 1916, in order to limit density in the new territories, the city's Board of Estimate approved a zoning resolution dividing New York into three types of zones: residential, business, and unrestricted. This specific and unusual mode of development allowed planners and savvy developers to design the construction of whole neighborhoods, both for a profit and with specific ways of life in mind.

The 7 train, for example, linked a succession of small towns—Long Island City, Newton, and Flushing—still separated by fields and marshes. In 1917, when the train reached 103rd Street in Corona, the president of the Queensboro Corporation, Edward A. MacDougall, had already bought most of the blocks north of Roosevelt Avenue and south of Jackson Avenue (now Northern Boulevard). Inspired by Ebenezer Howard's influential essay, *Garden Cities of Tomorrow*, MacDougall set out to build one of the country's first urban garden cities along the line.[18] Instead of single houses, as they also were built in Forest Hills and Sunnyside (along the 7), the Queensboro Corporation sold garden city apartments, an early form of cooperative housing. Middle- and upper-class buyers could live in an apartment surrounded by greenery and a nine-hole golf course a mere 23 minutes from midtown.[19]

In essence, MacDougall was selling the idea of bringing the city to the countryside in a suburban community. Queensboro developed three main arguments to convince buyers, all related to Wirth's definition of the city. First, regarding size, the apartments were part of the city's expansion outward. The main selling point was their quick subway connection to midtown and all the amenities of the city: "It is quiet as a country town but decidedly metropolitan in its taste."[20] Second, the development was much less dense than Manhattan's residential neighborhoods. In Jackson Heights, the early garden apartment buildings covered as little as 40 percent of the lot.[21] The gardens, enclosed in each block, gave the development a quiet, bucolic atmosphere. Richard Plunz, a historian of housing in New York City, wrote that the garden city apartment developed by the Queensboro Corporation represented the higher end of most of the interwar construction in the boroughs. Faced with competition because of the sudden availability of land within reach of the city center, developers drastically improved the quality of housing offered to even the lower and middle classes.

By 1920, developers in the outer boroughs had gone further than the requirements of the new tenement law, having realized that the affordability of the land opened to development did not require them to maximize density in order to make a profit. Notably, they shifted the scale of development from the usual lot of 25 by 100 feet to the entire block. This move allowed them to simplify the plan, save on construction costs per apartment, and transform the air shafts into actual garden spaces in the center of the development.[22]

If the first garden apartments in Jackson Heights were aimed at the middle and upper-middle classes, the next generation of apartments, inspired by the model, were targeting the more numerous working-class families looking to move out of Manhattan, where apartments in the tenements were often as expensive as those in the new buildings. In 1924, the Metropolitan Life Insurance Company, recently allowed by a state law to invest its profit in housing with limited rents, built fifty-four U-shaped buildings housing 2,125 working-class families in three districts of Queens along the 7 train, near Bliss Street and Woodside, and along the Astoria line near Ditmars Avenue. Density was a little higher than in Jackson Heights, but the land coverage, at 45 percent of the lot, was still much lower than in the tenement areas.[23] So-called garden apartments thus became ubiquitous along the dual-contract subway lines and made up the bulk of housing built until 1930.

The density in Jackson Heights and all the subway suburbs was lower than in the tenement neighborhoods of the Lower East Side and in the areas along the first subway line, but was higher than in the single-housing neighborhoods such as Forest Hills built earlier along the Long Island Rail Road. Through a combination of legislation, construction technology, architectural innovation, and market dynamics, the congestion problem was solved without abandoning the city's urbanity.

When Wirth wrote "Urbanism as a Way of Life" in 1938, the population of the most crowded neighborhoods in Manhattan had decreased dramatically, and density was no longer considered the city's main problem. Instead, population density was thought of as a variable in urban life that could be planned for and managed, especially through the development of mass transit.

Heterogeneity, in contrast, had reached unprecedented levels and accounted for, in Wirth's view, the disappearance of primary relations and the preeminence of secondary relations organized in a segmented fashion around the diverse interests of the individual. Unlike life in the village, the city person lacked a community in which to form a network of personal relations:

> It may easily be inferred, however, that the organizational framework which these highly differentiated functions call into being does not of itself insure the consistency and integrity of the personalities whose interest it enlists.

Personal disorganization, mental breakdown, suicide, delinquency, crime, corruption, and disorder might be expected under these circumstances to be more prevalent in the urban than in the rural community.[24]

The Queensboro real-estate developer Edward MacDougall also was concerned with the negative aspects of heterogeneity. He attempted to build a homogeneous community to ensure a form of social cohesion and stability in Jackson Heights, which would help keep prices high: "He conceived of Jackson Heights as a homogeneous suburb of like-minded middle-class residents who shared similar social backgrounds, occupational levels, and cultural values."[25] Even though some Italian and Irish families seem to have found their way into the development, the project's original orientation was decidedly Protestant and catered to buyers of northern European descent. Jews and blacks were expressly prohibited by these restrictive covenants. Elsewhere in the city, garden apartments were often quite homogeneous as well. In the Bronx, Jewish unions built many of the new cooperatives, forming like-minded urban communities around political or religious values.[26]

Large, dense and homogeneous, Jackson Heights with its garden city apartments was a resounding success in the 1920s. Between 1920 and 1925, eight apartment complexes, occupying one block each, were built and their apartments sold. From 1923 to 1930, the development rose from 3,800 to 44,500 residents distributed in 135 buildings grouped in thirteen complexes.[27] Contrary to Wirth's definition of the city, the garden subway suburbs in the 1920s succeeded in preserving both community and urbanity, by building medium-density housing organized like villages connected to the rest of the city by the subway.

In the 1930s, however, the Depression forced the Queensboro Corporation to subdivide the larger apartment into cheaper, smaller dwellings, and construction slowed dramatically. The corporation even rented furnished rooms to meet its financial obligations. By the beginning of World War II, developers along the 7 line had reverted to denser, more profitable, six-floor buildings rented to lower-income populations. Finally, after the war, to answer the pent-up demand for housing, the land left open was built up. The golf courses and other green areas in blocks adjacent to the building complexes disappeared. The covenants were modified, and Jewish families took up residence in large numbers. Density and heterogeneity rose, and Jackson Heights became more like the other apartment-house communities served by the subway. It was no longer the well-planned urban version of a garden community close to the city. It had become a far less planned, diverse, and dense urban neighborhood whose growth had been continually stimulated by a subway line linking it to a very large city.

The Moses Era and the Rise of the Automobile

In 1928, after much debates and protractions, the 7 train had finally reached Flushing.[28] But in the 1930s, as the subway was bringing greater density and heterogeneity to Jackson Heights and other nearby communities, families started moving out, going first to the lesser-developed areas of Queens, farther eastward along the line. Despite extension projects, the line never went any farther, leaving much of northeastern Queens accessible only by bus or car. Potential residents also moved to the more distant suburbs outside Queens, in Nassau and Westchester Counties.[29] In these areas, the automobile and appliance industries and builders of mass suburban tracts like Levittown were aggressively promoting single housing. These moves were facilitated by the opening of new roads under the direction of Robert Moses, who had managed to harness the federal financing of the New Deal.[30] On the north side of Jackson Heights, Grand Central Parkway offered a direct escape to Nassau County, and the new Triboro and Whitestone Bridges led to Westchester. In any case, the loss of population was minimal, since the Great Depression and then the war economy postponed the development of the suburbs. In 1946, however, everything was in place for the century's greatest shift in mode of transportation. The roads had been built; the car industry was back on track; and the federal government was underwriting mortgages for houses bought outside city limits.[31]

New Yorkers, too, were ready.

The World's Fair and Its Effects

In 1939/1940, the 7 train had seen an unusual peak in ridership (more than 8 million more rides) when many urbanites had flocked to the World's Fair, in what today is Flushing Meadows–Corona Park, near the end of the line. The fair's uncontested star was the Futurama pavilion, built by General

Motors to promote its vision of the country to come.[32] The visitors entering the pavilion took their place on a seat moving along a rail meandering around a huge model, where they were given a dramatic tour of a landscape governed entirely by cars and highways and where, ironically, trains and pedestrians had vanished.

Meanwhile, most of the housing construction in the city during the late 1930s and 1940s revolved around government-sponsored housing for the low-income population. Economies of scale and an ideology imported from the modernist European movement were used to lower lot coverage even more by constructing "towers in a park," following a famous motto made popular by the architect Le Corbusier. In Queens, the first major Federal Housing Administration (FHA)–sponsored housing development was the Queensbridge Houses built in Long Island City, just north of the Queensboro Bridge and subway station. As soon as 1940, 3,149 apartments were available to rent in six superblocks of about sixteen, six-story, Y-shaped units.[33] Inside the block, the distinction between the street and the garden was blurred by a continuous path leading from the subway to the street to the garden, mediating the encounter between the larger city and the community.

The Subway in Eclipse

Starting in 1946, the parallel between population growth and subway ridership suddenly stopped, with the population stagnating and ridership falling. Meanwhile, the rest of the country still was enjoying continuous economic growth.

Following the construction of the new highways and the municipally run independent subway lines (IND), new housing developments in the outer boroughs pursued the "tower in the park" trend. In 1949, Fresh Meadows, a housing complex, was built in the far reaches of northeastern Queens, just south of Flushing by the Long Island Expressway (LIE) and far from the subway. It housed 3,000 families in an "independent community for a middle-class estranged from the inner city urban condition"[34] and was not open to African Americans. In Lefrak City, just south of Elmhurst, near the E and D trains, was the most elaborate development, completed between 1962 and 1967, also along the LIE. Six X-shaped towers housed 800 families each, making this project the largest privately financed housing project in New York.[35]

The subway entered a period of slow decay. In the 1930s, the city had built its own municipal network, the IND, in order to compete with the private IRT and BMT companies, which were accused of profiteering.[36] In order to be profitable immediately, the new lines, with a few exceptions, were built in already well-served neighborhoods. Many urban-renewal housing projects were built along the lines in the less well-served areas such as Red Hook in Brooklyn and Far Rockaway in Queens. The competition was detrimental to both the new and the old companies. They all lost money, and by 1940, the city had taken over the two private companies and merged them with the IND into a unified system, hoping to raise efficiency and save on management costs. It did not happen.

The IRT and BMT lines had not been maintained for years. The elevated sections were becoming dangerous and were progressively deconstructed to make room for car traffic. In 1948, the fare, which had been set by contract at 5 cents since 1904 and used as a political argument in every municipal election, doubled to 10 cents. The increased revenues were supposed to help expand the system (for example, to build the Second Avenue line) and free the city from the financial burden of operating the subway. But the subway had never really been profitable. Any extra revenue was quickly used up to maintain the already aging system and to build much needed transfer points between the three networks (for example, at 74th Street).[37] As early as 1950, the system was losing money again. The dip in ridership slowed down in the 1960s as the federal government stepped in and allocated emergency funds for mass transit. Although the city regained some of its population, the financial crisis in the 1970s ended all hope of urban revitalization. Work on the Second Avenue line stalled once more, and both the population and the ridership dipped to an all-time low. Since 1946, the city had lost 1 million of its residents and half its ridership (from 2 billion to about 1 billion rides a year). Deindustrialization coupled with suburbanization had ended any hope that the city could maintain a self-sustaining social model linking urban ways of life and land development.

The Subway's Dark Decades

From 1976 to 1991, many New Yorkers avoided the subway. The number of riders per year fell to the lowest levels since World War II. The reasons for this have been discussed at length in histories of New York City covering the bleak years of the country's oil crisis, the city's financial crisis, the wave of disinvestment in public services, and the spike in crime.[38] The main reasons evoked by riders, in addition to people moving out of the city, was insecurity and the lack of reliability. Somehow New Yorkers had lost trust in the system on both social and technological grounds. The roughly 900 million to 1 billion trips taken every year seemed to represent an almost incompressible minimal level of "captive travel" by New Yorkers without any other commuting choice.

As the federal government sponsored the development of the distant suburbs by underwriting mortgages and subsidizing highway construction, Wirth began to doubt his 1938 article contrasting the city with the countryside. In "Rural-Urban Differences," written in 1948 but published posthumously in 1956, he wrote:

> From a sampling of a number of studies, including my own, of the ways in which rural and urban people are supposed to differ, I have found that if we allow for each of these fundamental factors, virtually all of the differences between rural and urban behavior are accounted for without any resorting to the alleged urban and rural natural dissimilarity.[39]

Even though Wirth did not give up the idea of urbanism completely, the urban way of life was no longer produced in the city. As people switched from the subway to a car or fled the city, Wirth's idea seemed to have lost its sociological pertinence.

In 1962, Herbert Gans went even further. In a famous rebuttal of Wirth's 1938 article, he denied the role of mass transportation in building a specific way of life and eliminated the line between urban and suburban:

> It is true that the upper-middle class housewife must become a chauffeur in order to expose her children to the proper educational facilities, but such differences as walking to the corner store and driving to its suburban equivalent seem to me of little emotional, social, or cultural import. In addition, the continuing shrinkage in the number of mass-transit users suggests that even in the city many younger people are now living a wholly auto-based way of life.[40]

In essence, Gans was stating that in the outer city as well as in the suburbs, the privacy of the car had replaced public spaces. Neighborhoods were now independent units detached from the rest of the city, which as a consequence had lost its unity. Gans observed that people tended to re-create ethnically and economically homogeneous communities in what he called the suburbs and the outer city.[41] This term, although not entirely clear, seems to include areas like Queens. According to Gans, what characterized a place and its sociability was neither secondary nor primary relationships, but some form in between that he called "quasi-primary" relationships, which developed between neighbors and were based on propinquity rather than density, size, or heterogeneity. In addition, because most Americans during the postwar period had the means to choose the location of their residence, they chose to live among people similar to themselves. Since homogeneity was a matter of choice, the social organization of neighborhoods depended more on the characteristics of its residents—such as their ethnicity and culture, their class and position in the life cycle—than on any trait of the spatial environment. Suburban tract housing served by the automobile and outer cities originally built along subway lines were similar. The inner city, although different, was for the people who had no choice, the captive poor, mostly African Americans and other racial minorities, who did not have the financial or legal means to escape.

Since the city had no specific urban quality to attract companies and the middle class, the city planners set out to change this. In New York, and in many other American cities, highways cut through neighborhoods to enable cars to reach the center:

> The principal strategy of the older cities in their battle for continued supremacy was to beat suburbia at its own game. To maintain preeminence, the aging hubs had to adapt to changing transportation technology and lifestyles. They would thereby acquire the advantages that suburbia boasted and retain middle-class residents and customers to balance the onslaught of poor minorities.[42]

William H. Whyte's "organization man," the title of an influential book published in 1956, was the typical target user of these new infrastructures. Living in the suburbs with his family, he could drive his car all the way to the office without ever setting foot on the street. Whether his office was in the city or in the suburbs made little difference, because so many companies had moved out of Manhattan. Accordingly, by 1980, except for a few lone voices, the very idea of the city as a specific mode of spatial settlement both integrative and innovative had almost disappeared.[43]

The Subway and City Return

Subway investments and improvements in service helped bring the city back. In the 1980s, the Metropolitan Transportation Authority (MTA), the public authority in charge of running the subways and suburban trains since 1969, obtained the right to borrow money and started an ambitious program of renovation and cleaning. In 1991, as the city was undergoing a new wave of immigration, ridership on the subway finally reversed. The number of rides taken every year rose from 930 million in 1990 to 1.6 billion rides in 2010, or about 670 million more rides (more than 72%).

What accounts for such a dramatic shift? First, there are more New Yorkers now than in 1990, in most part owing to the number of recent immigrants and their children.[44] Second, New Yorkers have been traveling more, pushed by a soaring economy until the early 2000s. Third, the subway has become a chosen means of transportation, accounting for a larger proportion of trips in the metropolitan area, mostly to the detriment of private cars. If only the first two reasons were the cause of the shift, it would mean that the new high levels of ridership were still the result of "captive travel." However, if the shift from car to subway is real and durable, it could signal a change in the relationship between the city and its public transportation system that could contribute to a less polluting and more sustainable way of life.

Private transportation consultant Bruce Schaller, then deputy commissioner for transportation for the city, was the first to report in a 2001 landmark study the shift from car to subway:

Subway ridership increased 34% during the 1990s while the number of autos owned by city residents increased by only 6%—a difference in growth rate of 28 percentage points in favor of the subway. . . . This represents a remarkable turnaround from trends in the 1950s through 1980s. In each of these decades, changes in auto ownership increased by 21% while subway ridership grew by only 2%. . . . The automobile's estimated mode share declined by 4 percentage points from 48% to 44% of all trips within New York

City in the 1990s, after increasing by 7 percentage points in the 1980s. The subway's estimated market share increased by 2 percentage points to 31% mode share in the 1990s after declining by 3 points in the 1980s.[45]

According to this report, six factors account for this shift: (1) public capital investment in the subway, (2) increased immigration, (3) the lower crime rate, (4) greater traffic congestion, (5) higher parking costs, and (6) changing patterns of economic growth and commercial and residential development. Some of these factors are directly related to the state of the subway system, others to car traffic, and a third category to more general urban trends, such as immigration, patterns of growth, and urban development. If they can be related to the shift from car to subway, since most manufacturing industries have left the city, they would point to an interesting relationship between the city and its transportation system. Did the characteristics of the city, size, density, and heterogeneity give it new life?

The Resilience of Medium-Density, Subway-Accessible Neighborhoods

The trends in ridership in the subway suburbs differ from the image of decay and later revival of the city. For example, ridership trends on the 7 train give a different account of postwar events.

While the general ridership curve and the 7 train ridership curve were almost exactly similar until 1946 (with a discrepancy due mostly to the 1939 World's Fair), the two lines changed markedly after 1946. For the next sixty years, ridership trends on the 7 were always significantly higher than the trends in the overall system (figure 8.2). That is, while general ridership fell drastically in the 1950s, the dip was much less severe on the 7, and while it decreased slowly during the 1960s, it went up on the 7 (with another peak due to the 1964 World's Fair). When it plateaued during the 1980s, it went up on the 7, and finally, when it rebounded in the whole system, it grew even faster on the 7. The only recent period during which the two curves were the same was in the 1970s, and the financial crisis was the only time when the population living along the line actually fell. The general result is a curve that suffered much less from suburbanization and deindustrialization than did the system as a whole. What explains this discrepancy? Why

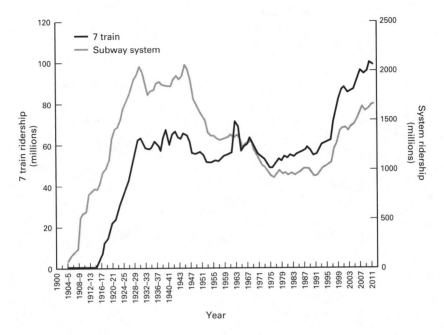

Figure 8.2 Ridership per year for the 7 train and for the whole system, 1903–2012.

did the 7 fare better than the rest of the system, and why is it growing faster today?

One hypothesis is that the "subway suburbs" built around the dual-contract lines in the 1920s offer an urban quality of life superior to that of the earlier tenement-law neighborhoods built along the old elevateds and the first IRT line and to the later developments along the IND lines. They also provide a density and a catchment area superior to those of the car suburbs that can sustain mass transit ridership. A comparison of ridership trends on the 7 with trends on the northern section of the original Broadway IRT in upper Manhattan and the Bronx (1 train from 103rd Street to Van Cortland Park, open in 1904) and on the Brooklyn part of the Coney Island IND (F train from York Street to Stillwell Avenue in Coney Island, open in 1933 as a subway) yields interesting indications.

Figure 8.3 depicts the competition among the different systems in the 1930s when the IND opened. Even though the 1 train and the F train are not next to each other, both faced competition with a nearby train, whereas

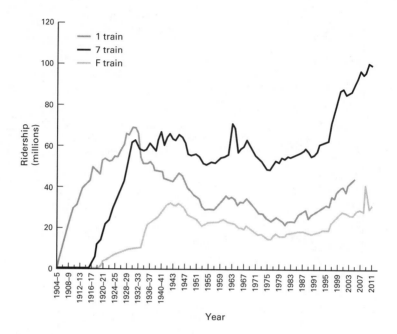

Figure 8.3 Ridership per year for the 7 train, the 1 train (in the Bronx and upper Manhattan), and the F train (in Brooklyn), 1904–2011.

the 7 was connected to the IND only at 74th Street/Roosevelt Avenue. (The A train was built three blocks from the 1 train, and the F was built close to the N and the Q trains.)

After the peak in 1946, all the lines suffered from the competition with the automobile. But whereas the neighborhoods along the 7 kept gaining residents, both the tenement neighborhoods of Washington Heights along the 1 line and the neighborhoods along the F route lost residents, which explains the loss of ridership. Not all the residents fleeing the dense neighborhoods went to the suburbs; a good proportion moved to the subway suburbs, which explains the resilience of the 7 train ridership. Starting after the war, Jackson Heights welcomed more Jews and Italians, and beginning in the 1960s, it started admitting Hispanics, first from Puerto Rico and then from Ecuador, Colombia, and Mexico. The garden city apartments, more comfortable than the tenements or the subdivided three-floor row houses along the F train, proved an affordable alternative to the suburbs.

In the 1980s, New York City started gaining population again, thanks to renewed immigration (mostly from South and East Asia in Jackson Heights and Flushing), but also to the birth of many immigrant children.[46] Subway ridership picked up and, by 2010, had reached levels close to its maximum in 1946. During that time, ridership growth for the 7 train was much stronger than that for the 1 and the F trains. The change came suddenly in 1998, just after the MTA introduced the MetroCard, a magnetic card that riders must swipe at the turnstile. For the first time, the MetroCard offered a free transfer from the bus to the subway, a policy that had an immediate effect in Queens, where many residents lived quite far from the subway stations. The policy halved the fare and brought many new riders to the 7 train. In particular, the stations in Jackson Heights and Flushing, with many bus lines, saw a huge increase in ridership, much higher than the growth in population.

While the quality of the garden apartments was related to density and heterogeneity, the bus-to-subway transfer was related to population size. The zones served by the 7 train are, on average, larger than the zone served by the F and 1 trains, because of their competition with other lines. These two factors have combined to providing good-quality and affordable housing to families that may not have the means to move into single-family housing and must rely on public transportation. These families often are recent immigrants, whose arrival in the subway suburbs helped these neighborhoods resist the flight to the suburbs. In both Jackson Heights and Flushing, the quality of housing also made more affluent residents, often white property owners, resist moving to the suburbs.[47] Thus the "invasion" by new populations (in Chicago school terms), was not immediately followed by a "succession" but by a superimposition of people of diverse origins. This is why neighborhoods like Elmhurst[48] and Jackson Heights have been called "hyperdiverse."[49] Norwood in north-central Bronx is another example of a subway suburb neighborhood that remained intact and became diverse. It was built around the last stations of the Jerome Avenue line, which opened in 1918. Farther down the line, in contrast, housing along the Grand Concourse suffered massive depopulation and decay in the 1950s, but Norwood presented a combination of size and density that kept it desirable. Along the Concourse, a new IND line had spurred a wave of sustained construction that dramatically raised density and contributed to its decay after the war.[50] In the end, the specific combination of medium-density housing characterized by the garden apartments and the street patterns may account for most of the resiliency of ridership on the dual-contract lines. Interestingly, residential density along the 7 train, which was much lower than that of the city as a whole throughout the twentieth century, is finally catching up with the average density of the entire city. The 7 line's density of 27,000 residents per square mile is slightly higher than the general density of Queens (20,000 per square mile), but still much lower than the density in Manhattan (69,000 per square mile).

A Ridership Greater Than the Sum of the Population

Since most of this recent growth took place in the subway suburbs, we next examined the relationship between the growth of population and the growth of ridership in these areas in order to identify possible patterns. For this, we looked at four segments of the 7 line in specific urban areas all developed in the 1920s. The first segment is the postindustrial section of Long Island City (Vernon–Jackson to Queensboro Plaza); the second segment is the neighborhoods of Sunnyside and Woodside, a mix of low- and medium-density housing (33rd Street to 69th Street); the third section is the Jackson Heights–Elmhurst–Corona area (74th Street/Roosevelt Avenue to 111th Street): and the fourth section is the lower-density commercial and residential area of Flushing (Flushing–Main Street).

In figure 8.4, we can see that most of the recent gain in subway ridership along the 7 train happened in the Jackson Heights–Elmhurst–Corona section of the line. Even though ridership in this section suffered massively from the postwar suburbanization, it did quite well throughout the 1960s and the bleak years of the financial crisis and rebounded quickly in the 1980s. Ridership in the Sunnyside–Woodside section also rallied during the dip of the 1960s, 1970s, and 1980s, when immigrants came to form more than half its population. But ridership took longer to rebound in Sunny-side–Woodside. The difference from Jackson Heights was based mostly on population size and density, since both areas had comparable housing structure and patterns of immigration. Jackson Heights–Elmhurst–Corona gained close to 60,000 new residents between 1980 and 2000, and its density shot up from 48,000 to more than 67,000 residents per square mile (table 8.1). In both areas, the relatively affordable and large number of apart-

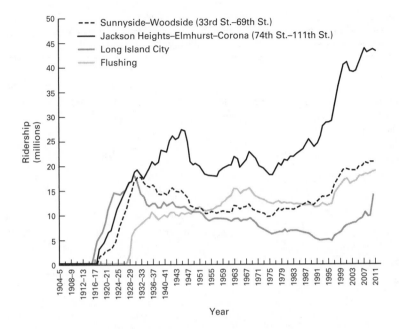

Figure 8.4   Ridership per year on four sections of the 7 line, 1917–2012.

ments, built in the 1920s and 1930s, were able to accommodate the greater than usual number of immigrant families. This explains the jump in population and density, despite the construction of relatively few new buildings.

The Long Island City section has lost a sizable number of riders since the early years. It suffered from the deindustrialization that began in the 1960s and started to regain riders only with the introduction of the Metro-Card in 1997. Since the resident population is very small (about 15,000), most living in the Queens River project, a high-density low-lot coverage complex in which residents' unemployment rate is particularly high, this trend suggests that the additional riders were workers coming to the area (table 8.2). Because they came by bus to the 7 train bound for Long Island City, workers may be coming from the farther reaches of Queens and then transferring to the 7 train at 74th Street/Roosevelt Avenue in Jackson Heights and Main Street in Flushing, the two stations with the highest increases in ridership in Queens since 1997 (see chapters 2 and 4). More recently, Long island City has seen an influx of new housing constructions and residents. Ridership has grown even faster.

TABLE 8.1
Evolution of Selected Population Characteristics over the Decennial Censuses 1970 to 2010 in Jackson Heights–Elmhurst–Corona and Sunnyside–Woodside

		Census Year				
		1970	1980	1990	2000	2010[a]
Jackson Heights–Elmhurst–Corona	Population	177,146	182,241	200,894	261,180	251,310
	Density (pop./sq. mile)	46,972.2	48,323.2	52,146.0	67,859.9	63,070.2
	Foreign born (%)	33.7	47.1	58.34	65.5	65.14
	Unemployment rate (%)	3.7	6.8	9.4	9.7	7.4
Sunnyside–Woodside	Population	75,757	74,188	79,287	90,463	87,838
	Density	49,296.1	44,120.7	46,702.8	53,232.4	56,544.3
	Foreign born (%)	31.3	45.4	54.5	62.1	58.9
	Unemployment rate (%)	3.5	6.9	7.8	6.9	7.5

[a]The data for the year 2010 are taken from the 2006–2010, five-year compounded American Community Survey (ACS). We used this survey instead of the decennial census because some of the questions relative to transportation and others disappeared from the 2010 questionnaire.

TABLE 8.2
Long Island City Population Characteristics, 1970–2010

	Census Year				
	1970	1980	1990	2000	2010
Population	15,442	14,164	12,994	13,084	14,713
Density	14,254.5	13,121.0	12,287.1	11,763.7	13,771.4
Foreign born (%)	13.3	17.7	16.7	24.4	30.2
Unemployment rate (%)	3.8	10.9	16.6	13.0	11.6

From 1980 to 2000, the number of subway riders entering the station at 74th Street/ Roosevelt Avenue and Flushing–Main Street has risen, respectively, 125 percent to 16.2 million and 50 percent to 18.6 million. Using those neighborhoods served by these stations, including the areas also served by local buses, to define the most probable catchment areas, we find that the populations of the concerned areas of Jackson Heights and Flushing grew, respectively, by 38 percent to 67,000 and 11 percent to 310,000 (table 8.3). The ratio of ridership growth to population growth is thus three to one at 74th Street and five to one in Flushing. In both cases, either residents started to

TABLE 8.3
Select Flushing Population Characteristics, 1970–2010

	Census Year				
	1970	1980	1990	2000	2010
Population	279,278	266,545	281,118	309,588	310,099
Density	17,632.3	16,828.4	17,803.5	19,599.8	19,521.4
Foreign born (%)	18.1	26.4	37.6	47.6	52.3
Unemployment rate (%)	2.8	5.3	5.9	5.2	8.7

take the subway a lot more, and/or many more visitors took the subway to the neighborhoods. The fact that as more residents move in, the more often they or visitors take the subway indicates an ecological property of the city. Whether size, density, heterogeneity, or more general trends are affecting the two areas is difficult to determine.

For example, the history and pattern of ridership is quite different in the Flushing section from that in the Jackson Heights section. Except during the 1970s and slightly during the 1980s and 1990s, ridership never dropped significantly. It even grew during the postwar suburbanization. Most of northeastern Queens was suburban, with single-family houses. Its proximity to the Flushing–Main Street station at the end of the line, as well as a couple of Long Island Rail Road stops, made it a desirable, low-density area of the city. Even more so than in Jackson Heights, many residents live quite far from the subway station, to which they must either drive or take a bus. This combination of low density and size accounts for the jump in ridership, visible in 1997 with the introduction of the free bus-to-subway transfer. Since 1980, the Flushing area also has gained more than 30,000 inhabitants, mostly of foreign origin, and residential and commercial density has increased, especially in the blocks around the subway station.

Despite the variations, one trend is common to all the sections of the 7 train in Queens. From 2000 to 2010, subway ridership grew when the population size actually stagnated or decreased. And except in Long Island City, more than 50 percent of the residents of all the neighborhoods along the line are foreign born. These numbers suggest that either many of the residents of these heterogeneous neighborhoods have started traveling more by subway (because they travel more and or because they switched from the car to the subway) and/or that the neighborhood themselves have become more attractive to workers and visitors from other areas of the city.

TABLE 8.4
Percentage of Use of Public Transportation in Neighborhoods Along the 7 Line, 1970–2010

		Census Year				
		1970	1980	1990	2000	2010
Long Island City	Public transportation (%)	60.00	58.7	62.9	68.5	68.3
	Subway only (%)	46.7	NA	51.3	60.3	59.5
Sunnyside–Woodside	Public transportation (%)	71.00	69.3	66.1	67.6	71.4
	Subway only (%)	56.7		57.3	59.7	65.1
Jackson Heights	Public transportation (%)	67.2	64.1	61.4	61.2	67.3
	Subway only (%)	57.2	NA	52.1	52.9	55.9
Flushing	Public transportation (%)	47.4	42.1	36.3	33.1	38.7
	Subway only (%)	33.9	NA	21.9	18.6	21.2

The statistics for the means of transportation to get to work for adults sixteen and older are helpful.

As seen in table 8.4, except for the residents of Long Island City, whose high numbers remained constant, the proportion of workers who took public transportation to work increased significantly (+6% in Jackson Heights–Elmhurst–Corona). This change does not, however, account for the growth in ridership during the 1990s, which was spurred more by the gain in population. In Flushing, for example, the proportion of workers who took the subway only as a means of transportation actually went down from 2000 to 2010. Since the population did not grow, the rise in subway ridership must therefore have been due either to trips taken for reasons other than work or to trips taken by workers and visitors from outside the station's catchment area. The latter reason is more probable. Flushing has recently emerged as a large commercial and business center for the Greater New York Area's East Asian community. Its growth and resilience as an urban center made possible by the combination of new immigration patterns, subway accessibility, and a relatively low density thus attracted investment in new constructions.

Urbanism: A Theory of Ecological Accessibility

Even though ridership on the 7 train outpaced the growth of the overall system, no clear single cause seems to be driving that growth. In Jackson

Heights, it was the combination of medium density, good-quality housing, and new immigration patterns that led to most of the new growth. In Flushing, it was a combination of immigration and low-density housing that enabled the recent commercial growth. All along the line, and indeed all over the city, immigration brought the cultural and economic heterogeneity of neighborhoods to levels unseen since the 1940s. As more residents born abroad move in, neighborhoods slowly acquire a new ethnic character or lose their older one when newcomers of diverse ethnicities converge. The "Irish" identity of Woodside and Sunnyside faded as east European, Chinese, Vietnamese, and other ethnicities asserted their presence. So too, "Indian" and "Pakistani" 74th Street has retained its South Asian commercial identity even as its residents have become more diverse; "Colombian" and "Ecuadoran" Jackson Heights now accommodates the shops and strollers of the young urban professionals moving in; and "Mexicans" (Corona) and "Chinese" and "Koreans" (Flushing) also host many other identifiable groups. Over the next generations, these groups will build their own organizations and institutions, and their members will also travel around the city. Heterogeneity has become a routine experience in the city, especially in the crowded conditions of mass transit. The heterogeneity of subway and bus passengers also has become taken for granted rather than wondered and stared at. In that sense, we have become urban.

The subway has become one of the main places where we experience urban diversity on a daily basis, but how is that diversity itself produced? In his influential theory of urbanism as the production of ever new subcultures and types of neighborhoods, Claude Fischer argued that the essential characteristic of the city is the heterogeneity it produces.[51] Although cities attract diverse populations of immigrants and migrants to the city, even more important, Fischer noted, cities produce new subcultural groups that did not exist before. He agreed with sociologist Herbert Gans that ethnic enclaves do not necessarily produce deviants and gangsters and may in fact provide a strong community for urbanites. He also agreed that the traits of this community were largely determined by the characteristics of its own people. Fischer contended, however, that the density and the heterogeneity of the city as a whole offered each urbanite more occasions to deviate from mainstream norms and to build and adopt distinct subcultures. Thus the city is a place for the recognition of nonconventional norms or, at least, nonmainstream norms.

Fischer's idea was not solely psychological, however, as it was for Simmel. Rather, it was "ecological" in the sense in which these two authors used the term to refer to variables of growth, density, heterogeneity, and other population parameters. If subcultures thrived in the city, it was because the number of people with specific nonconventional interests could reach a "critical mass" beyond which groups could form and even build local institutions and, in some cases, by their presence, create places associated with particular subcultures and specific influences. Think of the jazz scene on 52nd Street in the 1950s, the gay scene in the West Village at the time of the Stonewall riots, Harlem in the 1930s, Warhol's celebrity factory in the 1970s, or the contemporary hipsters of Williamsburg. These were scenes and subcultures always accessible by mass transit, so that not everyone associated with them lived in the local neighborhoods. Throughout the city, community and neighborhood social clubs, local newspapers, sports associations, and congregational groups attest to the presence of subcultures in less flamboyant but in infinite ways.[52] Moreover, the city's mass transit system allows these groups and organizations to draw their numbers from outside the local neighborhood or community. Mass transit also helps groups retain members who may have moved elsewhere in the city but still wish to remain members. Thus in a revisit of his subcultural theory of urbanism, twenty years after its first publication, Fischer moved a step closer to discovering what we might think of for New York and other major cities as a "subway theory of urbanism." He explained that what allowed the critical mass to arise, and presumably to flourish, was "intra-group accessibility".[53] "In our still-spatial world, larger places will be more unconventional than smaller ones only to the degree that group members have greater access to one another in larger places than in smaller places."[54]

The subway, along with other means of communication, is the urban institution that best affords this accessibility. The empirical finding that New York City's growth in ridership has grown beyond what one would expect from population growth alone supports Fischer's subcultural theory of urbanism, and it also calls our attention to the larger ecological sense of the meaning of subway transportation for urbanism.

A purely economic theory of accessibility, as presented in Edward Glaeser's *Triumph of the City: How Our Greatest Invention Makes Us Richer, Smarter, Greener, Healthier, and Happier*, advocates for the highest density possible.[55] We have seen that the medium-density subway suburbs along the 7 line (still a high density), are more resilient than the higher-density neighborhoods and that diversity also plays an important role in economic sustainability. Accessibility is therefore both an effect of density and heterogeneity, and the subway, combined with housing development, is its main driver.

We also saw in the previous chapters that the subway exerts powerful influences—planned and unplanned—on all the communities along its route and that almost every conceivable type of urban area can be found over or under its tracks. Fischer rightly emphasized the ways that a reliable transit system can positively affect accessibility, communication, and urban diversity. In addition, we have shown that the subway is an institution that shapes the human ecology of the entire city while it also exerts powerful influences on individual behavior. This duality returns us to Simmel's early argument that the city inevitably pushes urbanites toward both more heterogeneity (in his words, "eccentricity") and mass leveling (or equality). These two characteristics make the city's public spaces, and particularly the subway, the locale of bodily copresence where a multitude of different people must get along in order to go about their own business. And as we have consistently seen, urban copresence requires the ability to keep one's judgment to oneself in public and to tolerate the strangers in one's midst. Active toleration in public, as opposed to urban or rural people's attitudes of tolerance in surveys, is a behavioral skill honed and practiced in actual, everyday situations.

Subway Congestion: Are There Limits to Increasing Ridership?

In 2007, a report by the New York City Transit Authority found that seven subway lines (2, 3, 4, 5, 6, E, and L, with the 7 and F closely behind) were running at maximum capacity in both passenger load and the number of trains per hour.[56] Since then, the situation has not improved and represents a continuing, serious challenge to the quality of urban life for many New Yorkers.

The question is no longer only about population density in the apartments and in the neighborhoods but also about congestion and crowding in the subways that link them. As of this writing, we do not know the effects of the Second Avenue line on easing congestion in Manhattan. It is clear, however, that much depends on the subway's ability to take an ever-increasing number of passengers to their destination at an acceptable speed and in bearable conditions. How will New Yorkers cope with even more crowdedness and social diversity on the trains? In this regard, the 7 line will remain a good barometer of the larger system's success. In 1999, it was designated the most ethnically diverse train in the entire city, and the White House named it as a monument of the American immigration experience, which has only increased in the ensuing fifteen years. The processes we have uncovered in our empirical investigations of subway behavior are encouraging. We have seen that as density and heterogeneity increase both inside and outside the subway, New Yorkers become more competent at navigating not only the complicated technology and administration of the MTA but also the more unpredictable social mix of the subways and its social order. In turn, these competences help the system run better, with fewer incidents, and contribute to building the renewed trust that New Yorkers have in the system and in one another. Despite overcrowding, construction and mechanical delays, sweltering platforms in the summer, and endlessly broken escalators, the physically and socially competent urbanite chooses the subway. Will that always be the case? A subway theory of the city would argue the affirmative. Yet much will depend, as always, on the leadership capabilities of those who guide the system's future and on the willingness of citizens to pay for its increasing costs.

9 A World of Subway Citizens

Getting a seat on the train can be a New York rarity like a rent-controlled apartment or a late-night cab ride to the outer boroughs. But there are New Yorkers who know how to optimize their chances by staking out a spot on the platform. "On lines that use the same model train, figure out a spot where the doors open when the train stops. It gives you a leg up for getting a seat or at least a space on the car."

Gene Russianoff, attorney for the Straphangers Campaign

As its elevated tracks and stations expanded eastward in historic bursts, the 7 train spurred the real-estate deals that gradually increased the density and heterogeneity of the neighborhoods along the line. The placement of its stations created the communities of northern Queens. Today, the backgrounds and national origins of the people who live along the 7 line are global. As we have demonstrated in previous chapters, the least common denominators of their urbanity are their competence at circulating through the subway system and their trust that they will collectively reach their destination. These beliefs and competences are critical to the situational community in transit in which riders participate day after day throughout the system. This unique community also spills out onto the streets and enhances transit accessibility for everyone. None of these characteristics is unique to New York; throughout the world, the subway is a mode of transportation integral to dense urban living.

Subways are popular. In 2014, 160 cities had a subway system and the number is increasing. In the ten years leading up to 2015, twenty-nine new metro systems opened to the public in cities all around the world. China leads the trend with twenty-two subways already in operation and fifteen more under construction, and India is following closely behind. The systems of Shanghai, Guangzhou, and Shenzhen (in China) and Delhi (in India), built between 1993 and 2004, have quickly become among the world's most

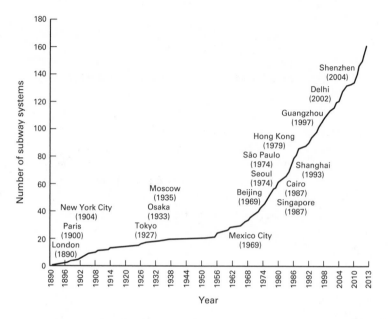

Figure 9.1 The number of subway systems built around the world from 1890 to 2014, and those with the largest riderships (800 million annual). ("Statistics Brief: World Metro Figures," October 2014, Union internationale des transports publics [UITP], http://www.uitp.org/sites/default/files/cck-focus-papers -files/Metro%2oreport%2oStat%2obrief-web_oct2014.pdf; "List of Metro Systems," January 15, 2015, Wikipedia, http://en.wikipedia.org/w/index.php?title= List_of_metro_systems&oldid=642060241)

trafficked subways, together with the older Western networks of London, Paris, and New York built almost exactly a hundred years earlier. Figure 9.1 traces the construction trend of metros around the world and clearly shows an acceleration starting in the 1960s. The construction of subway systems has correlated closely with the rise of the economic and political powers of large metropolises in the "emerging" countries of Asia and Latin America.

The Global Growth of Subway Studies

Social scientists throughout the world have gradually started paying more attention to how new transit infrastructure can affect their cities and their residents. The "mobility turn,"[1] led by geographers, and the sociology and anthropology of infrastructure[2] are recent and emerging fields that analyze the experience of movement in modern life. Despite this renewed interest, however, the number of studies, like ours, that have been conducted in the new subway systems, is small.[3] These few ethnographic works available in English or French focus on Delhi,[4] Taibei and Kaohsiung,[5] Moscow,[6] Mexico City,[7] and Cairo.[8]

In all these cities, the construction of a subway was invariably supported by claims that it would represent the city's entry into urban modernity. This optimistic claim often accompanied a larger assertion of national cultural superiority: Communist versus capitalist modernity for the Moscow subway, claimed in 1959 by the Soviet deputy premier, Frol Kozlov, to be vastly superior to the New York subway;[9] Indian versus Western modernity for the Delhi metro;[10] and clean and disciplined modernity in Taibei, as opposed to the grubby New York subway.[11] Modernity that also brings higher property values is particularly attractive to local financiers. Modernity in mass transit pertains as well to the supposed role of these "modern" transit technologies in encouraging order, cleanliness, and discipline, a role considered both positively and negatively.[12] In the end, subways represent a considerable collective achievement for municipal authorities and elites, and they seem to flourish best in nations with a centralized command over financial investment and political capital.

Just as in New York City, however, the behaviors that riders apply and enforce are not exactly in line with the official rules. In Taibei, Anru Lee conducted a detailed ethnography of the social consequences of the subway's effect. She showed that when the subway was opened, after years of excruciating surface disruptions of urban life and traffic, the authorities released a blitz of official messages instructing riders how to behave in the new system, where they should walk, how they should line up, and so forth. The strength of the riders' adherence to the new rules surprised even the authorities. In fact, most riders attributed their obedience to their feelings of national and local pride, and they were eager to show off their new metro at its best, despite the generally low esteem they had for their administration and its injunctions.[13]

In Delhi, the subway, which opened in 2002, was also supposed to lead to greater self-discipline and tolerance of difference.[14] Unfortunately for the women who ride the Delhi subway, research shows that gender neutrality and civil inattention, essential aspects of modern subway urbanity, have not become sufficiently accepted by the city's male population to ensure systemic security. Accordingly, separate cars for men and women had to be instituted as an option for women in 2010. Was it an acknowledgment that the people of Delhi were not yet ready for respectful intergender copresence? The horrible rape and murder in 2012 of a young student in a Delhi bus helped publicize the widespread sexist culture of violence against women.[15] In the city's new subway system, the problem arose in immediate and specific instances because it threatened trust and prevented the emergence of a functioning subway community, independent of more abstract discourses about modernity.

The New York Subway and the Situational Community in Transit

Scholars and managers of new subways around the world may be interested to learn that for a long time, New Yorkers did not view their system as representing either a utopian or a dystopian vision of modernity. Indeed, the New York City discourse of modernity was short-lived.[16] In 1905, only a year after its opening, the first IRT line was packed beyond capacity. Political and financial imbroglios delayed the construction of more lines for another ten years and prevented raising the fare from the initial 5 cents for forty years, effectively crippling maintenance and discouraging more investment. Following Bruno Latour, we suggest that the New York City subway has "never been modern" in its effects on New Yorkers.[17] It cannot be said to have "disciplined" its riders into respecting the official rules, nor has it taught them cleanliness. It has not brought about an era of generous finance or automatic good service. In fact, as we have seen, some subway lines may have accelerated urban disinvestment in the second half of the twentieth century by competing with already built lines rather than opening up new ones.

Conversely, the subway has helped make New York's subway riders more competent urbanites, adept at navigating diversity in public space, at scanning and reading the subway's human landscape, at adopting the right footing, and at participating in the social order of dense and diverse crowds. Those very practical skills and competences, especially visible on the 7 train, have helped produce a community in transit that displays civility and a necessary level of trust.[18] Rather than regard subways and the urban competences they engender among riders as a feature of modernity—a term fraught with confusing popular and academic connotations—we argue that social scientists and others should think of subways and riders' behaviors on a comparative empirical continuum that can measure what we understand as competences and urbanity.

We regard urbanity as a non-elite quality distributed unevenly among a city's residents. The urbane person interacts successfully in different milieus and knows how to "get around" in the city. But urbanity—at least in New York—also has a collective dimension in that among the skills of urbanity are those that look to enhancing the experience of all members of the city's situational community in transit. The generally shared expectation that riders' gender, age, and race are not immediately relevant to the role of subway passenger contributes a desirable equality of treatment. Urbanity in the community in transit becomes "subway city-zenship" in which the rider's competences are put to use for the greater good as well as for one's self. As we scan the crowds and watch for behavior, we can observe modest acts that foster cooperative mobility: giving way to another, offering a seat, stepping inside quickly, and more. We can also see competences at moving in the crowd exercised in the service of individual advantage as riders dart toward available seats or dash for the open elevator.

Generalizing from the 7 Train

A close study of 7 train riders and their interactions shows that the experience of diversity on the trains and in the stations is a consequence of who actually rides the trains over a given segment of the line. Demographic facts about the 7 line, such as the high volume of people of Chinese and Korean origin who get on in Flushing, or the Mexicans and other Latin Americans who enter the trains at the Corona and Jackson Heights stops, for example, naturally create specific contexts of interethnic mixing and interaction. The stereotype of the pushy Chinese ladies, discussed in chapter 2, thus originates in the particular environmental aspects of the Flushing–Main Street station and in the way that express and local trains are scheduled. The free and often boisterous behavior of Mets fans coming from Manhattan bars to a night game, versus the constrained behavior of recent

Asian and Latin American immigrants on the same trains, momentarily highlights the differences between riders who are citizens and those who are just beginning the long climb toward an American identity.

Becoming New Yorkers on the 7 Train, Really?

It is far easier to gain the sense that one is becoming a New Yorker on the 7 train and in the larger subway system—to feel that one is beginning to know how to get around the city and to grasp some of the variety of its regions and institutions—than it actually is to become an American. Yet the two are related in ways we have only begun to explore in this volume.

Since riders' actual experiences with diversity are the result of who gets on the trains at different stations, the 7 train is not at all representative of the entire New York subway system. It is not particularly helpful for studying encounters based on the more pre-global and binary, black-and-white forms of racial and class diversity. The 7 train does not serve a large population of African Americans or Puerto Ricans, as do the trains running sourth from the Bronx across Harlem and into lower Manhattan. Nor does it receive masses of affluent Manhattan apartment dwellers, as do the numbered trains along Broadway and Lexington Avenues. The IRT 6, for example, along Manhattan's East Side, crosses more of the city's venerable class and racial frontiers and would be a better site for studying racial and class encounters on the trains. So, for that matter, would be the Brooklyn subway lines, which converge at Flatbush and Atlantic Avenues, where black ethnicity—African American and West Indian—also often come into play. The A train from the Rockaways into central Brooklyn has historically been a line fraught with racial tensions and incidents.[19] In comparison, the 7 train deserves its reputation as the International Express, which also means that a distinct minority of its passengers are white, native-born Americans. Race relations on the Queens 7 line have their own interhemispheric particularities.

Students from the nations represented among 7 train riders shared their subway diaries with us. Without our prompting, they never failed to report on the gender, age, ethnicity, and race of people whose interactions they observed and chose to elucidate. At the same time that they were making these distinctions, they were behaving outwardly (especially if they were alone) as if none of it mattered. Except, of course, when it did matter, as when, boy and girl, students from the same class, flirted with each other on the train or at a station's gathering place. Otherwise, the categories of gender, ethnicity, and race that were in fact extremely salient to them had to remain secondary in the subway. It is in this pretending to not notice that we begin to take diversities for granted and gradually become blasé New Yorkers. But truly urbane New Yorkers can explain all these visible differences and comings and goings to newcomers; in this way, as riders who are good subway citizens, they will seek to apply this knowledge in the cause of civility and cooperative mobility.

Whatever the subway line, incidents that betray racial and ethnic prejudices occur all the time. So do imagined slights and unintended bumps. Any random interethnic or racial collision risks an essentialized interpretation: "That's how [they] are . . ." But generally, such mutterings are quickly lost in the shuffle of forward motion among the masses of daily riders. In contrast, major acts of racial or ethnic violence, like the racially inspired shooting by Bernhard Goetz on a Manhattan subway on December 22, 1984, at the nadir of subway security, can shock riders and do lasting damage to interpersonal trust in the subway system. Traumatized riders may even have a hard time going back to the subway and never again feel comfortable there. We have seen in various chapters of this study that from the dark low point of the 1980s, the system as a whole and the 7 line in particular have steadily gained riders. As a result, the major current concerns facing the public and transit authorities are about crowding, subway performance, and interpersonal conduct.

Trust and Performance: A New Subway Public Sphere?

Trust is not built on blind faith. It must be earned and maintained. On the transporter's side, it depends on the regularity of the actual train schedule and the provision of vital information in case of service disruption. In these areas of service and maintenance, the Metropolitan Transportation Authority (MTA) is facing multiple challenges. For one, ridership has been steadily climbing every year since the introduction of the Metro-Card. The free bus-to-subway transfer and the weekly and monthly cards have especially boosted ridership on the 7, where many riders transfer to the trains at Flushing–Main Street and 74th Street/Roosevelt Avenue. In order to cope with this influx, the MTA has tried to shorten the intervals between trains. But with the aging tracks, signal systems and rolling materials regularly break down, forcing partial line closures.

Since 2010, the MTA has also gradually implemented a new, real-time signaling system on the trains and tracks. New signs at select stations now will announce the wait time until the next train, helping riders cope with delays. When completed, this system will also help reduce the interval between trains at peak times and reduce crowding. In the meantime, the implementation of the new system creates additional delays and closures, especially on weekends.

Riders on the 7 line have been dealing with disruptions to service caused by track and signal work for longer than most can remember. While we have been writing this book, there have been systematic weekend closings of service between Queens and Manhattan. For eleven weekends in the spring of 2015, for example, riders of the 7 train had to figure out other ways to get to Manhattan. Thousands of men and women of Asian and Latin origin commute to work in Manhattan on Saturdays and Sundays. They labor in the 24/7 service businesses in the sleepless city where weekends are a luxury. There are buses and alternative trains for most. And the MTA does what it can to explain to all of us who rely on the 7 line why there is a need for the closings. But when on top of these necessary disruptions come increasing incidents of delays, accidents, and sudden line closings, the riding public becomes alarmed and begins to lose trust in the system.

On the elevated platforms above Roosevelt Avenue, riders feel the entire station sway back and forth as the trains rumble by. This is a routine experience for New Yorkers everywhere along the city's elevated lines. Many feel the swaying first as children. Parents often explain it as a tolerable engineering feature, like the sway of skyscrapers. But now we are not talking about some abstract "infrastructure" but whether we trust that adequate maintenance can ensure that the swaying structure does not one day just crash onto the street below. A growing incidence of accidents on subway and regional lines and the continual news articles about declining budgets for "infrastructure" do not shore up eroding trust.

Signal problems, work on the tracks, and overcrowding are in fact the three main causes of service disruption in the MTA system (as can be seen in the minutes of the monthly transit committee meeting, available online since 2012). Unfortunately, riders are usually never told about these disruptions until they discover a roped-off staircase or an overcrowded platform. But the information gaps and blind spots on the trains and at the stations are slowly responding to a combination of communication efforts and new technologies. The latter are also stimulating the rise of new "subway publics" on the social media, in which an informed and motivated public is demanding greater access to data about the system's performance. This is probably the most promising change affecting the entire system since we undertook this study. Now the direct connection of riders' cell phones with the Internet puts them in contact with most recent sources of information.[20] The 7 train is at an advantage compared with many other lines because it is elevated throughout most of its route, offering a good-quality signal. Riders can, for example, check out a Twitter feed dedicated to their line relaying all planned work and disruptions announced by the MTA. They can also participate online through innumerable local blogs, community newsletters, direct communications to the MTA, and much more. Just in 2015, a new advocacy Facebook group was created specifically about the 7 train. Based in Sunnyside, the "7 Train Blues" group aspires to act as the new watchdog for disruptions and improvements.

Technology also has transformed riders into potential informants about situations that disrupt or preserve or otherwise highlight the subway's community in transit. In effect, rather than talking out loud to their fellow riders, many passengers prefer to share their observations and feelings online, on Twitter, on a photo-sharing network, or on a more political website like Hollaback!, where one can report or discuss sexual harassment. They can also share their "subway horror stories" with the Riders Alliance, a new organization aimed at relaying the lived experience of subway riders to the state legislature in Albany.

New York is not a national capital like Paris, Moscow, London, and Delhi where the urban transportation system is viewed as a matter of countrywide pride. The New York system, for which about one-half of the needed revenue comes from actual fares, has for decades received additional public funding from what former MTA head Richard Ravitch called "a cyclical political circus."[21] To end the dispiriting bickering and stalemate between governors and the state legislature, the commission that Ravitch headed in 2008 proposed a series of needed revenue streams, including an MTA takeover of the city-owned Harlem River and East River Bridges, which historically have been free to drivers. The new tolls would be collected electronically, without toll booths. The Ravitch Commission also recommended that a new tax be dedicated to financing the regular operation of the whole urban mass transit system.[22] This proposal, as well as the later congestion tax proposed by Mayor Michael Bloomberg, was struck down by the state legislature. In 2015, when the single subway fare increased by 25 cents, to $2.75, Governor Andrew Cuomo blasted the proposed MTA budget, and the usual Albany to New York City political circus went into full swing. The dispiriting impasse prompted planner and public transit advocate Roxanne Warren to write that

> Gov. Andrew M. Cuomo has called the M.T.A.'s capital plan "bloated" and that he has not addressed the funding gap, instead publicly drawing attention to other infrastructure projects, including a new Tappan Zee Bridge and his proposal for an AirTrain to LaGuardia Airport.
>
> The governor seems to have a preference for funding transportation infrastructure that serves cars and air travel, but has much less interest in the rail network of our city—which happens to be the economic engine of the entire region.
>
> Passenger rail of all kinds—intracity and intercity—has been expected to somehow be self-sustaining. The irony is that the automobile and airline modes are the most space-consuming per passenger, and are thereby the least vital and appropriate for special treatment in high-density cities like New York.[23]

Until the subway and suburban mass transit are recognized as public services, just as schools, fire stations, and roads are, the city will not likely be able to renovate and improve the service. It will be also hard-pressed to build more lines to ease crowding and reduce car traffic. Even if the whole city depends on it, mass transit will lag behind other systems in the world in quality of service, thus slowing down the progress toward a more sustainable metropolis. When it opens, the Second Avenue line will ease some of the current crowding, especially in midtown Manhattan, but more capacity will be needed as the central city continues to expand and densities mount. Our study points to the need to expand the subway beyond the boroughs in order to build more subway suburbs just like Jackson Heights and Flushing. Having extended the 7 train into Manhattan's Far West Side, where new luxury towers are sprouting like mushrooms, the city would be well advised to expand it eastward into Long Island and thus complete the job envisioned a century earlier. It would build more subway suburbs, dense but not too dense, and open to diversity, both ethnic and economic. It would also help the new New Yorkers share in the urbane values of the situational community in transit.

Will the emergence of a new public sphere organized around the technologies of communication and the media make a difference? Will it help transform the situational community in transit into a subway public sphere? Under the leadership of founder Gene Russianoff, the Straphangers Campaign remains the subway system's foremost political advocacy group, addressing the crippling budgetary impasse faced by the MTA and the riding public. Perhaps additional voices will be raised as the system's problems continue to worsen with aging, increasing urban density, and overcrowding. We have seen throughout this volume that the new media increasingly give voice to the millions of riders who daily make up the subway's situational community of transit. This trend renews hope for effective communication with the relevant managerial and political actors and institutions. At this writing, the MTA has embarked on a snappy visual campaign of subway ads that aim to educate its riders about many of the behavioral issues we discussed in previous chapters. These include eating and drinking on the trains, manspreading into adjacent seats, pole leaning, dancing around the poles, blocking the entrances, and holding open the doors.[24] Clearly, the system's managers have been reading the angry blogs and raised voices of passengers at public meetings. It would seem from this recent evidence—the civility campaign—that the MTA has learned from riders' organizations and feminist organizations that they can only help reinforce those norms of civility already widely accepted, but often flaunted, in the subway's situational community in transit. Such a hopeful assertion brings us again to consider the place of social science in the operation of the subway. Or should we say the nonplace of social science in MTA operations?

Public operating agencies like the MTA, the Port Authority of New York and New Jersey, and the New York City Department of Transportation vary somewhat in the degree to which they apply methods of social science to the issues they face. None of them is especially keen to share with the public what they may know from application of these methods through internal, proprietary studies. None of them is particularly interested in sponsoring public research, such as appears in this volume, thanks to funding largely by the City University itself. This is in contrast to the New York Police Department, which is a pioneer in applying social scientific methods to understanding crime and its conceivable control in the city. The police department is also a pioneer in cooperating with research institutions and has developed a number of model programs, like CompStat, to show for its efforts (although regrettably, data from the Transit Bureau are still unavailable). As social scientists and members of the riding public, we may ask: When the MTA opens an ambitious public education campaign like the one just described, does it have any way of knowing and incorporating the results? Has it collected any before- and after-data? Is it interested, as it appears to be, in enhancing rider competences, subway citizenship, and trust in the system? If so, it is also to be desired that research on and conceptualization of the behavioral issues such as those we have examined here might become far more developed in the future. The more we all know about the human dimensions of mass transit, the more the entire city will benefit.

Appendix

Mixed Methods in Subway Research

*Now, the ethnographic task has sometimes been designated "mere" descrip-
tion. A new generation of ethnographers rejects the "mere," and sees in the
formulation of an adequate ethnographic description a truly theoretical
task, the development of a theory adequate to a particular case. Inference,
hypothesis, and prediction are equally involved in accounting for a body of
behavior, whether the universe is all communities or one.*

Dell H. Hymes, "A Perspective for Linguistic Anthropology"

For this project, we relied on a set of mixed methods in order to approach our subject, the 7 train, from several perspectives. Participant
observation and distant observation were our modes of access to the field.
As we discuss here, observation yields rich data but is not exempt from
bias, especially in an environment dominated by nonverbal communication, as is the subway. To complement this method we also conducted about
thirty interviews with riders; twenty-five interviews with on-the-ground
subway workers, both Metropolitan Transportation Authority (MTA) employees and others (such as vendors and buskers); and fourteen institutional interviews with individuals working in jobs related to the subway.
We also used quantitative data from the U.S. Census, to learn more about
the neighborhoods along the line, and from the MTA, for information
about ridership trends. Police data were not reliable, as the Transit Bureau
does not make its records public, and our freedom of information requests
were not granted.

In addition to these traditional methods, we used three more innovative techniques that we thought were well adapted to our field. Twenty-one
walking, or go-along, interviews helped us determine what riders actually
do when they take the subway, rather than what they think they do when
they are interviewed in other locations, such as their home. The subway
diaries kept by twelve high school students gave us a unique perspective on

the subway from the vantage point of this specific subset of riders. Finally, online data, collected from forums and responses to online articles about sexual harassment, revealed gender relations on the subway.

Next we will examine the most innovative of these methods. We will start with observation and its limits before discussing walking interviews, subway diaries, and the use of online data.

Observation on the Subway

When does simply riding the subway qualify as ethnographic research? Throughout this volume we refer to our own experiences on the 7 train and other New York City subway lines. But what makes our observations any more reliable or "scientific" than those of bloggers or journalists or anyone else who has ridden on the subway? One answer has to do with the number of years and seasons we have spent riding trains and observing the stations. Another pertains to the systematic recording of our experiences and observations on the subway. As researchers and fare-paying subway riders, we are acting as "participant observers" in the classic mode of ethnographic research. But how do we know that our observations are contributing to objective evaluations rather than subjective moral judgments? And what constitutes "systematic observation," as opposed to anecdotal evidence? Clearly, these questions raise far larger issues of epistemology in the social sciences than we can address here.

For a more detailed discussion of ethnographic methods, we refer readers to *Writing Ethnographic Field Notes*.[1] As the title suggests, recording experiences from "the field" is both an art and a science. The observations we chose to describe seemed noteworthy if they told us about the particulars of human behavior in the subway system. We tried to pay close attention and remember the essential details. As soon as possible, we wrote down the details of behavior—facial expressions; the things people said, even very quickly; the looks and stares; the embraces; and the fist bumps—always noting the degree of crowding, the time of day, and other relevant contextual aspects of the setting. We avoided imputing our feelings or motives that we could not know. Unless these were outwardly expressed or revealed later in an interview, we had to be careful not to project our own feelings on the situation except, of course, if we were observing our own experiences and feelings. Our notes inevitably include separate passages in which we make judgments about what we were seeing. We expressed our hunches about meaning and significance of acts or events that we observed and then looked for more confirming examples or variations on the themes.

Ethnographic Teamwork

To conduct the fieldwork, we hired three research assistants, for which we are grateful for a CUNY Collaborative grant. At that time, Richard Ocejo, Amalia Leguizamon, and Chi-Hsin Chiu all were graduate students in sociology and environmental psychology at the CUNY Graduate School. Hailing from Staten Island, Argentina, and China, respectively, they added Spanish and Mandarin to the languages (English and French) we used to talk to the riders. But more important, they each wrote their own field notes and enlarged the perspectives of the two principal investigators. Rich Ocejo was more involved in the research with the high school students, and chapter 7 is based on an article that he and Stéphane wrote for the journal *Ethnography*. Amalia Leguizamon was in charge of inquiring about the street vendors immediately around the 74th Street/Roosevelt Avenue station, and chapter 4 relies heavily on her field notes. Finally, Chi-Hsin Chiu talked to the street vendors in the pedestrian passage in Flushing's Lipmann Plaza, which leads from the municipal parking lot to the Flushing–Main Street subway station and thus forms a transitional space for commuters. For lack of space, however, we did not include this part of the work in this book. In Flushing, Chi-Hsin also conducted (and translated) walking interviews in Mandarin.

Avoiding the Subway Ethnographic Trap

Following the lead of anthropologists like Marc Augé, who has written extensively about the Paris metro,[2] contemporary scholars of subway behavior tend to rely heavily on hypotheses that they see confirmed by their own observations of interactions on the trains and stations. Scholars of the "mobility turn" have identified the subway and commuter trains as mostly a place of the masses' silent suffering and restraint.[3] While laudable as a method when practiced over adequate time and space, participant observation on the subway—riding the trains and watching behavior in different situations—faces empirical limitations due to the tendency to see what one is looking for. This bias is especially strong in the subway. There, the pre-eminence of nonverbal communication seems to invite riders and research-ers to freely interpret their fellow riders' intentions, thoughts, and even dreams. Augé readily admits this in his original study of the Paris metro in 1986 and his revisit in 2008.

In his earlier work, Augé described the Paris subway as a truly "mod-ern" institution in the Beaudelairian sense that new ways of acting in pub-lic arose out of the encounter of new technologies with traditions, marry-ing the new with the old.[4] As he rode the Paris trains, he felt that he could read the city's history in the different lines and stations and their riders.[5] In 2008, though, when he revisited the Paris subway, twenty years after his first book was published, he was struck by the evidence among youthful riders of poverty, solitude and sullenness, and self-involvement.[6] But Augé readily admits that his books are auto-ethnographies. The subway let him read a multitude of details about other riders that he was able to assemble into a personal narrative of change, including his own aging: "Like all in-formants, I started with me and then proceeded to generalize; I laid out what I thought I knew and hid what I didn't know."[7]

Riding the 7 train as passenger-observers, we also have fallen into this trap and also have sought to avoid it by making methodological choices that add perceptual depth to the observations. When we began our field-work, we were persuaded by a hopeful hypothesis about subways and pub-lic behavior. From our late colleague the sociologist Isaac Joseph, we inher-ited the desire to explore the subway as an essentially civilizing technology.[8] Places of frequent heterogeneity, the Paris and New York City subways, were, for Joseph, crucibles that formed cosmopolitan urbanites. Observing people from so many of the world's countries getting along, or seeming to do so, on the 7 train, it was easy for us to imagine that we were observing the assimilating effects of the experience. Some of our informants eagerly confirmed our wishful hypothesis. For example, Roger, a middle-class Indian American living in Jackson Heights, told us that "each car of the 7 train is a mini United Nations."

Yet if people are simply traveling in one another's' presence, does that mean they are becoming tolerant New Yorkers, outside of assimilating the larger values of democracy? Could it be that each rider sees in the subway what is most important to her at the moment, falling into the same sub-way ethnographic trap as we had? This was our first hint that we needed to know more about what riders were actually thinking and feeling, for better and for worse, as they encountered others on the 7 train. We acquired these subjective accounts from riders through walking interviews, student diaries, and conversations with riders, and from the voices of subway riders on the blogosphere. These became essential data sources, as were the more quantitative measures of rider diversity and frequency of subway use. The walking interviews, for example, showed us that each rider has particular concerns, pleasures, worries, prejudices, and memories, which the outward civility of subway competencies often masks. We learned, however, that as they approach the station and enter the subway system, individuals become riders as they switch codes to subway mode. We saw in chapter 3 that as they assumed the role of rider, our informants began to apply more universal ideas about how one acts in the subway's community in transit in order to make the ride as uneventful as possible.

Walking Interviews: What Are the Limits of the Subway?

In chapter 3, "Walking to the Stations, Code Switching, and the I-We-You Shift," we used a specific method to explore how riders adapt to the changing social and spatial environment as they walk from their home to the subway. At what point does one leave the neighborhood to enter the more public realm of mass transit? We chose to answer this apparently simple question by using walking interviews with inhabitants who lived around the 74th Street/Roosevelt Avenue station at the junction of Jackson Heights and Elmhurst, two Queens neighborhoods on either side of the 7 train's elevated tracks.

The Go-Along or *parcours commenté*

In order to refine the protocol, we relied on a method inspired by the "go-along" developed by Margarethe Kusenbach,[9] which consists of interviewing a subject while walking in the urban context being examined. Urban walks already have a short history in the social sciences. Michel de Certeau, for example, thought that they would display the everyday tactics and resistance to an environment way too oppressive (especially when gridded).[10] With a different theoretical approach but somewhat similar objectives of resistance, Guy Debord and the Situationists developed a theory of "derive" (drifting) aimed at uncovering the "psychogeography" of urban neighborhoods otherwise hidden behind the deadening routine of everyday life.[11] More recently, thanks to the efforts of field researchers such as Setha Low, new methods such as "transect walks"[12] and "guided tours"[13] have been used to gather systematic data. Transect walks are adapted from the environmental sciences, in which community consultants are asked to give a spatialized overview of the community's problems. Guided tours are aimed at giving voice to a deeply personal and historical relation of residents' "dwelling" or anchoring in the spatial environment. Another method, the *parcours commenté*, elaborated by our colleagues Jean-Yves Petiteau and Jean-Paul Thibaud,[14] was designed to explore the "ambience" of urban environments. These French scholars regard interviewees as receptors who, through their descriptions, reveal a place's specific characteristics that interact with users. Their assumption is that a direct connection among circulating, perceiving, and describing makes the walking interview very efficient at collecting the residents' direct experiences while bypassing representations. The ambience is the result of recurring descriptions by different walkers who help the researchers identify what may be called a "place effect."

In an important article, Kusenbach summed up the advantages of these "go-along" interview methods.[15] Using her own materials collected from residents in two different neighborhoods of Los Angeles, she uncovered five themes that go-alongs are particularly suited to explore: environmental perception, spatial practices, biographies, social architecture, and social realms. The way that commuters perceive the social realms they traverse on their routine trips is precisely what we set out to explore. According to Kusenbach, go-alongs can help researchers identify whether the interview takes place in a private space, a familiar neighborhood, or a public domain: "'Hanging out' and moving along with a range of informants permits ethnographers to examine the naturally occurring patterns and variations of social encounters which they could not fully access as outside observers, nor as practitioners."[16] For example, while walking along, one can observe instances of "friendly recognition" indicating that the informant considers the environment as familiar. Conversely, demonstrations of "civil inattention" point to a public social realm. Thus the go-along can help uncover the transition between the subway and the neighborhood.

Identifying Thresholds

The clues that Kusenbach identified are discrete gestures that signify only the type of social realm one is in at a given moment. They do not point to the limits or let us see any precise boundaries or thresholds between domains. We would also add that the connection between walking and talking is more than a simple way of collecting direct experiences, as it also can be seen as the coming together of two distinct concepts of public space. The first one is a space of circulation and mobility, much in the spirit of the Chicago school, the main analyzer of which is Georg Simmel's stranger.[17] The second one is a space of dialogue, more like the public sphere of Jürgen Habermas.[18] In this regard, our hypothesis is that public space itself contains some procedural constraints bearing on the communication of walkers and subway riders. Thus "walking interviews" can be more than a way to describe ambience or social realms. They can also help us identify what John J. Gumperz and Jan-Petter Blom called "situational code switching,"[19] which is triggered by an element of context such as the setting (space), a social occasion, or a social event and which puts the speaker on another "footing."[20]

We thus have tried to identify two levels of clues in the interviews. The first level relates to two aspects of recognition as defined by Axel Honneth.[21] On the one hand, inhabitants recognize their own community in the neighborhood. This is important, as it pertains directly to self-esteem: "The 'honor,' 'dignity' or, to use the modern term, 'status' of a person can be understood to signify the degree of social acceptance forthcoming for a person's method of self-realization within the horizon of cultural traditions in a given society."[22] As Paola, one of the interviewees, says: "Here this just like in Bogotá, I feel home." The reading of cultural signs in the environment works as the recognition of the member of a given community as a valuable person whose values are publicly displayed.[23] In the same way, manifestations of "friendly recognition" demonstrate the resident's belonging to a certain neighborhood and mark the area as a "parochial domain."

On the other hand, the subway is the site of a priori anonymous and even alien copresence. In order to circulate, passersby must grant one another the "right" to pass and go about their own business as persons defined with nothing more in common than being a member of the larger society. According to Honneth, rights, recognized or not, are what makes an individual a full-fledged member of society or, conversely, a second-rate citizen. In the subway, this right is better expressed as a combination of two normative patterns, cooperative mobility and civil inattention, that, according to Lyn Lofland,[24] regulate behaviors in the urban public realm.

This second level of clues is to be found not only in the words of the interviewee but also in the modes of speech that denote a change of context, such as an event happening in the vicinity or, in our case, the passage from the neighborhood to the public realm of the subway. This code switching is observable in various instances, both verbal and nonverbal. Its most important characteristic is that it should not be punctual but mark different "moments" in the larger social occasion of the interview.

Recruiting, Walking, and Filming

We conducted twenty-one walking interviews with thirteen residents in Jackson Heights and eight in Flushing.[25] We recruited the residents through posters placed in public spaces and restaurants around the subway stations[26] and, for the teenagers, through a high school teacher. Each interviewee was compensated $30 for his or her time spent.

The interviews followed a standard procedure. One interviewer filmed the walk and the surroundings while the other asked the questions. We conducted the interviews in English, except when the participant was not fluent enough in this language, in which case we used Spanish, French, or Mandarin. We met in front of the interviewee's home where we asked about his or her residential career, including immigration to New York City. We inquired about the interviewee's occupation and how often he or she used the subway. We also asked for a description of the neighborhood before beginning the walk. At this point, the residents generally explained their idea of diversity, which, after we started walking, we then compared with how they related to the neighborhood diversity. The interviewee took us to the train station, where we both boarded the 7 train to Manhattan for one stop, got off, and walked under the elevated track back to the departure station. During the walk, we asked the informant to describe the immediate environment and to explain his or her choices of direction. The walk was set by the talk, irregular in its pace. Finally, we stopped at a local café and asked the informant to trace the walk on a neighborhood map and identify its different parts, before we reviewed the video (figure A.1).[27] This last step also allowed us to collect more background data about the interviewee. Each interview lasted from 1 to 2 hours.

Figure A.1 Walking from home to the station: map and excerpts from two walking interviews in Jackson Heights, 2007.

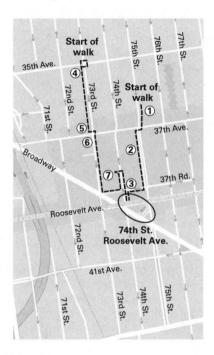

START OF WALK

1 The State Department has people who . . . brings people here from countries around the world to try and explain to them that you can live with different people without killing one another and somehow we don't do that in Jackson Heights, we're able to get along very well. And I make the point of how varied the people are and I'm always trying to point it out to them when they get here and they say, well, they notice. It's the most obvious thing in the world to them, the variety.

2 Well, coming up here is this parking lot that was one of my . . . one of the issues that was before our community board recently. They need a variance to have this place here because it's in a residential zone so they had to come before us and they have these lights that are in there and they shine into my apartment. So I was trying to make the point that they shouldn't have these lights. They should have some type of shade on them or something so they don't shine into the neighborhood, which is the rule. We have a big problem with that, and we were trying to get them to plant a little ivy here so that it would grow on the fence and it's not the nicest fence in the world.

3 74th St.'s just a bit too many twists and turns to get through there.
And obviously the stores are all servicing people who are from South Asia, and we're here. And obviously everybody's from someplace else. It's quite apparent. If I open my eyes to it. You know you get used to it after a while.

(continued)

START OF WALK (*continued*)

4 There's all sorts of nationalities here. I would say, myself, I'm in the minority. A
   very . . . I remember the other day, I was talking to my father who lives in Florida and
   he's very much in an all-white area, and I said, "You know as I walk down the street, I
   could see like 20 people here and maybe one what I will call Caucasian." . . . I guess
   the people from India are also Caucasian, I guess, I don't know about that. But in
   terms of a white America, I would say as I walk down the street, I was about one out
   of 20. For every 20 people I would see I would see another white person, or like that.

5 I got to know one of the Chinese women that sells things on a table over here, she lived
   downstairs. They had like a downstairs area here where they had rooms all sharing the same
   kitchen. They had like six rooms around a central kitchen and a bathroom. And she had,
   because one time I was helping her load her stuff down there, carrying it down the stairs.
   There's a lady who came here and set up a booth over, not a booth, but a table.

6 See . . . [*Woman passes by*] She's probably Chinese.
   How do you know?
   I can just, I got to actually be able to tell the difference by looking between Koreans,
   Chinese, and Japanese. . . . Because I got a glimpse of her face. It's one of those things
   where, well, I had a Korean girlfriend too when I first moved in here. And you can see
   there's a difference. It's not easy to explain.

7 These two are hot properties because they're right around the corner from the subway.
   These two co-ops. . . . People I think like it because they come out of the subway and
   they walk right around the corner and they're in their apartment. . . . I think, to tell
   you the truth, I think, generally speaking, from just their appearance, they seem to be
   more wealthy. And they're not that interested in the neighborhood. They're working
   in Manhattan, you know.

Coding

We looked for clues in the interviews that would identify the two social
realms, public and parochial, and would mark observable switches in the
interviewee's behavior and expressions. How did the informants define and
recognize their own group in the environment, and how did they recognize
and deal with the presence of others? How did they move from a familiar
neighborhood to the less familiar environment of the subway?

In our analysis, we first attempted to identify those traits found in all
the interviews based on the distance to the station. But this comparative
approach didn't yield any common observations across the sample, maybe
because of its size, but also because of the large variety of interviewees. We
overcame this problem by considering each interview as a case to be viewed
as a whole sequence.[28] We then compared each interview with the next one,
to find any recurring phenomena independent of spatial location. Since

the protocol was designed to probe the limits of social realms, this method of analysis was better adapted to uncovering not only the interviewees' location but also their variations. We reached saturation when new interviews didn't bring any new variation in the way that the participants moved from one realm to the next. In this regard, the method is similar to Pascal Amphoux's "recurring observation" of urban public spaces, where saturation was obtained after about a dozen cases.[29] This small-sample analysis thus demonstrates logical ways of acting in specific contexts, which in turn offers significant information about the setting.

Findings

The specific findings from this method are explained in chapter 3. Mainly they show that each interviewee had a dominant concern around which he or she organized the descriptions of the interviewee's environment. Some were linked to race, others to housing tenure, class, a recent immigration experience, and more.

Despite the diversity of experiences, all the interviewees switched at some point in the walk, from using the pronoun "we" or "I" and "them," typical in their neighborhood, to using the more impersonal pronoun "you" when getting closer to the subway station. We interpreted this shift as an adaptation to the passage from a familiar environment to a more anonymous one. Each interviewee switched at a different distance from the station. This means that for some, the anonymous realm started farther away from the station, whereas for others, it went all the way into the station. As a result, we found that the station and its environment superimposed different social realms, making it a zone of uncertainty and possibilities.

Subway Diaries: How Do Immigrant Teenagers Describe Their Subway Rides?

In chapter 7, "Teenagers on the 7 Train," we analyze the subway riding experience of twelve relatively recent immigrant high school students, as described in the diaries that they kept for one month. The goal was to understand their own conception of subway rules and how enjoyable or stressful riding the subway was for them.[30]

Recruitment

In order to inquire about teenagers' experience of the subway, we built on other innovative ethnographic studies that have used youth as "coresearchers" in collecting data.[31] We contacted a teacher at a school located near the 7 train, who announced to the students that we were seeking participants in a research study. Ten of the twelve high school students we recruited attended this highly diverse public school in Queens for immigrant students who have been in the country for five years or less.[32] Four of the students were boys from China, Mexico, Bangladesh, and Colombia, and six were girls from Bangladesh, Haiti, Mauritius, China, and Argentina. We selected them from an honors class, and each was relatively proficient in English. We also recruited two Colombian girls who had come to the United States when they were young and attended a different high school, also along the 7 train line.[33] The twelve students ranged in age from fifteen to eighteen, and each took the 7 train at some point in their commute. Like many immigrant youths in cities, these students lived and socialized with people from their own ethnic group, in either large enclaves or important spaces within their multicultural neighborhoods (for example, certain streets, buildings, and businesses). Our research with these students took place over one month, June 2006, for which they each received an honorarium of $200 ($100 at the beginning of the project and $100 at the end) for their work as our "research assistants."

Accounts of Lived Situations

Due to our differences (such as age and culture) and the difficulties of conducting immersive and sustained participant observation with young people on the subway (that is, impracticalities of the setting), we chose a method that would reveal their *in situ* experiences. After describing the general project to the students, we gave them journals with log sheets and instructed them to keep a daily report of their trips—indicating the date and departure time, the reason for the trip, if they were with other people or alone, any transfers to buses or other trains, and where and when they exited—and to write an entry in their journals for every trip that they took (figure A.2). This diary method allowed the participants to document and describe their lived experiences in a manner less mediated than oral narration.[34] That is, we wanted the teenagers to "tell us the code"[35] of the subway and how they experienced it through their own account of lived situations.

A trip began when they left their starting point and ended when they arrived at their destination (usually home or school but sometimes work or places for leisure). We asked them to describe their experiences in as much detail as possible, and we met with them several times a week to read over and discuss their journals. The purpose of the meetings was threefold. First, we wanted to interview each student and learn more about his or her background. Second, we wanted to guide the students in their note taking and improve their ethnographic skills by adding as many details to their entries as possible. We explained the importance of social context and showed them how to describe a setting. After a few sessions of instruction, the students became better at observing and writing. Our discussions focused on the substance of their entries, which was the third purpose of the meetings. Since it was the students who made the observations, we wanted to understand their own interpretations of their experiences. We read their journals with them, asked them questions about the episodes they docu-

Subway trip log
Name _____

7 train project
page number: 1

Date / time departure	Reason for trip	Other people traveling along and leg number if partial trip together	Leg 1 Station and line number (or bus)	Leg 2 Transfer point and next line	Leg 3 Transfer point, next line (or bus)	Exit station and time
6/2/06 3:50pm	HOME	3 friends	7 train 33rd street	74th street	Q 47	74th street 4:07pm
6/5/06 8:45a.m	School	Alone	74 street 7 train	-	-	33rd street 8:58a.m
6/5/06 4:45pm	HOME	Alone	7 train 33rd street	74th street	Q 47	74th street 4:34pm
6/6/06 8:48am	School	Alone	7 train 74th street	-	-	33rd street 9:06a.m
6/6/06 4:20pm	HOME	1 friend	7 train 33rd	74th street	Q47	74th 4:36pm
6/7/06 8:40pm	SCHOOL	ALONE	7 train 74th	-	-	33rd 8:54a.m
6/7/06 4:40pm	HOME	2 friends	7 train 33rd	74th	Q47	74th 4:56pm
6/9/06 5:15pm	HOME	1 friend (with his 2 friends)	7 train 33rd	74th	Q47	74th 5:30pm
6/12/06 8:35a.m	School	ALONE	7 train 74th	-	-	33rd 8:45a.m
6/13/06 7:35a.m	School	1 friend	7 train 74th	-	-	33rd 7:51a.m
6/13/06 3:45pm	HOME	3 friends	7 train 33rd	74th	Q47	74th 3:58pm
6/14/06 8:43a.m	School	Alone	7 train 74th	-	-	33rd 9:17a.m
6/16/06 around 4pm	HOME	With Gaelle + Stephane + 2 friends	7 train 33rd	74th	Q47	74th 4:50pm
6/28/06 9:45a.m	School	Alone	7 train 74th	-	-	33rd 10:30 a.m
6/28/06 2:15pm	HOME	2 friends	7 train 33rd	74th	Q47	74th 2:29pm
6/29/06 11:30a.m	Northern Boulevard	Mother	R train Northern Blv.	-	-	Northern 11:37a.m

Figure A.2   A student's subway trip log, June 2006.

mented, and allowed them to explain what they thought about what they saw and did. From the beginning of these sessions, we noticed that descriptions of the subway's normative order through depictions, emotional expressions, and moral judgments of events and people pervaded their journals. Our subsequent conversations with them often explored their interpretations of these norms. While we tried not to influence them to concentrate on any one aspect of their experiences, we acknowledge that our interest in their observations of social norms may have led them to emphasize such episodes in their entries.

Toward the end of the month of diary keeping, we rode the subway with the students in groups organized by language (English, French, Spanish, and Mandarin) in order to illustrate, in place, some of the salient aspects of their commute.

We also organized a collective debriefing meeting at the CUNY Graduate Center. All the students traced their routes on a large map and commented on a series of pictures that they had taken with a disposable camera.

Analysis: Norms and Emotions

We overcame problems that afflict small-sample qualitative studies by regarding each diary as a case consisting of several smaller cases—that is, the entries themselves.[36] Ethnography contains many examples of small-sample studies. Although Mitchell Duneier and Harvey Molotch's study of street vendors who "harass" passersby is part of a long-term research project involving many dozens of participants, and although they recorded hundreds of hours of conversations between the men and people on the sidewalk, they based their article on only two episodes from their data collection that were suitable for their immediate purpose.[37] Despite the small quantity, they argued that these episodes contained richly textured exchanges that served their purpose of applying conversation analysis to understand the "interactional vandalism" between disparate groups on city streets. In our study, we applied our central research question to each entry in each diary. Each entry provided us with findings and questions that helped us with the next case until we achieved "saturation," or the point when the cases ceased to offer new information.[38] With the journal entry as our unit of analysis, we expanded our sample. The logs indicate that the twelve students documented a total of 245 trips in their journals: an average of 20 trips per student, for a total of 518 pages or an average of approximately 43 pages per student.[39]

We coded the diaries by looking for emotional expressions, both negative and positive, and then related the emotion to the situation described and determined the rule that was being expressed. This method, consistent with the appraisal theory of emotions,[40] considers these as normative

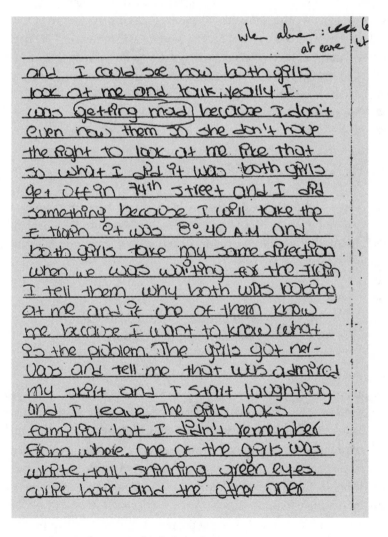

Figure A.3 Excerpt from a student's diary, June 2006.

reactions that reveal the expectations of individuals and guide their answers.

In the extract shown in figure A.3, the student explains that she was getting mad (emotional descriptor) because two girls were staring at her. The incident shows that when she is riding alone, this student is sensitive to being looked at and considers no staring to be a strict rule.

Besides participant observation and interviewing, the students' journals allowed us to understand the workings of their experiences in a public space. Journal writing is an effective way of making more explicit the tacit and otherwise undocumented accounts of social experience.[41] The students revealed many of the aspects of being a rider on the subway that people ordinarily take for granted, specifically observing others. For instance, in a journal entry, Ana, a sixteen-year-old from Argentina, described adults on the train staring at a young couple who were kissing:

> For me that is just something normal and if I wouldn't be doing this [journaling] I wouldn't even have noticed them.

All riders make observations and have interactions and encounters similar—and often identical—to those that the students documented. The diary method brings out the hidden meanings and interpretations of this tacit behavior.

Working with Online Data About Sexual Harassment on the Subway

As we saw in chapter 6, "Gender Relations on the Subway," much of the discussion about gender takes place outside the transportation system. Gendered interactions among strangers on the trains or platforms usually are silent and, when they are verbal, are difficult to observe.

Violations of subway norms produce great emotional stress in riders, who rarely vent their frustrations on the spot. As a result, most reports and comments are made in conversations with friends and colleagues, in diaries, and, increasingly, online.

Forums on the Internet offer a popular and anonymous way for riders to complain about and comment on situations they have been involved in. This is an outlet that started early in the twentieth century in songs, plays, and newspapers[42] and more recently moved to online forums and announcement sites. As a result, many of the concerns of subway riders can be found on the web. Accordingly, the virtual network of New York City–based websites dealing with the subway has become an echo chamber reverberating the thoughts, frustrations, and desires of many riders and New Yorkers.

Online Data Collection

Recently, the social, management, and medical sciences have adopted methods to collect data online. Basically, they have transposed traditional collection methods such as surveys and polling to the World Wide Web.[43] Arguably, this method is cheaper than traditional data collection and is supposed to reach a wider sample of the population. But because the respondents must be adept at using the Internet, the online collection of data has been criticized for not reaching people unable or unwilling to participate because of the "digital divide" separating those people who have and those who do not have access to technology.[44] Online sample biases are difficult to determine because they may not follow usual distinctions of class, levels of education, age, and the like. Notably, online surveys often are open to everybody, which means that one person can answer several times or that only those people concerned with the issue at hand will take the time to answer. As a result, this type of survey risks overrepresenting the incidence of the phenomenon under inquiry or having very low response rates.

In chapter 6, we cited an online survey specifically designed to study the incidence of sexual harassment on the subway. Called "Hidden in Plain Sight," it was conducted in 2007 by the office of the Manhattan borough president.[45] This survey offers a general quantitative snapshot of sexual harassment and, more important, of the weak relationship between harassment and complaints to the police. The survey was sent to 25,000 e-mail addresses via the Borough President listserv and distributed through the weblogs of activist organizations concerned with riders or women. A total of 1,790 people answered the survey, a rather low response rate. Since the survey was open access, the kinds of people who responded versus those who did not are not known, although the respondents gave us some useful information. For example, most of them lived in Manhattan. Because of the biases inherent in the data collection method, any numbers must be used with caution and confirmed by other means. As the organizers acknowledge, the survey reached only those people already connected online to one of the organizations that promoted it. In addition, it also seems likely that the people who filled out the questionnaire did it because they had been sexually harassed on the train or had witnessed harassment. On the one hand, as we discussed in chapter 6, online forums provide a place to express feelings otherwise difficult to get off one's chest. On the other hand, many women who have been harassed may have refused to participate, despite the anonymity of the response. One reason is that they may not want to relive a traumatic event. As a result, the incidence of sexual harassment is difficult to assess from an online survey. The information about women's reactions is more telling. The fact that a vast majority of women who declared to have been harassed also wrote that they had not contacted the New York Police Department (96%) or the MTA (86%) is telling. Also, most incidents happened during the morning (69%) or afternoon (51%) rush hour.

Working with Existing Online Data

We decided not to collect our own data for our research but instead to use existing information publicly available online.[46] In addition to observation, interviews, and diary methods, we used two main digital sources to better understand gender relations on the subway. The first one is the online forum maintained by the feminist organization Hollaback! (http://www .ihollaback.org/), where we found thirty-four testimonies about groping on the New York City subway. The second one is the comments posted by readers of the *New York Times* in answer to two articles on groping on the subway. The article that drew the most comments is an opinion-page testimony, published in 2013, written by a twenty-nine-year-old woman named Kimberly Matus.[47] A total of 492 readers commented on it, 51 of whom also described an episode of groping. Karen Zraick wrote the second article, "A Personal Story of Sexual Harassment," in 2010.[48] It elicited 74 comments, including 17 testimonies of groping.

Contributors to these forums have to register on the site. Although the registration is free, it is a substantial barrier to participation that we cannot evaluate. Arguably, the forums we did use also have the same digital divide as more traditional online data collection. In addition, the forums' managers, such as the *New York Times* editors and the Hollaback! website manager, filter public contributions in ways that are not always known. For instance, we learned in an interview that they erase posts deemed offensive, such as those that contain racial epithets. Because of these limitations, the sample of contributions we have collected online is not representative of riders in general. Nonetheless, the testimonies of victims of groping that we analyzed enabled us to identify typical reactions and their consequences. In this regard, the existing forums on the subway lend themselves better to qualitative than to quantitative analysis. In our analysis, we looked for patterns of development linked to the woman's reaction to sexual abuse, that is, for the internal consistency of the testimony rather than for its representativeness. When a pattern occurs in several testimonies, it probably is happening with some regularity on the trains, but it does not indicate how prevalent it is. The main finding from this type of source is the patterns themselves, which indicate how events can unfold in specific situations.

Looking for Internal Logics in Online Responses to Groping

Caution must be used when evaluating the veracity of declarations made online. Some of the messages about missed encounters on Craigslist that we cited describe situations that may have never happened. For example, the author of a post could hope that the situation he has described is vague enough so that a female rider may think it actually happened. Or it may just be a fantasy. This is why we used these messages to evaluate fantasies on or about the subway rather than regarding them as actual missed encounters. This is not to say that these encounters do not happen but that the information available is not sufficient to understand how they work and, much less, how commonly they occur.

The testimonies of women who have been groped on the subway give more detailed accounts of the events than do the missed-encounter messages on Craigslist. The testimonies explain the circumstances, the actions, and their consequences. Notably, they link emotions to specific developments. The following is an example taken from the comments by Kimberley Matus in the *New York Times*:

> About eight years ago, after stepping on a packed train at Grand Central station, a man came up behind me and pressed himself against me. Even when the crowd started to thin out, he continued to do so and whenever I moved so did he.
>
> This went on for some time and for about several minutes, no one on the train did or said anything. Not even the two women, sitting in front of me, who I was making eye contact with while it was happening. It was not until

a young man, standing at the door, called out and asked me if I wanted to come and stand next to him that it all stopped. The whole ordeal lasted for about three to four minutes; and the entire time, all I could do was pray for him to get away.

What's crazy is that about two weeks earlier, my cousin had the same experience. However, much like the author's friends, I too was certain that I would had done something to defend myself. But when it did actually happened to me, all I could do was just stand there with fear.

May 13, 2013, 9:35 P.M.[49]

We believe that the internal organization of this testimony is quite different from fantasized or made-up encounters, as it has a descriptive consistency that can be used for analysis.[50] We built a database of all such reactions and coded them for four types of descriptors. The first category was the context, for which we looked for words like "crowd," "rush hour," "train," "pole," and "platform." The second category was about the action, for which we coded words like "groping," "touch," "hand," and "humping." The third category was for the victim's reaction, for which we coded words like "silent," "move," "scream," "yell," "say," "talk," and "elbow." The last category was about emotions such as fear, anger, frozen, and disbelief. Our analysis of the testimonies with these categories allowed us to link specific emotions to specific reactions. We then subdivided these reactions into four types with their associated emotions: (1) silent and passive, (2) silent and active, (3) direct confrontation, and (4) talking out loud. The first two types maintain the appearance of normality by pretending that nothing unusual is happening, whereas the latter two imply the participation of witnesses.

The patterns identified in online testimonies must be confirmed via other means, such as interviews or direct observation. We managed to gather some confirmation, especially when women remain silent and when they speak out, but we need to do more research to confirm these findings.

Working with Quantitative Data on Subway Ridership

In chapter 2, "Coping with Diversity Aboard the 'International Express,'" and chapter 8, "Subway City: The 7 Train as an Engine of Urbanism," we relied heavily on quantitative data obtained from the U.S. Census and the MTA.

We did not use quantitative data to identify correlations or run regression analyses. Instead, we used quantitative data as a complement to qualitative methods in order to build a contextual portrait of ridership and neighborhood populations on which we could rely to locate our observations. We also used quantitative data for two basic comparative purposes: between subway riders and inhabitants, and between ridership on different subway lines.

Comparing Residential and Ridership Populations

In chapter 2, we used census data by census blocks from the compounded 2006–2011 American Community Survey (ACS) data sets and from the 2000 decennial census in order to compare the population living in neighborhoods along the 7 line with the composition of the ridership on the train.

Our first task was to select the census blocks most likely to send their residents to a specific subway stop. We chose the blocks immediately around the subway station and added the blocks along bus lines serving the station.

We then compared the composition of the population living in the selected areas according to the census with the proportion of this population stating that they used public transportation to go to work. This comparison worked only for the population eighteen years old and older and is possible only using the decennial census.

Unfortunately, the ACS dropped "means of transportation to work" from the questionnaire. In order to compensate for this lack of information, we did our own counting at the turnstiles during morning peak time at the Flushing–Main Street and 74th Street/Roosevelt Avenue stations from 8:00 to 9:00 A.M. on two different weekdays. We were a team of four counters, and we covered all the main entries. At the 74th Street station, this meant that one side entry was not counted. We organized the counting in sets of 10 minutes. For each set, we counted all riders entering the turnstile with a clicker held in our left hand, and a subset of this population with a clicker in our right hand. The subsets were chosen to match the census categories as closely as possible. They were female, Hispanic, African American or black, non-Hispanic white, South Asian, and East Asian. We controlled for errors by counting a few times together at the same gates. The margin of error among us was a few percentage points, not significant enough to alter the comparison.

We did not count enough times to be able to generalize. But the fact that the results match the census data, except for the white category, is a good indication that the population using the subway is representative of the residents in the surrounding neighborhood, at least in terms of gender, ethnicity and race, with the significant exception of non-Hispanic white riders being less well represented on the subway than in the neighborhoods around the line.

We used the same counting method to get a picture of the distribution of riders according to gender, ethnicity, and race in the 74th Street/Roosevelt Avenue station complex. This allowed us to study the mixing taking place as riders transferred from one line to another. This kind of information is entirely missing from the MTA data sets, even in absolute numbers.

Ridership Data per Station per Year, 1904–2012

In 2007, the MTA was not willing to share its ridership data collected through the turnstiles at every station, but this has since changed, and the MTA is now eager to partner with companies and individuals who develop applications to graphically represent flows and, possibly, model rider behaviors.

We first obtained ridership data from the Straphangers Campaign in the form of a large Excel table listing yearly ridership per station from the opening year in 1904 to 2007. We later received an additional table with the years 2008 to 2012 from the Regional Planning Association.

We used these data to compare the evolution of ridership across different lines over time. This is how we realized the lines did not suffer equally during the post–World War II years of suburbanization and subsequent deindustrialization. We also used these data to compare the evolution of ridership per station and line with the growth of the population in the adjacent neighborhoods. This comparison helped us identify periods of ridership growth or loss that are not proportional to the variation in the population in absolute numbers.

Notes

Acknowledgments

1. We highly recommend reading the published version of his doctoral dissertation: Richard E. Ocejo, *Upscaling Downtown: From Bowery Saloons to Cocktail Bars in New York City* (Princeton, N.J.: Princeton University Press, 2014).

1. Becoming New Yorkers on the 7 Train

1. According to the Metropolitan Transportation Authority (MTA), the New York City (NYC) subway has 21 interconnected subway routes spanning four out of the five boroughs via 660 track miles and 469 stations. In 2015, the NYC subway officially registered 1,763 million rides, an average of 5.7 million per weekday and the highest number since 1948. The fare, including a free bus-to-subway transfer when using a magnetic MetroCard, is $2.75 per trip.
2. According to data released by the New York Police Department (NYPD) and the MTA to the *Daily News*, the crime rate in the subway is at an all-time low of 0.6 crime per 100,000 rides. See Sarah Ryley and Pete Donohue, "How Safe Is Your Subway?" *Daily News*, June 22, 2014, http://www.nydailynews.com/new-york/nyc-crime/daily-news-analysis-reveals-crime-rankings-city-subway-system-article-1.1836918.
3. Ido Tavory, *Summoned: Identification and Religious Life in a Jewish Neighborhood* (Chicago: University of Chicago Press, 2016).
4. Alfred Schutz, *Alfred Schutz on Phenomenology and Social Relations*, ed. Helmut R. Wagner (Chicago: University of Chicago Press, 1970), 112–13.

5. Ulf Hannerz, *Transnational Connections: Culture, People, Places* (London: Routledge, 1996).
6. Susie J. Tanenbaum, *Underground Harmonies: New York City Subway Music and Its Implications for Public Space* (Ithaca, N.Y.: Cornell University Press, 1996).
7. Isaac Joseph, *La ville sans qualités* (La Tour d'Aigues: Éditions de l'Aube, 1998), 124 (our translation).
8. Clifton Hood, *722 Miles: The Building of the Subways and How They Transformed New York* (New York: Simon & Schuster, 1993).

2. Coping with Diversity Aboard the "International Express"

1. Arun Peter Lobo and Joseph J. Salvo, *The Newest New Yorkers, 2000: Immigrant New York in the New Millennium* (New York: Department of City Planning, Population Division, 2004).
2. Arun Peter Lobo and Joseph J. Salvo, *The Newest New Yorkers: Characteristics of the City's Foreign-born Population*, 2013 ed. (New York: Department of City Planning, Office of Immigrant Affairs, 2013), https://www1.nyc.gov/site/planning/data-maps/nyc-population/newest-new-yorkers-2013.page.
3. Michael Walzer, *What It Means to Be an American: Essays on the American Experience* (New York: Marsilio, 1996).
4. Steven Gregory, *Black Corona: Race and the Politics of Place in an Urban Community* (Princeton, N.J.: Princeton University Press, 1998).
5. Hsiang-Shui Chen, *Chinatown No More: Taiwan Immigrants in Contemporary New York* (Ithaca, N.Y.: Cornell University Press, 1992).
6. Jorge Duany, "Hispanas de Queens: Latino Panethnicity in a New York City Neighborhood," *Centro Journal* 15, no. 2 (2003): 256–67.
7. Madhulika Shankar Khandelwal, *Becoming American, Being Indian: An Immigrant Community in New York City* (Ithaca, N.Y.: Cornell University Press, 2002).
8. Roger Sanjek, *The Future of Us All: Race and Neighborhood Politics in New York City* (Ithaca, N.Y.: Cornell University Press, 1998).
9. Another celebration of diversity, this time environmental diversity, connected by the 7 train was presented by the Urban Landscape Lab at Columbia University under the name "Safari 7." In this case, too, the train is a connector, not a real place. See "Safari 7," Urban Landscape Lab at Columbia University and MTWTF, last modified 2016, http://www.safari7.org/.
10. Quoted in Jeff Pearlman, "At Full Blast," *CNN/Sports Illustrated*, December 23, 1999, http://sportsillustrated.cnn.com/features/cover/news/1999/12/22/rocker/.
11. In 2012, the MTA reported 234,00 entering swipes per average weekday in stations of the 7 line, not including Manhattan and the two major transfer points in Queens, 74th Street/Roosevelt Avenue and Queensboro Plaza. Considering that most riders make a return trip, this amounts to more than 450,00 riders each weekday in Queens alone.
12. James Clifford, *Routes: Travel and Translation in the Late Twentieth Century* (Cambridge, Mass.: Harvard University Press, 1997).
13. Ibid., 11.

14. Philip Kasinitz, John H. Mollenkopf, and Mary C. Waters, eds., *Becoming New Yorkers: Ethnographies of the New Second Generation* (New York: Russell Sage Foundation, 2004).

15. Philip Kasinitz, John H. Mollenkopf, and Mary C. Waters, "Worlds of the Second Generation," in ibid., 7.

16. We used the data from the five-year compounded 2006–2010 ACS because it matches the time of our observations and interviews. In addition, since 2010, the decennial census has not included questions about means of transportation, thus making it less useful for our purposes. The margin of error in the five-year ACS is significant, but not enough to alter our interpretation of the data, since we are trying to get only an approximate picture. Indeed, the composition of the riders aboard the 7 train varies throughout the day, the week, and even the year. Therefore, even an exact survey gives only an average picture of the population over the five-year period.

17. Luca M.'s Yelp page, edited May 25, 2013, http://www.yelp.com/biz/the-7-subway-train-flushing?hrid=wviaeJWJkKn8hFYeKHwj6Q&utm_campaign=www_review_share_popup&utm_medium=copy_link&utm_source=(direct).

18. Ling Z.'s Yelp page, edited January 13, 2011, http://www.yelp.com/user_details_reviews_self?userid=lx4g7ip8sv4nb4HrlKqZug&rec_pagestart=130.

19. Anahad O'Connor and Terry Pristin, "Bloomberg Unveils Plan to Redevelop Willets Point," *New York Times*, May 1, 2007, http://www.nytimes.com/2007/05/01/nyregion/01cnd-willets.html. See also Véréna Paravel and J. P. Sniadecki, *Foreign Parts* [documentary film] (New York: Kino International, 2010).

20. Sanjek, *Future of Us All*.

21. Ridership at the Vernon-Jackson station, the first stop in Queens, has risen dramatically since 2010, from an average of 10,028 riders entering each weekday to 14,819 in 2015. See "Average Weekday Subway Ridership," MTA, http://web.mta.info/nyct/facts/ridership/ridership_sub.htm.

22. Sam Roberts, *Grand Central: How a Train Station Transformed America* (New York: Grand Central Publishing, 2013).

23. Isaac Joseph, *La ville sans qualités* (La Tour d'Aigues: Éditions de l'Aube, 1998), 124.

24. Colson Whitehead, *The Colossus of New York: A City in Thirteen Parts* (New York: Anchor Books, 2004), 57.

25. Roger Sanjek, "Color-Full Before Color Blind: The Emergence of Multiracial Neighborhood Politics in Queens, New York City," *American Anthropologist* 102, no. 4 (2000): 762–72.

3. Walking to the Stations, Code Switching, and the I-We-You Shift

1. Margarethe Kusenbach, "Street Phenomenology: The Go-Along as Ethnographic Research Tool," *Ethnography* 4, no. 3 (2003): 455–85.

2. Jean-Paul Thibaud, "La méthode des parcours commentés," and Jean-Yves Petiteau and Élisabeth Pasquier, "La méthode des itineraires: Recits et parcours," both

in *L'espace urbain en méthodes*, edited by Michèle Grosjean and Jean-Paul Thibaud, Collection Eupalinos (Marseille: Éditions parenthèses, 2001), 79–100, 63–78.

3. Kusenbach, "Street Phenomenology."

4. Ibid., 476.

5. Albert Hunter, "Private, Parochial, and Public Social Orders: The Problem of Crime and Incivility in Urban Communities," in *The Challenge of Social Control: Citizenship and Institution Building in Modern Society—Essays in Honor of Morris Janowitz*, ed. Gerald D. Suttles and Mayer N. Zald (Norwood, N.J.: Ablex, 1985), 230–42; Lyn H. Lofland, *The Public Realm: Exploring the City's Quintessential Social Territory* (Hawthorne, N.Y.: Aldine de Gruyter, 1998).

6. Philip Kasinitz, Mohamad Bazzi, and Randal Doane, "Jackson Heights, New York," *Cityscape* 4, no. 2 (1998): 161–77.

7. Erving Goffman, *Forms of Talk* (Philadelphia: University of Pennsylvania Press, 1981).

8. Jan-Petter Blom and John J. Gumperz, "Social Meaning in Linguistic Structure: Code-Switching in Norway," in *The Bilingualism Reader*, ed. Li Wei (London: Routledge, 2000), 111–36.

9. Anita Konzelmann Ziv, "L'intentionnalité collective: Entre sujet pluriel et expérience individuelle," in *Qu'est-ce qu'un collectif? Du commun à la politique*, ed. Laurence Kaufmann and Danny Trom, Raisons pratiques 20 (Paris: Éditions de l'École des hautes études en sciences sociales, 2010), 103–33 (our translation).

10. Louis Quéré and Dietrich Brezger, "L'étrangete mutuelle des passants: Le mode de coexistence du public urbain," *Annales dela recherche urbaine*, nos. 57–58 (1992): 89–99.

11. Reference to Liisa Malkki's "accidental community of memory," in "News and Culture: Transitory Phenomena and the Fieldwork Tradition," in *Anthropological Locations: Boundaries and Grounds of a Field Science*, ed. Akhil Gupta and James Ferguson (Berkeley: University of California Press, 1997), 86–101.

12. Ulf Hannerz, *Exploring the City: Inquiries Toward an Urban Anthropology* (New York: Columbia University Press, 1980).

13. This is a view consistent with John Dewey's definition of the public, in *The Public and Its Problems* (New York: Holt, 1927). Although he was concerned about social problems, he posited that the condition for problems to become public was that they reach people who were "indirectly concerned" with the problem. In the same way, the space around subway stations becomes public as it grants access to people who are indirectly concerned with the neighborhood or "parochial" social order.

14. Ines M. Miyares, "From Exclusionary Covenant to Ethnic Hyperdiversity in Jackson Heights, Queens," *Geographical Review* 94, no. 4 (2004): 462–83; Kasinitz, Bazzi, and Doane, "Jackson Heights, New York."

15. Daniel Cefaï and Isaac Joseph, *L'héritage du pragmatisme: Conflits d'urbanité et épreuves de civisme* (La Tour d'Aigues: Éditions de l'Aube, 2002).

4. The 74th Street/Roosevelt Avenue Station

1. Peter Bearman, *Doormen* (Chicago: University of Chicago Press, 2005).
2. Gilles Jeannot and Isaac Joseph, *Métiers du public: Les compétences de l'agent et l'espace de l'usager* (Paris: CNRS Editions, 1995).
3. For a great presentation of life in this neighborhood, see Frederick Wiseman, *In Jackson Heights* [documentary film] (Cambridge, Mass.: Zipporah Films, 2016).
4. The fieldwork on vendors was conducted in the winter and spring of 2007 with Amalia Leguizamon, then a doctoral student in sociology at the CUNY Graduate School. We rely heavily on her notes in this chapter. All the names have been changed.
5. There now are concession stands on both the ground floor and the lower mezzanines. They were not open in 2007, at the time of our observations.
6. Jane Jacobs, *The Death and Life of Great American Cities* (New York: Random House, 1961).
7. Boris Herrera Barrera, "Knowledge as an Effective Tool to Improve Economic Performance in Micro and Small Enterprises" (Ph.D. diss., Universidad Ramón Llull, ESADE School of Business, 2008), 135–43.
8. Fernanda Santos, "A Prime Retail Spot, but No Takers," *City Room* (blog), *New York Times*, November 8, 2010, http://cityroom.blogs.nytimes.com/2010/11/08/a-prime-retail-spot-but-no-takers/.
9. Angy Altamirano, "Famous Famiglia Opens at Jackson Heights Subway Station," *Queens Courier*, December 9, 2013, http://queenscourier.com/famous-famiglia-opens-at-jackson-heights-subway-station/.
10. In reality, the MTA is responsible for managing the space three feet outside the subway doors. In the case of 74th Street/Roosevelt Avenue, where the station occupies a whole city block, the MTA is responsible for the entire block.
11. Robert W. Snyder, *Transit Talk: New York's Bus and Subway Workers Tell Their Stories* (New York: New York Transit Museum; New Brunswick, N.J.: Rutgers University Press, 1997).
12. Mark Moore and David Eddy Spicer, *The New York City Transit Authority Station Manager Program* (Cambridge, Mass.: John F. Kennedy School of Government, 1995), http://www.thecasecentre.org/educators/products/view?id=7607.
13. Joshua Benjamin Freeman, *In Transit: The Transport Workers Union in New York City, 1933–1966* (New York: Oxford University Press, 1989), 344.
14. Metropolitan Transportation Authority, "MTA Financial Plan" (MTA, New York, November 2008).
15. Sewell Chan and Steven Greenhouse, "M.T.A. and Union Clash on Pensions and Roving Conductors as Deadline Closes In," *New York Times*, December 7, 2005, http://www.nytimes.com/2005/12/07/nyregion/07mta.html.
16. Freeman, *In Transit*.
17. Steven Greenhouse, "City Seeks Stiff Fines for Workers and Transit Union If They Strike," *New York Times*, December 14, 2005, http://www.nytimes.com/2005/12/14/nyregion/14strike.html.

18. Jennifer Steinhauer, "Citywide Strike Halts New York Subways and Buses," *New York Times*, December 21, 2005, http://www.nytimes.com/2005/12/21/nyregion/nyregionspecial3/21strike.html.

19. Janny Scott and Sewell Chan, "Transit Strike into 2nd Day; Stakes Climb," *New York Times*, December 22, 2005, http://www.nytimes.com/2005/12/22/nyregion/nyregionspecial3/22strike.html.

20. Richard Pérez-Peña, "Businesses Tally Losses from Strike," *New York Times*, December 24, 2005, http://www.nytimes.com/2005/12/24/nyregion/nyregionspecial3/24fallout.html.

21. In December 2006, a year after the strike, the Partnership for New York City, an organization of businesses in New York City, released a report, *Growth or Gridlock? The Economic Case for Traffic Relief and Transit Improvement for a Greater New York* (http://www.pfnyc.org/reports/Growth%20or%20Gridlock.pdf), announcing that traffic congestion and gridlock cost the city about $13 billion a year in lost revenues because of lost time and missed opportunities (not counting the health costs of pollution).

22. Corey Kilgannon, "Along No. 7 Line, It Can Be Hard to Stand the Quiet," *New York Times*, December 22, 2005, Academic OneFile.

23. Benjamin Kabak, "Straphangers Poll Finds Support for Station Agents," *2nd Ave. Sagas* (blog), June 18, 2009, http://secondavenuesagas.com/2009/06/18/straphangers-poll-finds-support-for-station-agents/.

24. Marian Swerdlow, *Underground Woman: My Four Years as a New York City Subway Conductor* (Philadelphia: Temple University Press, 1998).

25. Harvey Molotch, *Against Security: How We Go Wrong at Airports, Subways, and Other Sites of Ambiguous Danger* (Princeton, N.J.: Princeton University Press, 2012), esp. chap. 3, coauthored with Noah McClain, "Below the Subway: Taking Care Day In and Day Out," 50–84.

26. Brett G. Stoudt, Michelle Fine, and Madeline Fox, "Growing Up Policed in the Age of Aggressive Policing Policies," *New York Law School Law Review* 56 (2011): 1331.

27. George L. Kelling, *A Strategic Perspective on Policing the New York City Subway* (Boston: St. Germain Group, 1988); George L. Kelling and William J Bratton, "Declining Crime Rates: Insiders' Views of the New York City Story," *Journal of Criminal Law and Criminology* 88, no. 4 (1998): 1217–32.

28. In New York State, a police officer can consider "theft of service" as either an infraction, sanctioned by a ticket, or a class-A misdemeanor, leading to an arrest and a trial. Since the data released by the surface precincts do not indicate any arrests for the years 2006 to 2012, the probability that most of the arrests were conducted by officers of the Transit Bureau is high (N.Y. Pen. Law §165.15: Theft of services). Unfortunately, we were unable to obtain arrest data from the Transit Bureau, despite a Freedom of Information request. See Barry Paddock and Sarah Ryley, "Exclusive: Arrests for Transit Fare Evasion Surge in Recent Years, Putting It Among City's Top Offenses Leading to Jail: *Daily News* Analysis," *Daily News*, August 18, 2004, http://www.nydailynews.com/new-york/nyc-crime/fare-evasion-arrests-surge-years-article-1.1906667.

29. Alice Goffman, "On the Run: Wanted Men in a Philadelphia Ghetto," *American Sociological Review* 74, no. 3 (2009): 339–57.

30. Andy Newman, "Finding Stress, and Some Friction," *New York Times*, March 29, 2005, http://www.nytimes.com/2005/03/29/nyregion/29scientology.html.
31. Susie J. Tanenbaum, *Underground Harmonies: New York City Subway Music and Its Implications for Public Space* (Ithaca, N.Y.: Cornell University Press, 1996).
32. Elijah Anderson, *The Cosmopolitan Canopy: Race and Civility in Everyday Life* (New York: Norton, 2011).

5. Trust in the Subway

1. Marc Santora, "Woman Is Held in Death of Man Pushed onto Subway Tracks in Queens," *New York Times*, December 29, 2012, http://www.nytimes.com/2012/12/30/nyregion/woman-is-held-in-death-of-man-pushed-onto-subway-tracks-in-queens.html.
2. J. David Goodman and Sandra E. Garcia, "Routine Trip Turns Fatal as a Man Is Pushed in Front of a Subway Train," *New York Times*, November 16, 2014, http://www.nytimes.com/2014/11/17/nyregion/man-killed-by-train-was-pushed-onto-tracks-police-say.html.
3. Stanley Milgram, "The Familiar Stranger: An Aspect of Urban Anonymity," in *The Individual in a Social World: Essays and Experiments* (Reading, Mass.: Addison-Wesley, 1977), 51–53.
4. Anthony Giddens, *The Consequences of Modernity* (Stanford, Calif.: Stanford University Press, 1991).
5. Kate Ascher, *The Works: Anatomy of a City* (New York: Penguin, 2005).
6. Erving Goffman, *The Presentation of Self in Everyday Life* (Garden City, N.Y.: Doubleday, 1959).
7. Quoted in Sewell Chan, "A Subway Seat Is No Footstool, Transit Officials Say," *New York Times*, December 19, 2004.
8. Transit Adjudication Bureau, "Rules of Conduct & Fines," Metropolitan Transportation Authority, New York, http://web.mta.info/nyct/rules/rules.htm.
9. Nina Bernstein, "When a Metrocard Led Far out of Town: Post-9/11, Even Evading Subway Fares Can Raise the Prospect of Deportation," *New York Times*, October 11, 2004.
10. Chan, "Subway Seat Is No Footstool."
11. Ted Botha, "Welcome to My Home. Watch the Closing Doors," New York Observed, *New York Times*, December 12, 2004, http://query.nytimes.com/gst/fullpage.html?res=940DE3D91131F931A25751C1A9629C8B63&sec=&spon=&pagewanted=all.
12. William Neuman, "Between-Cars Crackdown Adds to Arrests on Subways," *New York Times*, March 27, 2007, http://www.nytimes.com/2007/03/27/nyregion/27crime.html.
13. Joshua Robin, "MTA Fails to Pass Subway Photo Ban," *Newsday*, March 14, 2005.
14. Sewell Chan, "Want Shots Like These? Get a Permit. Ban on Subway Photography Would Defy a Tradition," *New York Times*, January 7, 2005.
15. Walker Evans, *Many Are Called*, intro. James Agee (1966; New Haven, Conn.: Yale University Press, 2004).
16. Chan, "Want Shots Like These?"

17. For examples of his photographs, taken as he commuted to and from his job, see www.travisruse.com.
18. Quoted in Steven Kurutz, "When the Muse Is a Train," *New York Times*, December 25, 2005.
19. Michael Lipsky, *Street-Level Bureaucracy: Dilemmas of the Individual in Public Service* (New York: Russell Sage Foundation, 1980).
20. Erving Goffman, *Behavior in Public Places: Notes on the Social Organization of Gatherings* (New York: Free Press, 1963).
21. Matthew L. Fried and Victor J. DeFazio, "Territoriality and Boundary Conflicts in the Subway," *Psychiatry* 37 (1974): 47–59.
22. Gary W. Evans and Richard E. Wener, "Crowding and Personal Space Invasion on the Train: Please Don't Make Me Sit in the Middle," *Journal of Environmental Psychology* 27, no. 1 (2007): 90–94, doi: 10.1016/j.jenvp.2006.10.002.
23. Gary H. Winkel and D. Geoffrey Hayward, "Some Major Causes of Congestion in Subway Stations. Research Report to the Transit / Land Use Committee" (Environmental Psychology Program, City University of New York, 1971).
24. Randy Kennedy, *Subwayland: Adventures in the World Beneath New York* (New York: St. Martin's Griffin, 2004), 180.
25. Lyn H. Lofland, *The Public Realm: Exploring the City's Quintessential Social Territory* (Hawthorne, N.Y.: Aldine de Gruyter, 1998).
26. Lofland uses the word "motility," but we use the word "mobility," in order to differentiate it from the meaning of the word "motility" proposed by Vincent Kauffman, Manfred Max Bergman, and Dominique Joye in "Motility: Mobility as Capital," *International Journal of Urban and Regional Research* 28, no. 4 (2004): 745–56, which is now widely accepted as a capital of mobility.
27. Goffman, *Behavior in Public Places*, 83–84.
28. Sewell Chan, "Ad Discourages Subway Door-Holding," *City Room* (blog), *New York Times*, September 4, 2009, http://cityroom.blogs.nytimes.com/2009/09/04/ad-discourages-subway-door-holding/.
29. Ibid.
30. Janey Levine, Ann Vinson, and Deborah Wood, "Subway Behavior," in *People in Places: The Sociology of the Familiar*, ed. Arnold Birenbaum and Edward Sagarin (New York: Praeger, 1973), 208–16.
31. Marc Augé, *Un ethnologue dans le métro*, Textes du 20e siècle (Paris: Hachette, 1986.
32. Lofland, *Public Realm*, 30. Although these principles were not written specifically with the subway in mind, it is interesting that mass transit facilities often come to represent the most illustrative case of public space for sociologists who look for telling examples, from the founding fathers to contemporaries. They are often evoked as an extreme anonymous environment where the social norms governing public space are becoming more obvious. For example, issues of "civil inattention" are often illustrated with examples drawn from the subway or, sometimes, relatively similar environments such as buses or elevated trains. Indeed, the subway is associated with the growth of Western cities around the turn of the century, when the immigrant populations of New York, Chicago, Berlin, and Paris grew rapidly over only a few decades. Then subways and buses appeared as the biggest contrast with the villages from which many immigrants had come.

The flows of urban masses pointed to the inadequacies of the norms imported from the rural world. Politeness even in 1901, according to Gabriel Tarde, was put to test:

> Conversation is the mother of politeness. This is true even when being polite means not talking. To a new urbanite recently arrived from the province, nothing seems as peculiar and against nature as seeing a bus loaded with people who refrain from talking. Silence among strangers seems rude, just as silence among acquaintances is a sign of misunderstanding. (*L'opinion et la foule* [Paris: Felix Alcan, 1901] [our translation])

33. Stanley Milgram and John Sabini, "On Maintaining Urban Norms: A Field Experiment in the Subway," in *Advances in Environmental Psychology*, ed. Andrew Baum, Jerome E. Singer, and Stuart Valins (Hillsdale, N.J.: Erlbaum, 1978), 1:31–40.
34. Irving M. Piliavin, Judith Rodin, and Jane A. Piliavin, "Good Samaritanism: An Underground Phenomenon?" *Journal of Personality and Social Psychology* 13, no. 4 (1969): 289–99.
35. Botha, "Welcome to My Home."
36. Isaac Joseph, *La ville sans qualités* (La Tour d'Aigues: Éditions de l'Aube, 1998).
37. Martin Aranguren and Stéphane Tonnelat, "Emotional Transactions in the Paris Subway: Combining Naturalistic Videotaping, Objective Facial Coding and Sequential Analysis in the Study of Nonverbal Emotional Behavior," *Journal of Nonverbal Behavior* 38, no. 4 (2014): 1–27.
38. Andrea Swalec, "'Snackman' Who Stopped Subway Fight Now Has His Own Bat-Symbol," April 11, 2012, DNAinfo New York, http://www.dnainfo.com/new-york/20120411/greenwich-village-soho/snackman-who-stopped-subway-fight-now-has-his-own-bat-symbol/.
39. Ibid.
40. Georg Simmel, "The Metropolis and Mental Life" (1903), in *The Sociology of Georg Simmel*, trans. and ed. Kurt Wolff (New York: Free Press, 1950), 409–24.
41. Michèle Jolé, "Trouver une place. Prendre son tour," *Annales de la recherche urbaine*, nos. 57–58 (1992): 83.
42. Louis Quéré and Dietrich Brezger, "L'étrangeté mutuelle des passants: Le mode de coexistence du public urbain," *Annales de la recherche urbaine*, nos. 57–58 (1992): 96 (our translation).
43. Harvey Sacks, "Lecture Eleven on Exchanging Glances," *Human Studies*, 1964–1965 Lectures, 12, nos. 3–4 (1989): 345.
44. Ibid.
45. David Maines, "Tactile Relationships in the Subway as Affected by Racial, Sexual, and Crowded Seating Situations," *Environmental Psychology and Nonverbal Behavior* 2, no. 2 (1977): 100–108, and "Ecological and Negotiation Processes in New York Subways.," *Journal of Social Psychology* 108, no. 1 (1979): 29–36.
46. Sacks, "Lecture Eleven on Exchanging Glances," 345.
47. But see Claudia Rankine, *Citizen: An American Lyric* (Minneapolis: Graywolf Press, 2014).
48. Giddens, *Consequences of Modernity*, 99–100.

49. Anne Warfield Rawls, "The Interaction Order Sui Generis: Goffman's Contribution to Social Theory," *Sociological Theory* 5, no. 2 (1987): 139, doi: 10.2307/201935.
50. Goffman, *Presentation of Self in Everyday Life*, 10, quoted in ibid.
51. Rawls, "Interaction Order Sui Generis," 140.
52. Ibid., 142.
53. Erving Goffman, *Interaction Ritual: Essays on Face-to-Face Behavior* (Garden City, N.Y.: Anchor Books, 1967), 1:135, quoted in ibid., 139.
54. Veronika Belenkaya, "Riders Take a 'No Pants Subway Ride,'" *Daily News*, January 13, 2008, http://www.nydailynews.com/news/2008/01/13/2008-01-13_riders_take_a_no_pants_subway_ride.html.
55. Charlie Todd, "No Pants 2k8," January 16, 2008, Improv Everywhere: We Cause Scenes, http://improveverywhere.com/2008/01/16/no-pants-2k8/.
56. Ibid.
57. Isaac Joseph, *Le passant considérable* (Paris: Librairie des Méridiens, 1984), 106.
58. Kennedy, *Subwayland*, 125; Edmund Love, "Subways Are for Sleeping," *Harper's*, March 1956, http://harpers.org/archive/1956/03/subways-are-for-sleeping/.
59. Botha, "Welcome to My Home."

6. Gender Relations on the Subway

1. In 2013, our Parisian colleague Marion Tillous identified seventeen subway systems in the world that have or have had cars reserved for women.
2. Claire Hancock, "Une lecture de politiques urbaines genrées dans des pays émergents," *EchoGéo*, October 10, 2012, doi: 10.4000/echogeo.13145.
3. Clifton Hood, *722 Miles: The Building of the Subways and How They Transformed New York* (1993; repr., Baltimore: Johns Hopkins University Press, 2004).
4. Sunny Stalter, "The Subway Crush: Making Contact in New York City Subway Songs, 1904–1915," *Journal of American Culture* 34, no. 4 (2011): 321–31, doi: 10.1111/j.1542-734X.2011.00783.x.
5. Clifton Hood, "Changing Perceptions of Public Space on the New York Rapid Transit System," *Journal of Urban History* 22, no. 3 (1996): 308–31.
6. Kerry Segrave, *Policewomen: A History* (Jefferson, N.C.: McFarland, 1995), 54.
7. Dorothy M. Schulz and Susan Gilbert, "Women and Transit Security: A New Look at an Old Issue" (speech presented at the Women's Travel Issues Second National Conference, Federal Highway Administration, Washington, D.C., 1996).
8. Hood, "Changing Perceptions of Public Space."
9. George L. Kelling and William J. Bratton, "Declining Crime Rates: Insiders' Views of the New York City Story," *Journal of Criminal Law and Criminology* 88, no. 4 (1998): 1217–32.
10. Quoted in Jennifer 8. Lee, "Sexual Harassment Is 'No. 1 Quality of Life Offense' on Subways, Police Say," *City Room* (blog), *New York Times*, November 19, 2009, http://cityroom.blogs.nytimes.com/2009/11/19/sexual-harassment-is-no-1-quality-of-life-offense-on-subways-police-say/.

11. Janice D. Yoder et al., "Exploring Moderators of Gender Differences: Contextual Differences in Door-Holding Behavior," *Journal of Applied Social Psychology* 32, no. 8 (2002): 1682–86, doi: 10.1111/j.1559–1816.2002.tb02769.x.

12. Peter Donohue, "Chivalry Takes Front Seat on City's Buses," *Daily News*, March 14, 2005.

13. Peter Donohue, "N.Y. Stand-up Town. Mom-to-Be Finds City Has Heart as Straphangers Let Her Sit Down. Pregnant Question: Will Jaded New Yorkers Part with a Seat?," *Daily News*, March 13, 2005.

14. Candace West and Don H. Zimmerman, "Doing Gender," *Gender & Society* 1, no. 2 (1987): 125–51, doi: 10.1177/0891243287001002002.

15. David Francis and Stephen Hester, "Le genre selon l'ethnométhodologie et l'analyse de conversation," *Réseaux* 18, no. 103 (2000): 215–51, doi: 10.3406/reso.2000.2277.

16. Harvey Sacks, "Lecture Eleven on Exchanging Glances," *Human Studies*, 1964–1965 Lectures, 12, nos. 3–4 (1989): 333–48.

17. Carol Brooks Gardner, *Passing By: Gender and Public Harassment* (Berkeley: University of California Press, 1995). Even though this fear is real, it does not correspond to the distribution of violence against women. As Fabienne Malbois pointed out to us, domestic space (the family) remains the place where women are most susceptible to fall victim to aggression (e.g., violence, rape). On this, see the debate between Joan W. Scott, "The Evidence of Experience," *Critical Inquiry* 17, no. 4 (1991): 773–97, and "The Tip of the Volcano," *Comparative Studies in Society and History* 35, no. 2 (1993): 438–43; and Laura Lee Downs, "If 'Woman' Is Just an Empty Category, Then Why Am I Afraid to Walk Alone at Night? Identity Politics Meets the Postmodern Subject," *Comparative Studies in Society and History* 35, no. 2 (1993): 414–37.

18. Martha J. Smith and Ronald V. Clarke, *Men Taking Up Too Much Space on the Train* (blog), last edited June 13, 2016, http://mentakingup2muchspaceonthetrain.tumblr.com/.

19. David Maines, "Tactile Relationships in the Subway as Affected by Racial, Sexual, and Crowded Seating Situations," *Environmental Psychology and Nonverbal Behavior* 2, no. 2 (1977): 100–108.

20. West and Zimmerman, "Doing Gender," 136.

21. Erving Goffman, "The Arrangement Between the Sexes," *Theory and Society* 4, no. 3 (1977): 329, doi: 10.2307/656722.

22. Ibid.

23. Craigslist lists the posters for only the past seven days.

24. Frank Beau, "L'amour mobile: Une étude en cinq actes des récits de coup de foudre dans le métro" (Régie autonome des transports parisiens [RATP], n.d.).

25. William H. Whyte, *The Social Life of Small Urban Spaces* (Washington, D.C.: Conservation Foundation, 1980).

26. Such as the man who posted a drawing of a missed encounter and who was thus able to meet the lady and date her. The success of the drawing on social networks made a television network devote a show to the event. See http://nygirlof mydreams.com/; and Alan Feuer, "If You See Someone, Say Something," *New York Times*, June 28, 2009, http://www.nytimes.com/2009/06/28/nyregion/28 poetry.html.

27. Anne Beller, Sanford Garelik, and Sydney Cooper, "Sex Crimes in the Subway," *Criminology* 18, no. 1 (1980): 35–52.
28. Martha J. Smith and Ronald V. Clarke, "Crime and Public Transport," *Crime and Justice* 27 (2000): 169–233.
29. Beller, Garelik, and Cooper, "Sex Crimes in the Subway," 41.
30. Smith and Clarke, "Crime and Public Transport," 189.
31. Lee, "Sexual Harassment."
32. For more on Hollaback!, a "non-profit and movement to end harassment in public spaces," see http://www.hollabacknyc.blogspot.com/.
33. Office of Manhattan Borough President Scott Stringer, "Hidden in Plain Sight: Sexual Harassment and Assault in the New York City Subway System," July 2007, http://www.nytimes.com/packages/pdf/nyregion/city_room/20070726_hidden-inplainsight.pdf.
34. Isaac Joseph, "Le reclus, le souci de soi et la folie dans la place," in *Erving Goffman et les institutions totales*, ed. Charles Amourous and Alain Blanc (Paris: L' Harmattan, 2001), 79–92.
35. Hood, "Changing Perceptions of Public Space."
36. Beller, Garelik, and Cooper, "Sex Crimes in the Subway," 47.
37. Lee, "Sexual Harassment."
38. Tracy Connor, "Hunt Perv Caught in a Flash: Fone Gives Cops Pic of Subway Suspect," *Daily News*, August 27, 2005, 5.
39. Quoted in Russell Scott Smith, "Onan the Vegetarian: The Story of a Raw-Food Guru Turned 'Subway Perv,'" *New York*, April 10, 2006, http://nymag.com/news/features/16576/.
40. For more on this website, see Hollaback! You Have the Power to End Harassment, http://www.ihollaback.org/.
41. Emily May, interview with author, September 11, 2013.
42. Jack Katz, *How Emotions Work* (Chicago: University of Chicago Press, 1999).
43. Patrick Gallahue, "Posters Rub MTA Wrong," *New York Post*, July 15, 2008, http://nypost.com/2008/07/15/posters-rub-mta-wrong/; Emily May and Sam Carter, "MTA Must Crack Down on Epidemic of Subway Groping," *Daily News*, July 19, 2007, http://www.nydailynews.com/opinion/mta-crack-epidemic-subway-groping-article-1.348236.
44. Sewell Chan, "Fighting Sexual Harassment on the Subways," *City Room* (blog), *New York Times*, October 2, 2008, http://cityroom.blogs.nytimes.com/2008/10/02/fighting-sexual-harassment-on-the-subways/.
45. Kimberly Matus, "I Was Groped on the Subway," *Opinionator* (blog), *New York Times*, May 13, 2013, http://opinionator.blogs.nytimes.com/2013/05/13/i-was-groped-on-the-subway/.
46. Robert Emerson and Carol Gardner, "Bus Troubles: Public Harassment and Public Transportation," *Perspectives on Social Problems* 9 (1997): 265–74.
47. Diana, "Everyone Is on Your Side," July 31, 2007, Hollaback!, http://www.ihollaback.org/blog/2007/07/.
48. Molly, "Subway Groper on the 6 Train," October 10, 2006, Hollaback!, http://www.ihollaback.org/blog/2006/10/10/subway-groper-on-the-6-train/.
49. Jill P. Dimond et al., "Hollaback!: The Role of Storytelling Online in a Social Movement Organization," in *Proceedings of the 2013 Conference on Computer Sup-*

ported *Cooperative Work* (New York: Association for Computing Machinery, 2013), 477–90.

50. Michael W. Brooks, *Subway City: Riding the Trains, Reading New York* (New Brunswick, N.J.: Rutgers University Press, 1997), 179, http://www.h-net.org/review /hrev-a0a5f0-aa.

51. Karen Zraick, "A Personal Story of Sexual Harassment," *City Room* (blog), *New York Times*, November 10, 2010, http://cityroom.blogs.nytimes.com/2010/11/10 /a-personal-story-of-sexual-harassment/.

52. Matus, "I Was Groped on the Subway"; see, especially, the comment by Follitics, *Opinionator* (blog), *New York Times*, May 13, 2013, http://opinionator.blogs.nytimes .com/2013/05/13/i-was-groped-on-the-subway/?_r=1#permid=157.

53. Max Gluckman, "Gossip and Scandal," *Current Anthropology* 4 (1963): 307–I5.

54. Debra, "It Is Currently 94 Degrees in New York City," June 8, 2008, Hollaback!, http://www.ihollaback.org/blog/2008/06/.

55. John Brookshire Thompson, *Political Scandal: Power and Visibility in the Media Age* (Cambridge: Polity Press, 2000).

56. Damien de Blic and Cyril Lemieux, "Le scandale comme épreuve," *Politix*, September 1, 2005, 9–38, doi: 10.3917/pox.071.0009.

57. Judith Butler, *Undoing Gender* (New York: Routledge, 2004).

7. Teenagers on the 7 Train

This chapter is a reworked and shortened version of Richard E. Ocejo (then a research assistant for the subway project and now an assistant professor at John Jay College of Criminal Justice, CUNY) and Stéphane Tonnelat, "Subway Diaries: How People Experience and Practice Riding the Train," *Ethnography*, November 17, 2014, doi: 10.1177/1466138113491171.

1. The financing of the student MetroCards is an ongoing point of contention between the MTA and the city and state legislature. Until 1995, the discounts were entirely funded by the city and the state, but since 1995, they each have contributed an equal lump sum of $45 million a year. This sum, however, was never increased, whereas the fare more than doubled, from $1.25 to $2.75 in 2015, leaving the MTA to pay for the extra cost. The city and the state have repeatedly decided to cut the funding altogether. But each time, the MTA threatened to eliminate the program completely, letting families foot a bill estimated at $750 per year per student, a threat that so far has forced the state and city to back off.

2. Alex Napoliello, "Group of About 20 Teenage Girls Attack a NYC Subway Rider, Report Says," January 21, 2014, NJ.com, http://www.nj.com/news/index.ssf/2014 /01/group_of_about_20_teenage_girls_attack_a_nyc_subway_rider_report _says.html.

3. Larry Celona, Kirstan Conley, and Rebecca Harshbarger, "Teen Seriously Hurt, Loses Eye Subway Surfing," *New York Post*, November 5, 2013, http://nypost. com/2013/11/05/man-suffers-head-injury-while-train-surfing/.

4. "Subway Kills Teen on Upper West Side," Fox 4 News, http://www.fox4news.com /story/21801699/subway-kills-person-uws.

5. "I'm 13 Years Old and I Live in NYC, Do You Think I'm Too Young to Ride the Subway?" Yahoo! Answers, https://answers.yahoo.com/question/index?qid=2007 0716140737AAh5rnL.

6. Gill Valentine, *Public Space and the Culture of Childhood* (Burlington, Vt.: Ashgate, 2004).

7. Colin Symes, "Coaching and Training: An Ethnography of Student Commuting on Sydney's Suburban Trains," *Mobilities* 2, no. 3 (2007): 443–61, doi: 10.1080/17450100701597434.

8. Hugh Matthews et al., "The Unacceptable Flaneur," *Childhood* 7, no. 3 (2000): 279–94; Iain Borden, *Skateboarding, Space and the City: Architecture and the Body* (New York: Berg, 2001).

9. Cindi Katz, *Growing Up Global: Economic Restructuring and Children's Everyday Lives* (Minneapolis: University of Minnesota Press, 2004); Hugh Matthews, Melanie Limb, and Mark Taylor, "Reclaiming the Street: The Discourse of Curfew," *Environment and Planning A* 31 (1999): 1713–30.

10. Mats Lieberg, "Teenagers and Public Space," *Communication Research* 22, no. 6 (1995): 720–44.

11. Erving Goffman, *Behavior in Public Places: Notes on the Social Organization of Gatherings* (New York: Free Press, 1963), 84.

12. A study of the Delhi subway also showed that teenagers gathered in the subway and had very different experiences. See Melissa Butcher, "Cultures of Commuting: The Mobile Negotiation of Space and Subjectivity on Delhi's Metro," *Mobilities* 6, no. 2 (2011): 237.

13. Mario Luis Small, "'How Many Cases Do I Need?': On Science and the Logic of Case Selection in Field-Based Research," *Ethnography* 10, no. 1 (2009): 25.

14. Jean-Paul Thibaud, "La methode des parcours commentes," in *L'espace urbain en méthodes*, ed. Michèle Grosjean and Jean-Paul Thibaud, Collection Eupalinos (Marseille: Éditions parenthèses, 2001), 79–100.

15. Margarethe Kusenbach, "Street Phenomenology: The Go-Along as Ethnographic Research Tool," *Ethnography* 4, no. 3 (2003): 455–85.

16. Howard S. Becker, "Photography and Sociology," *Studies in the Anthropology of Visual Communication* 1, no. 1 (1974): 3–26; Douglas Harper, "The Visual Ethnographic Narrative," *Visual Anthropology* 1, no. 1 (1987): 1–19.

17. Javier Auyero and Debora Alejandra Swistun, *Flammable: Environmental Suffering in an Argentine Shantytown* (New York: Oxford University Press, 2009).

18. Goffman, *Behavior in Public Places*, 64–78.

19. Lyn H. Lofland, *A World of Strangers: Order and Action in Urban Public Space* (New York: Basic Books, 1973).

20. Elijah Anderson, *The Cosmopolitan Canopy: Race and Civility in Everyday Life* (New York: Norton, 2011).

21. For a good analysis of the work of subway musicians, see Susie J. Tanenbaum, *Underground Harmonies: New York City Subway Music and Its Implications for Public Space* (Ithaca, N.Y.: Cornell University Press, 1996).

22. Anderson, *Cosmopolitan Canopy*.

23. Erving Goffman, *Relations in Public: Microstudies of the Public Order* (New York: Basic Books, 1971).

8. Subway City

1. John R. Logan and Harvey L. Molotch, *Urban Fortunes: The Political Economy of Place* (Berkeley: University of California Press, 2007).
2. Peter Derrick, *Tunneling to the Future: The Story of the Great Subway Expansion That Saved New York* (New York: New York University Press, 2001).
3. Jacob Riis, *How the Other Half Lives: Studies Among the Tenements of New York* (1890; repr., New York: Penguin, 1997).
4. Richard Plunz, *A History of Housing in New York City* (New York: Columbia University Press, 1990), 47–48.
5. Derrick, *Tunneling to the Future*, 95.
6. Ibid., 45.
7. Clifton Hood, *722 Miles: The Building of the Subways and How They Transformed New York* (New York: Simon & Schuster, 1993), 159.
8. Kenneth T. Jackson, *Crabgrass Frontier: The Suburbanization of the United States* (New York: Oxford University Press, 1985).
9. Louis Wirth, "Urbanism as a Way of Life," *American Journal of Sociology* 44, no. 1 (1938): 8.
10. Isaac Joseph, *La ville sans qualités* (La Tour d'Aigues: Éditions de l'Aube, 1998).
11. Robert Ezra Park, Ernest W. Burgess, and Roderick D. McKenzie, *The City* (Chicago: University of Chicago Press, 1967).
12. Frederic M. Thrasher, *The Gang: A Study of 1,313 Gangs in Chicago* (Chicago: University of Chicago Press, 1927).
13. Charles Horton Cooley, *On Self and Social Organization* (New York: Scribner, 1902).
14. Charles Horton Cooley, "The Theory of Transportation," *Publications of the American Economic Association* 9, no. 3 (1894): 13–148.
15. Ernest W. Burgess, "The Growth of the City: An Introduction to a Research Project," in Park, Burgess, and McKenzie, *City*, 47–62.
16. Brian J. Cudahy, *Under the Sidewalks of New York: The Story of the Greatest Subway System in the World* (Brattleboro, Vt.: Greene Press, 1979); Peter Derrick, "The Dual System of Rapid Transit: The Role of Politics and City Planning in the Second Stage of Subway Construction in New York City, 1902 to 1913" (Ph.D. diss., New York University, 1979); Derrick, *Tunneling to the Future*; Hood, *722 Miles*; Stan Fischler, *Uptown, Downtown: A Trip Through Time on New York's Subways* (New York: Hawthorne Books, 1976).
17. Hood, *722 Miles*, 179.
18. Ebenezer Howard, *Garden Cities of Tomorrow: Being the Third Edition of "To-Morrow: A Peaceful Path to Real Reform"* (London: Sonnenschein, 1902).
19. In the ads printed by the Queensboro Corporation, the commuting times vary by a few minutes. At least four stops served the Jackson Heights area (74th Street, 82nd Street, 90th Street, and Junction Boulevard).
20. Quoted in Hood, *722 Miles*.
21. Daniel Karatzas, *Jackson Heights: A Garden in the City* (New York: Jackson Heights Beautification Group, 1990), 57–69.
22. Plunz, *History of Housing in New York City*, 135.

23. Ibid., 151.
24. Wirth, "Urbanism as a Way of Life."
25. Hood, *722 Miles*, 176.
26. Plunz, *History of Housing in New York City*, 151–63.
27. Karatzas, *Jackson Heights*, 117.
28. Joseph B. Raskin, *The Routes Not Taken: A Trip Through New York City's Unbuilt Subway System* (New York: Fordham University Press, 2013).
29. Ines M. Miyares, "From Exclusionary Covenant to Ethnic Hyperdiversity in Jackson Heights, Queens," *Geographical Review* 94, no. 4 (2004): 462–83.
30. Robert A. Caro, *The Power Broker: Robert Moses and the Fall of New York* (New York: Knopf, 1974).
31. Dolores Hayden, *Building Suburbia: Green Fields and Urban Growth, 1820–2000* (New York: Vintage Books, 2004).
32. Roland Marchand, "The Designers Go to the Fair II: Norman Bel Geddes, the General Motors 'Futurama,' and the Visit to the Factory Transformed," *Design Issues* 8, no. 2 (1992): 23–40, doi: 10.2307/1511638.
33. Plunz, *History of Housing in New York City*, 238–40.
34. Ibid., 282.
35. Ibid., 285.
36. Derrick, *Tunneling to the Future*.
37. Andrew J. Sparberg, *From a Nickel to a Token: The Journey from Board of Transportation to MTA* (New York: Fordham University Press, 2016).
38. John H. Mollenkopf, *The Contested City* (Princeton, N.J.: Princeton University Press, 1983), and *A Phoenix in the Ashes: The Rise and Fall of the Koch Coalition in New York City Politics* (Princeton, N.J.: Princeton University Press, 1994).
39. Louis Wirth, "Rural-Urban Differences," in *Classic Essays on the Culture of Cities*, ed. Richard Sennett (New York: Appleton-Century-Crofts, 1969), 224.
40. Herbert J. Gans, "Urbanism and Suburbanism as Ways of Life: A Reevaluation of Definitions," in *Human Behavior and Social Processes*, ed. Arnold M. Rose (Boston: Houghton Mifflin, 1962), 636–37.
41. Herbert J. Gans, "The Balanced Community: Homogeneity or Heterogeneity in Residential Areas?" *Journal of the American Institute of Planners* 27, no. 3 (1961): 176–84, doi: 10.1080/01944366108978452.
42. Jon C. Teaford, *The Rough Road to Renaissance: Urban Revitalization in America, 1940–1985* (Baltimore: Johns Hopkins University Press, 1990), 7.
43. For a visionary discussion of this idea, see Jane Jacobs, *The Death and Life of Great American Cities* (New York: Random House, 1961).
44. Arun P. Lobo and Joseph J. Salvo, *The Newest New Yorkers, 2000: Immigrant New York in the New Millennium* (New York: Department of City Planning, Population Division, 2004), and *The Newest New Yorkers: Characteristics of the City's Foreign-born Population*, 2013 ed. (New York: Department of City Planning, Office of Immigrant Affairs, 2013), http://www.nyc.gov/html/dcp/html/census/nny.html.
45. Bruce Schaller, *Mode Shift in the 1990s: How Subway and Bus Ridership Outpaced the Auto in Market Share Gains in New York City* (New York: Schaller Consulting, August 8, 2001), 1.
46. Lobo and Salvo, *Newest New Yorkers, 2000*.

47. Philip Kasinitz, Mohamad Bazzi, and Randal Doane, "Jackson Heights, New York," *Cityscape* 4, no. 2 (1998): 161–77.
48. Roger Sanjek, *The Future of Us All: Race and Neighborhood Politics in New York City* (Ithaca, N.Y.: Cornell University Press, 1998).
49. Miyares, "From Exclusionary Covenant to Ethnic Hyperdiversity."
50. Derrick, *Tunneling to the Future*, 260.
51. Claude S. Fischer, "Toward a Subcultural Theory of Urbanism," *American Journal of Sociology* 80, no. 6 (1975): 1319–41.
52. William B. Helmreich, *The New York Nobody Knows: Walking 6,000 Miles in the City* (Princeton, N.J.: Princeton University Press, 2013).
53. Claude S. Fischer, "The Subcultural Theory of Urbanism: A Twentieth-Year Assessment," *American Journal of Sociology* 101, no. 3 (1995): 549.
54. Ibid., 550.
55. Edward Glaeser, *Triumph of the City: How Our Greatest Invention Makes Us Richer, Smarter, Greener, Healthier, and Happier* (New York: Penguin, 2014).
56. William Neuman, "Between-Cars Crackdown Adds to Arrests on Subways," *New York Times*, March 27, 2007, http://www.nytimes.com/2007/03/27/nyregion/27crime.html.

9. A World of Subway Citizens

1. Mimi Sheller and John Urry, "The New Mobilities Paradigm," *Environment and Planning A* 38, no. 2 (2006): 207–26; John Urry, *Mobilities* (Cambridge: Polity Press, 2007); Tim Cresswell, "Mobilities I: Catching Up," *Progress in Human Geography*, November 5, 2010, doi: 10.1177/0309132510383348; "Mobilities II: Still," *Progress in Human Geography* 36, no. 5 (2012): 645–53, doi: 10.1177/0309132511423349; and "Mobilities III: Moving On," *Progress in Human Geography* 38, no. 5 (2014): 712–21, doi: 10.1177/0309132514530316.
2. Marc Augé, *Un ethnologue dans le métro* (Paris: Hachette, 1986), and *Le métro revisité* (Paris: Seuil, 2008); Bruno Latour, *Aramis, or the Love of Technology*, trans. Catherine Porter (Cambridge, Mass.: Harvard University Press,1996); Susan Leigh Star, "The Ethnography of Infrastructure," *American Behavioral Scientist* 43, no. 3 (1999): 377–91, doi: 10.1177/00027649921955326; Isaac Joseph, *Météor, les métamorphoses du métro* (Paris: Economica, 2004); Julie Kleinman, "Adventures in Infrastructure: Making an African Hub in Paris," *City & Society* 26, no. 3 (2014): 286–307, doi: 10.1111/ciso.12044.
3. This gap maybe closed soon. In 2016, Stéphane Tonnelat and Rashmi Sadana organized an international workshop on "ethnographies of mass transportation in a globalized world." Their call for proposal received many applications from researchers working in many cities of the world.
4. Rashmi Sadana, "On the Delhi Metro: An Ethnographic View," *Economic and Political Weekly*, November 13–19, 2010, 77–83, and "The Metro and the Street," *Seminar*, no. 646 (2012): 16–20; Melissa Butcher, "Cultures of Commuting: The Mobile Negotiation of Space and Subjectivity on Delhi's Metro," *Mobilities* 6, no. 2 (2011): 237.

5. Anru Lee, "Subways as a Space of Cultural Intimacy: The Mass Rapid Transit System in Taipei, Taiwan," *China Journal*, no. 58 (2007): 31–55.

6. Alaina Lemon, "Talking Transit and Spectating Transition: The Moscow Metro," in *Altering States: Ethnographies of Transition in Eastern Europe and the Former Soviet Union*, ed. Daphne Berdahl, Matti Bunzl, and Martha Lampland (Ann Arbor: University of Michigan Press, 2000), 15–39, https://www.academia.edu/4564168/Talking_Transit_and_Spectating_Transition_The_Moscow_Metro; Oksana Zaporozhets, "Becoming a Subway User: Managing Affects and Experiences," SSRN Scholarly Paper (Social Science Research Network, Rochester, N.Y., May 6, 2014), http://papers.ssrn.com/abstract=2433951.

7. Claire Hancock, "Une lecture de politiques urbaines genrées dans des pays émergents," *EchoGéo*, October 10, 2012, doi: 10.4000/echogeo.13145.

8. Jean-Charles Depaule and Philippe Tastevin, "Deux ethnologues dans le métro," *Égypte/Monde arabe*, December 31, 2006, 23–34.

9. Clifton Hood, *722 Miles: The Building of the Subways and How They Transformed New York* (New York: Simon & Schuster, 1993), 257.

10. Sadana, "On the Delhi Metro."

11. Lee, "Subways as a Space of Cultural Intimacy."

12. Michel Foucault, *Discipline and Punish: The Birth of the Prison*, trans. Alan Sheridan (New York: Pantheon Books, 1978); Garrett Ziegler, "Subjects and Subways: The Politics of the Third Rail," *Space and Culture* 7, no. 3 (2004): 283–301.

13. Lee, "Subways as a Space of Cultural Intimacy."

14. Sadana, "On the Delhi Metro."

15. Dean Nelson, "Rape Cases in Delhi Double After Gang Rape of Student on Bus," *Telegraph* (London), October 31, 2013, http://www.telegraph.co.uk/news/world news/asia/india/10417749/Rape-cases-in-Delhi-double-after-gang-rape-of-student -on-bus.html.

16. Stefan Höhne, "The Birth of the Urban Passenger: Infrastructural Subjectivity and the Opening of the New York City Subway," *City* 19, nos. 2–3 (2015): 313–21, doi: 10.1080/13604813.2015.1015276.

17. Bruno Latour, *We Have Never Been Modern*, trans. Catherine Porter (Cambridge, Mass.: Harvard University Press, 2012).

18. Lyn H. Lofland, *The Public Realm: Exploring the City's Quintessential Social Territory* (Hawthorne, N.Y.: Aldine de Gruyter, 1998).

19. William Kornblum and Kristen Van Hooreweghe, "The Changing Traditional Uses of Jamaica Bay" (U.S. Department of the Interior, National Park Service, Washington, D.C., 2012).

20. A notable source of information online is Benjamin Kabak's blog, *2nd Ave. Sagas*, http//: secondavenuesagas.com.

21. Quoted in Sewell Chan and William Neuman, "Ravitch Unveils M.T.A. Rescue Plan," *City Room* (blog), *New York Times*, December 4, 2008, http://cityroom.blogs.nytimes.com/2008/12/04/ravitch-unveils-mta-rescue-plan/.

22. Richard Ravitch, "Report to Governor David A. Paterson" (Commission on Metropolitan Transportation Authority Financing, New York, 2008).

23. Roxanne Warren, "Subway Fares Rise, as Do Riders' Gripes," *New York Times*, March 24, 2015, http://www.nytimes.com/2015/03/24/opinion/subway-fares-rise -as-do-riders-gripes.html.

24. Peter Tuckel, William Milczarski, and Michael Benediktsson, "Etiquette of Riders on New York City Subways," An Observational Study Conducted by Students at Hunter College, The City University of New York, Spring 2016, http://silo-public.hunter.cuny.edu/798320a76b1c330347bb7155d717c86bdf278c0f/Behavior-of-New-York-City-Subway-Riders_v.8.pdf.

Appendix

1. Robert M. Emerson, Rachel I. Fretz, and Linda L. Shaw, *Writing Ethnographic Fieldnotes*, 2nd ed. (Chicago: University of Chicago Press, 2011).
2. Marc Augé, *Un ethnologue dans le métro* (Paris: Hachette, 1986), and *Le métro revisité* (Paris: Seuil, 2008).
3. John Urry, *Mobilities* (Cambridge: Polity Press, 2007); Tim Cresswell, "Mobilities I: Catching Up," *Progress in Human Geography* 35, no 4 (2011): 550–58, doi: 10.1177/0309132510383348; David Bissell, "Encountering Stressed Bodies: Slow Creep Transformations and Tipping Points of Commuting Mobilities," *Geoforum* 51 (2014): 191–201, doi: 10.1016/j.geoforum.2013.11.007.
4. Augé, *Un ethnologue dans le métro.*
5. Many subway buffs—passionate about the history of the subway, its rolling stock, and anecdotal evidence that make great stories—also subscribe to this view. They like to reminisce about the infrastructure that ushered them into modernity.
6. Augé, *Le métro revisité.*
7. Ibid., 25.
8. Norbert Elias, *The Civilizing Process*, vol. 1, *The History of Manners* (New York: Pantheon Books, 1978).
9. Margarethe Kusenbach, "Street Phenomenology: The Go-Along as Ethnographic Research Tool," *Ethnography* 4, no. 3 (2003): 455–85.
10. Michel de Certeau, *The Practice of Everyday Life*, trans. Steven F. Rendall (Berkeley: University of California Press, 1984).
11. Ken Knabb, ed., *Situationist International Anthology* (Berkeley, Calif.: Bureau of Public Secrets, 1995).
12. Setha M. Low, Dana Taplin, and Suzanne Scheld, *Rethinking Urban Parks: Public Space and Cultural Diversity* (Austin: University of Texas Press, 2005).
13. Gabrielle Bendiner-Viani, "Walking, Emotion, and Dwelling," *Space and Culture* 8, no. 4 (2005): 459; Sarah Pink, "An Urban Tour: The Sensory Sociality of Ethnographic Place-Making," *Ethnography* 9, no. 2 (2008): 175–96.
14. Jean-Yves Petiteau and Élisabeth Pasquier, "La méthode des itineraires: Recits et parcours," and Jean-Paul Thibaud, "La méthode des parcours commentés," both in *L'espace urbain en méthodes*, ed. Michèle Grosjean and Jean-Paul Thibaud, Collection Eupalinos (Marseille: Éditions parenthèses, 2001), 63–78, 79–100.
15. Kusenbach, "Street Phenomenology."
16. Ibid., 476.
17. Georg Simmel, *The Sociology of Georg Simmel*, trans. and ed. Kurt Wolff (New York: Free Press, 1950).

18. Jürgen Habermas, *The Structural Transformation of the Public Sphere: An Inquiry into a Category of Bourgeois Society* (Cambridge, Mass.: MIT Press, 1989).
19. John J. Gumperz and Jan-Petter Blom, "Social Meaning in Linguistic Structures: Code Switching in Norway," in *Directions in Sociolinguistics*, ed. John J. Gumperz and Dell H. Hymes (New York: Holt, Rinehart and Winston, 1972), 407–34.
20. Erving Goffman, *Forms of Talk* (Philadelphia: University of Pennsylvania Press, 1981).
21. Axel Honneth, *The Struggle for Recognition: The Moral Grammar of Social Conflicts* (Cambridge, Mass.: MIT Press, 1996); Low, Taplin, and Scheld, *Rethinking Urban Parks*.
22. Axel Honneth, "Integrity and Disrespect: Principles of a Conception of Morality Based on the Theory of Recognition," *Political Theory* 20, no. 2 (1992): 191.
23. Low, Taplin, and Scheld, *Rethinking Urban Parks*.
24. Lyn L. Lofland, *The Public Realm: Exploring the City's Quintessential Social Territory* (Hawthorne, N.Y.: Aldine de Gruyter, 1998).
25. The interviews were conducted in 2006 and 2007. All the names have been changed, and all the participants signed a consent form validated by the institutional review board at the CUNY Graduate Center.
26. In Jackson Heights, our posters did not remain for long on the walls or poles under the elevated train. Both MTA personnel and residents took them down after a couple of hours at the most. As a result, it was not easy to recruit random riders. We used this method because we were trying to avoid recruiting people through institutional contacts, such as community centers, worried that they would try to convey the opinion of their official group rather than their own perceptions.
27. We also sent a DVD of the film to an address provided by the participants and told them that they could ask that we delete any part of it.
28. Mario Luis Small, "'How Many Cases Do I Need?': On Science and the Logic of Case Selection in Field-Based Research," *Ethnography* 10, no. 1 (2009): 5–38.
29. Pascal Amphoux, "L'observation récurrente," in *L'espace urbain en méthodes*, ed. Michèle Grosjean and Jean-Paul Thibaud, Collection Eupalinos (Marseille: Éditions parenthèses, 2001), 153–69.
30. The diary method was explained in Richard E. Ocejo (then a research assistant for the subway project) and Stéphane Tonnelat, "Subway Diaries: How People Experience and Practice Riding the Train," *Ethnography*, November 17, 2014, doi: 10.1177/1466138113491171.
31. Caitlin Cahill, "Doing Research with Young People: Participatory Research and the Rituals of Collective Work," *Children's Geographies* 5, no. 3 (2007): 297–312, and "Street Literacy: Urban Teenagers' Strategies for Negotiating Their Neighbourhood," *Journal of Youth Studies* 3, no. 3 (2000): 251–77; Terry Williams and William Kornblum, *Growing Up Poor* (Lexington, Mass.: Lexington Books, 1985).
32. We met with a group of twenty-six students, explained the project, and asked them to fill out a form giving their age, country of origin, commuting route, and a few words about why they were interested in the project. We asked eleven of them if they would agree to participate in our project. We selected them because

we wanted as even a number of boys and girls as possible and not too many students from a single ethnic group.

33. We recruited them through another participant, who was the mother of one of the girls. All the students and at least one of their parents agreed to participate by signing an institutional review board–approved consent form (when necessary, we translated the form into the parents' native language).

34. Don H. Zimmerman and D. Lawrence Wieder, "The Diary: Diary-Interview Method," *Journal of Contemporary Ethnography* 5, no. 4 (1977): 479–98.

35. D. Lawrence Wieder, "Telling the Code," in *Ethnomethodology*, ed. Roy Turner (New York: Penguin, 1974), 144–72; Jason B. Jimerson and Matthew K. Oware, "Telling the Code of the Street: An Ethnomethodological Ethnography," *Journal of Contemporary Ethnography* 35, no. 1 (2006): 24–50.

36. Small, "'How Many Cases Do I Need?,'" 24.

37. Mitchell Duneier and Harvey Molotch, "Talking City Trouble: Interactional Vandalism, Social Inequality, and the 'Urban Interaction Problem,'" *American Journal of Sociology* 104, no. 5 (1999): 1263–95.

38. Small, "'How Many Cases Do I Need?,'" 25.

39. The entries range from a single page to ten pages, but most are about two or three pages long. They cover a broad range of topics, such as descriptions of people and places seen during daily routines, particular episodes that they were involved in or witnessed, reflections on their experiences and encounters, personal stories involving their friends, and general comments on the subway. Most of the journals contain a mixture of these, and some of the students also used illustrations to help describe the scene of a particular episode. But mainly the students described daily routines and their reactions to episodes they experienced.

40. Klaus R. Scherer, Angela Schorr, and Tom Johnstone, *Appraisal Processes in Emotion: Theory, Methods, Research* (New York: Oxford University Press, 2001), https://books.google.com/books?hl=en&lr=&id=IWLnBwAAQBAJ&oi=fnd&pg =PT14&dq=appraisal+theory+of+emotions+scherer&ots=tdtTKO8PSX&sig=3X SUSt_GY8B-pwwJiLz9ODi5vIE.

41. Zimmerman and Wieder, "Diary"; Amy Shuman, *Storytelling Rights: The Uses of Oral and Written Texts by Urban Adolescents* (New York: Cambridge University Press, 1986).

42. Sunny Stalter-Pace, "Underground Theater: Theorizing Mobility Through Modern Subway Dramas," *Transfers* 5, no. 3 (2015): 4–22, doi:10.3167/TRANS.2015.050302; Sunny Stalter, "The Subway Crush: Making Contact in New York City Subway Songs, 1904–1915," *Journal of American Culture* 34, no. 4 (2011): 321–31, doi: 10.1111 /j.1542-734X.2011.00783.x.

43. Darcy Haag Granello and Joe E. Wheaton, "Online Data Collection: Strategies for Research," *Journal of Counseling & Development* 82, no. 4 (2004): 387–93, doi: 10.1002/j.1556-6678.2004.tb00325.x.

44. Pippa Norris, *Digital Divide: Civic Engagement, Information Poverty, and the Internet Worldwide* (New York: Cambridge University Press, 2001).

45. Office of Manhattan Borough President Scott Stringer, "Hidden in Plain Sight: Sexual Harassment and Assault in the New York City Subway System," July 2007, http://www.nytimes.com/packages/pdf/nyregion/city_room/20070726_hidden inplainsight.pdf.

46. Tom Boellstorff et al., *Ethnography and Virtual Worlds: A Handbook of Method* (Princeton, N.J.: Princeton University Press, 2012).

47. Kimberly Matus, "I Was Groped on the Subway," *Opinionator* (blog), *New York Times*, May 13, 2013, http://opinionator.blogs.nytimes.com/2013/05/13/i-was-groped -on-the-subway/?comments&_r=0#permid=110.

48. Karen Zraick, "A Personal Story of Sexual Harassment," *City Room* (blog), *New York Times*, November 10, 2010, http://cityroom.blogs.nytimes.com/2010/11/10 /a-personal-story-of-sexual-harassment/.

49. Matus, "I Was Groped on the Subway."

50. For the relation between description and analysis, see Jack Katz, "From How to Why: On Luminous Description and Causal Inference in Ethnography (Part 1)," *Ethnography* 2, no. 4 (2001): 443–73, and "From How to Why: On Luminous Description and Causal Inference in Ethnography (Part 2)," *Ethnography* 3, no. 1 (2002): 63–90.

Bibliography

Altamirano, Angy. "Famous Famiglia Opens at Jackson Heights Subway Station." *Queens Courier*, December 9, 2013. http://queenscourier.com/famous-famiglia -opens-at-jackson-heights-subway-station/.

Amourous, Charles, and Alain Blanc, eds. *Erving Goffman et les institutions totales*. Paris: L'Harmattan, 2001.

Amphoux, Pascal. "L'observation récurrente." In *L'espace urbain en méthodes*, edited by Michèle Grosjean and Jean-Paul Thibaud, 153–72. Collection Eupalinos. Marseille: Éditions parenthèses, 2001.

Anderson, Elijah. *The Cosmopolitan Canopy: Race and Civility in Everyday Life*. New York: Norton, 2011.

Aranguren, Martin, and Stéphane Tonnelat. "Emotional Transactions in the Paris Subway: Combining Naturalistic Videotaping, Objective Facial Coding and Sequential Analysis in the Study of Nonverbal Emotional Behavior." *Journal of Nonverbal Behavior* 38, no. 4 (2014): 1–27.

Ascher, Kate. *The Works: Anatomy of a City*. New York: Penguin, 2005.

Augé, Marc. *Le métro revisité*. Paris: Seuil, 2008.

——. *Un ethnologue dans le métro*. Paris: Hachette, 1986.

Auyero, Javier, and Debora Alejandra Swistun. *Flammable: Environmental Suffering in an Argentine Shantytown*. New York: Oxford University Press, 2009.

Bearman, Peter. *Doormen*. Chicago: University of Chicago Press, 2005.

Beau, Frank. "L'amour mobile: Une étude en cinq actes des récits de coup de foudre dans le métro." Régie autonome des transports parisiens (RATP), n.d.

Becker, Howard S. "Photography and Sociology." *Studies in the Anthropology of Visual Communication* 1, no. 1 (1974): 3–26.

Belenkaya, Veronika. "Riders Take a 'No Pants Subway Ride.'" *Daily News*, January 13, 2008. http://www.nydailynews.com/news/2008/01/13/2008-01-13_riders_take_a _no_pants_subway_ride.html.

Beller, Anne, Sanford Garelik, and Sydney Cooper. "Sex Crimes in the Subway." *Criminology* 18, no. 1 (1980): 35–52. doi: 10.1111/j.1745–9125.1980.tb01346.x.

Bendiner-Viani, Gabrielle. "Walking, Emotion, and Dwelling." *Space and Culture* 8, no. 4 (2005): 459.

Bernstein, Nina. "When a MetroCard Led Far out of Town: Post-9/11, Even Evading Subway Fares Can Raise the Prospect of Deportation." *New York Times*, October 11, 2004.

Bissell, David. "Encountering Stressed Bodies: Slow Creep Transformations and Tipping Points of Commuting Mobilities." *Geoforum* 51 (2014): 191–201. doi: 10.1016/j.geoforum.2013.11.007.

Blom, Jan-Petter, and John J. Gumperz. "Social Meaning in Linguistic Structure: Code-Switching in Norway." In *The Bilingualism Reader*, edited by Li Wei, 111–36. London: Routledge, 2000.

Boellstorff, Tom, Bonnie Nardi, Celia Pearce, and T. L. Taylor. *Ethnography and Virtual Worlds: A Handbook of Method.* Princeton, N.J.: Princeton University Press, 2012.

Borden, Iain. *Skateboarding, Space and the City: Architecture and the Body.* New York: Berg, 2001.

Botha, Ted. "Welcome to My Home. Watch the Closing Doors." New York Observed, *New York Times*, December 12, 2004. http://query.nytimes.com/gst/fullpage.html?res=940DE3D91131F931A25751C1A9629C8B63&sec=&spon=&pagewanted=all.

Brooks, Michael W. *Subway City: Riding the Trains, Reading New York.* New Brunswick, N.J.: Rutgers University Press, 1997.

Burgess, Ernest W. "The Growth of the City: An Introduction to a Research Project." In Robert Ezra Park, Ernest W. Burgess, and Roderick D. McKenzie, *The City*, 47–62. Chicago: University of Chicago Press, 1967.

Butcher, Melissa. "Cultures of Commuting: The Mobile Negotiation of Space and Subjectivity on Delhi's Metro." *Mobilities* 6, no. 2 (2011): 237.

Butler, Judith. *Undoing Gender.* New York: Routledge, 2004.

Cahill, Caitlin. "Doing Research with Young People: Participatory Research and the Rituals of Collective Work." *Children's Geographies* 5, no. 3 (2007): 297–312.

——. "Street Literacy: Urban Teenagers' Strategies for Negotiating Their Neighbourhood." *Journal of Youth Studies* 3, no. 3 (2000): 251–77.

Caro, Robert A. *The Power Broker: Robert Moses and the Fall of New York.* New York: Knopf, 1974.

Cefaï, Daniel, and Isaac Joseph. *L'héritage du pragmatisme: Conflits d'urbanité et épreuves de civisme.* La Tour d'Aigues: Éditions de l'Aube, 2002.

Certeau, Michel de. *The Practice of Everyday Life.* Translated by Steven F. Rendall. Berkeley: University of California Press, 1984.

Chan, Sewell. "Ad Discourages Subway Door-Holding." *City Room* (blog). *New York Times*, September 4, 2009. http://cityroom.blogs.nytimes.com/2009/09/04/ad-discourages-subway-door-holding/.

——. "Fighting Sexual Harassment on the Subways." *City Room* (blog). *New York Times*, October 2, 2008. http://cityroom.blogs.nytimes.com/2008/10/02/fighting-sexual-harassment-on-the-subways/.

——. "A Subway Seat Is No Footstool, Transit Officials Say." *New York Times*, December 19, 2004.

——. "Want Shots Like These? Get a Permit. Ban on Subway Photography Would Defy a Tradition." *New York Times*, January 7, 2005.

Chan, Sewell, and Steven Greenhouse. "M.T.A. and Union Clash on Pensions and Roving Conductors as Deadline Closes In." *New York Times*, December 7, 2005. http://www.nytimes.com/2005/12/07/nyregion/07mta.html.

Chan, Sewell, and William Neuman. "Ravitch Unveils M.T.A. Rescue Plan." *City Room* (blog). *New York Times*, December 4, 2008. http://cityroom.blogs.nytimes.com/2008/12/04/ravitch-unveils-mta-rescue-plan/.

Chen, Hsiang-Shui. *Chinatown No More: Taiwan Immigrants in Contemporary New York*. Ithaca, N.Y.: Cornell University Press, 1992.

Clifford, James. *Routes: Travel and Translation in the Late Twentieth Century*. Cambridge, Mass.: Harvard University Press, 1997.

Connor, Tracy. "Hunt Perv Caught in a Flash: Fone Gives Cops Pic of Subway Suspect." *Daily News*, August 27, 2005, 5.

Cooley, Charles Horton. *On Self and Social Organization*. New York: Scribner, 1902.

——. "The Theory of Transportation." *Publications of the American Economic Association*, May 1, 1894, 13–148.

Cresswell, Tim. "Mobilities I: Catching Up." *Progress in Human Geography* 35, no. 4 (2011): 550–58. doi: 10.1177/0309132510383348.

——. "Mobilities II: Still." *Progress in Human Geography* 36, no. 5 (2012): 645–53. doi: 10.1177/0309132511423349.

——. "Mobilities III: Moving On." *Progress in Human Geography* 38, no. 5 (2014): 712–21. doi: 10.1177/0309132514530316.

Cudahy, Brian J. *Under the Sidewalks of New York: The Story of the Greatest Subway System in the World*. Brattleboro, Vt.: Greene, 1979.

de Blic, Damien, and Cyril Lemieux. "Le scandale comme épreuve." *Politix* 71, no. 3 (2005): 9–38. doi: 10.3917/pox.071.0009.

Depaule, Jean-Charles, and Philippe Tastevin. "Deux ethnologues dans le métro." *Égypte/Monde arabe*, December 31, 2006, 23–34.

Derrick, Peter. "The Dual System of Rapid Transit: The Role of Politics and City Planning in the Second Stage of Subway Construction in New York City, 1902 to 1913." Ph.D. diss., New York University, 1979.

——. *Tunneling to the Future: The Story of the Great Subway Expansion That Saved New York*. New York: New York University Press, 2001.

Dewey, John. *The Public and Its Problems*. New York: Holt, 1927.

Dimond, Jill P., Michaelanne Dye, Daphne Larose, and Amy S. Bruckman. "Hollaback! The Role of Storytelling Online in a Social Movement Organization." In *Proceedings of the 2013 Conference on Computer Supported Cooperative Work*, 477–90. New York: Association for Computing Machinery, 2013.

Donohue, Peter. "Chivalry Takes Front Seat on City's Buses." *Daily News*, March 14, 2005.

——. "N.Y. Stand-Up Town. Mom-to-Be Finds City Has Heart as Straphangers Let Her Sit Down. Pregnant Question: Will Jaded New Yorkers Part with a Seat?" *Daily News*, March 13, 2005.

Downs, Laura Lee. "If 'Woman' Is Just an Empty Category, Then Why Am I Afraid to Walk Alone at Night? Identity Politics Meets the Postmodern Subject." *Comparative Studies in Society and History* 35, no. 2 (1993): 414–37.

Duany, Jorge. "Hispanas de Queens: Latino Panethnicity in a New York City Neighborhood." *Centro Journal* 15, no. 2 (2003): 256–67.

Duneier, Mitchell, and Harvey Molotch. "Talking City Trouble: Interactional Vandalism, Social Inequality, and the 'Urban Interaction Problem.'" *American Journal of Sociology* 104, no. 5 (1999): 1263–95.

Elias, Norbert. *The Civilizing Process.* Vol. 1, *The History of Manners.* New York: Pantheon Books, 1978.

Emerson, Robert M., Rachel I. Fretz, and Linda L. Shaw. *Writing Ethnographic Fieldnotes.* 2nd ed. Chicago: University of Chicago Press, 2011.

Emerson, Robert M., and Carol B. Gardner. "Bus Troubles: Public Harassment and Public Transportation." *Perspectives on Social Problems* 9 (1997): 265–74.

Evans, Gary W., and Richard E. Wener. "Crowding and Personal Space Invasion on the Train: Please Don't Make Me Sit in the Middle." *Journal of Environmental Psychology* 27, no. 1 (2007): 90–94. doi: 10.1016/j.jenvp.2006.10.002.

Evans, Walker. *Many Are Called.* Introduction by James Agee. 1966. New Haven, Conn.: Yale University Press, 2004.

Feuer, Alan. "If You See Someone, Say Something." *New York Times,* June 28, 2009. http://www.nytimes.com/2009/06/28/nyregion/28poetry.html.

Fischer, Claude S. "The Subcultural Theory of Urbanism: A Twentieth-Year Assessment." *American Journal of Sociology* 101, no. 3 (1995): 543–77.

——. "Toward a Subcultural Theory of Urbanism." *American Journal of Sociology* 80, no. 6 (1975): 1319–41.

Fischler, Stan. *Uptown, Downtown: A Trip Through Time on New York's Subways.* New York: Hawthorne Books, 1976.

Foucault, Michel. *Discipline and Punish: The Birth of the Prison.* Translated by Alan Sheridan. New York: Pantheon Books, 1978.

Francis, David, and Stephen Hester. "Le genre selon l'ethnométhodologie et l'analyse de conversation." *Réseaux* 18, no. 103 (2000): 215–51. doi: 10.3406/reso.2000.2277.

Freeman, Joshua Benjamin. *In Transit: The Transport Workers Union in New York City, 1933–1966.* New York: Oxford University Press, 1989.

Fried, Matthew L., and Victor J. DeFazio. "Territoriality and Boundary Conflicts in the Subway." *Psychiatry* 37 (1974): 47–59.

Gallahue, Patrick. "Posters Rub MTA Wrong." *New York Post,* July 15, 2008. http://nypost.com/2008/07/15/posters-rub-mta-wrong/.

Gans, Herbert J. "The Balanced Community: Homogeneity or Heterogeneity in Residential Areas?" *Journal of the American Institute of Planners* 27, no. 3 (1961): 176–84. doi: 10.1080/01944366108978452.

——. "Urbanism and Suburbanism as Ways of Life: A Reevaluation of Definitions." In *Human Behavior and Social Processes,* edited by Arnold M. Rose, 625–48. Boston: Houghton Mifflin, 1962.

Gardner, Carol Brooks. *Passing By: Gender and Public Harassment.* Berkeley: University of California Press, 1995.

Giddens, Anthony. *The Consequences of Modernity.* Stanford, Calif.: Stanford University Press, 1991.

Glaeser, Edward. *Triumph of the City: How Our Greatest Invention Makes Us Richer, Smarter, Greener, Healthier, and Happier.* New York: Penguin, 2011.

Gluckman, Max. "Gossip and Scandal." *Current Anthropology* 4 (1963): 307–15.

Goffman, Alice. "On the Run: Wanted Men in a Philadelphia Ghetto." *American Sociological Review* 74, no. 3 (2009): 339–57.

Goffman, Erving. "The Arrangement Between the Sexes." *Theory and Society* 4, no. 3 (1977): 301–31. doi: 10.2307/656722.

——. *Behavior in Public Places: Notes on the Social Organization of Gatherings.* New York: Free Press, 1963.

——. *Forms of Talk.* Philadelphia: University of Pennsylvania Press, 1981.

——. *Interaction Ritual: Essays on Face-to-Face Behavior.* Garden City, N.Y.: Anchor Books, 1967.

——. *The Presentation of Self in Everyday Life.* Garden City, N.Y.: Doubleday, 1959.

——. *Relations in Public: Microstudies of the Public Order.* New York: Basic Books, 1971.

Goodman, J. David, and Sandra E. Garcia. "Routine Trip Turns Fatal as a Man Is Pushed in Front of a Subway Train." *New York Times*, November 16, 2014. http://www.nytimes.com/2014/11/17/nyregion/man-killed-by-train-was-pushed-onto-tracks-police-say.html.

Granello, Darcy Haag, and Joe E. Wheaton. "Online Data Collection: Strategies for Research." *Journal of Counseling & Development* 82, no. 4 (2004): 387–93. doi: 10.1002/j.1556-6678.2004.tb00325.x.

Greenhouse, Steven. "City Seeks Stiff Fines for Workers and Transit Union If They Strike." *New York Times*, December 14, 2005. http://www.nytimes.com/2005/12/14/nyregion/14strike.html.

Gregory, Steven. *Black Corona: Race and the Politics of Place in an Urban Community.* Princeton, N.J.: Princeton University Press, 1998.

Gumperz, John J., and Jan-Petter Blom. "Social Meaning in Linguistic Structures: Code Switching in Norway." In *Directions in Sociolinguistics: The Ethnography of Communication*, edited by John J. Gumperz and Dell H. Hymes, 407–34. New York: Holt, Rinehart and Winston, 1972.

Habermas, Jürgen. *The Structural Transformation of the Public Sphere: An Inquiry into a Category of Bourgeois Society.* Cambridge, Mass.: MIT Press, 1989.

Hancock, Claire. "Une lecture de politiques urbaines genrées dans des pays émergents." *EchoGéo*, October 10, 2012. doi: 10.4000/echogeo.13145.

Hannerz, Ulf. *Exploring the City: Inquiries Toward an Urban Anthropology.* New York: Columbia University Press, 1980.

——. *Transnational Connections: Culture, People, Places.* London: Routledge, 1996.

Harper, Douglas. "The Visual Ethnographic Narrative." *Visual Anthropology* 1, no. 1 (1987): 1–19.

Hayden, Dolores. *Building Suburbia: Green Fields and Urban Growth, 1820–2000.* New York: Vintage Books, 2004.

Helmreich, William B. *The New York Nobody Knows: Walking 6,000 Miles in the City.* Princeton, N.J.: Princeton University Press, 2013.

Herrera Barrera, Boris. "Knowledge as an Effective Tool to Improve Economic Performance in Micro and Small Enterprises." Ph.D. diss., Universidad Ramón Llull, ESADE School of Business, 2008.

Höhne, Stefan. "The Birth of the Urban Passenger: Infrastructural Subjectivity and the Opening of the New York City Subway." *City* 19, nos. 2–3 (2015): 313–21. doi: 10.1080/13604813.2015.1015276.

Honneth, Axel. "Integrity and Disrespect: Principles of a Conception of Morality Based on the Theory of Recognition." *Political Theory* 20, no. 2 (1992): 187–201.

——. *The Struggle for Recognition: The Moral Grammar of Social Conflicts.* Cambridge, Mass.: MIT Press, 1996.

Hood, Clifton. "Changing Perceptions of Public Space on the New York Rapid Transit System." *Journal of Urban History* 22, no. 3 (1996): 308–31.

——. *722 Miles: The Building of the Subways and How They Transformed New York.* New York: Simon & Schuster, 1993.

——. *722 Miles: The Building of the Subways and How They Transformed New York.* Reprint. Baltimore: Johns Hopkins University Press, 2004.

Howard, Ebenezer. *Garden Cities of Tomorrow: Being the Third Edition of "To-Morrow: A Peaceful Path to Real Reform."* London: Sonnenschein, 1902.

Hunter, Albert. "Private, Parochial, and Public Social Orders: The Problem of Crime and Incivility in Urban Communities." In *The Challenge of Social Control: Citizenship and Institution Building in Modern Society—Essays in Honor of Morris Janowitz*, edited by Gerald D. Suttles and Mayer N. Zald, 230–42. Norwood, N.J.: Ablex, 1985.

Hymes, Dell H. "A Perspective for Linguistic Anthropology." *Journal of Sociolinguistics* 14, no. 5 (2010): 569–80.

Jackson, Kenneth T. *Crabgrass Frontier: The Suburbanization of the United States.* New York: Oxford University Press, 1985.

Jacobs, Jane. *The Death and Life of Great American Cities.* New York: Random House, 1961.

Jeannot, Gilles, and Isaac Joseph. *Métiers du public: Les compétences de l'agent et l'espace de l'usager.* Paris: CNRS Éditions, 1995.

Jimerson, Jason B., and Matthew K. Oware. "Telling the Code of the Street: An Ethnomethodological Ethnography." *Journal of Contemporary Ethnography* 35, no. 1 (2006): 24–50.

Jolé, Michèle. "Trouver une place. Prendre son tour." *Annales de la recherche urbaine*, nos. 57–58 (1992): 82–88.

Joseph, Isaac. *La ville sans qualités.* La Tour d'Aigues: Éditions de l'Aube, 1998.

——. *Le passant considerable.* Paris: Librairie des Méridiens, 1984.

——. "Le reclus, le souci de soi et la folie dans la place." In *Erving Goffman et les institutions totales*, edited by Charles Amourous and Alain Blanc, 79–92. Paris: L' Harmattan, 2001.

——. *Météor, les métamorphoses du métro.* Paris: Economica, 2004.

Kabak, Benjamin. *2nd Ave. Sagas* (blog). http://secondavenuesagas.com/.

Karatzas, Daniel. *Jackson Heights: A Garden in the City.* New York: Jackson Heights Beautification Group, 1990.

Kasinitz, Philip, Mohamad Bazzi, and Randal Doane. "Jackson Heights, New York." *Cityscape* 4, no. 2 (1998): 161–77.

Kasinitz, Philip, John H. Mollenkopf, and Mary C. Waters, eds. *Becoming New Yorkers: Ethnographies of the New Second Generation.* New York: Russell Sage Foundation, 2004.

Katz, Cindi. *Growing Up Global: Economic Restructuring and Children's Everyday Lives.* Minneapolis: University of Minnesota Press, 2004.

Katz, Jack. "From How to Why: On Luminous Description and Causal Inference in Ethnography (Part 1)." *Ethnography* 2, no. 4 (2001): 443–73.

———. "From How to Why: On Luminous Description and Causal Inference in Ethnography (Part 2)." *Ethnography* 3, no. 1 (2002): 63–90.

———. *How Emotions Work*. Chicago: University of Chicago Press, 1999.

Kaufmann, Vincent, Manfred Max Bergman, and Dominique Joye. "Motility: Mobility as Capital." *International Journal of Urban and Regional Research* 28, no. 4 (2004): 745–56.

Kelling, George L. *A Strategic Perspective on Policing the New York City Subway*. Boston: St. Germain Group, 1988.

Kelling, George L., and William J. Bratton. "Declining Crime Rates: Insiders' Views of the New York City Story." *Journal of Criminal Law and Criminology* 88, no. 4 (1998): 1217–32.

Kennedy, Randy. *Subwayland: Adventures in the World Beneath New York*. New York: St. Martin's Griffin, 2004.

Khandelwal, Madhulika Shankar. *Becoming American, Being Indian: An Immigrant Community in New York City*. Ithaca, N.Y.: Cornell University Press, 2002.

Kilgannon, Corey. "Along No. 7 Line, It Can Be Hard to Stand the Quiet." *New York Times*, December 22, 2005.

Kleinman, Julie. "Adventures in Infrastructure: Making an African Hub in Paris." *City & Society* 26, no. 3 (2014): 286–307. doi: 10.1111/ciso.12044.

Knabb, Ken, ed. *Situationist International Anthology*. Berkeley, Calif.: Bureau of Public Secrets, 1995.

Konzelmann Ziv, Anita. "L'intentionnalité collective: Entre sujet pluriel et expérience individuelle." In *Qu'est-ce qu'un collectif? Du commun à la politique*, edited by Laurence Kaufmann and Danny Trom, 103–33. Raisons pratiques 20. Paris: Éditions de l'École des hautes études en sciences sociales, 2010.

Kornblum, William, and Kristen Van Hooreweghe. "The Changing Traditional Uses of Jamaica Bay." U.S. Department of the Interior, National Park Service, Washington, D.C., 2012.

Kurutz, Steven. "When the Muse Is a Train." *New York Times*, December 25, 2005.

Kusenbach, Margarethe. "Street Phenomenology: The Go-Along as Ethnographic Research Tool." *Ethnography* 4, no. 3 (2003): 455–85.

Latour, Bruno. *Aramis, or the Love of Technology*. Translated by Catherine Porter. Cambridge, Mass.: Harvard University Press, 1996.

———. *We Have Never Been Modern*. Translated by Catherine Porter. Cambridge, Mass.: Harvard University Press, 2012.

Lee, Anru. "Subways as a Space of Cultural Intimacy: The Mass Rapid Transit System in Taipei, Taiwan." *China Journal*, no. 58 (2007): 31–55.

Lee, Jennifer 8. "Sexual Harassment Is 'No. 1 Quality of Life Offense' on Subways, Police Say." *City Room* (blog). *New York Times*, November 19, 2009. http://cityroom.blogs.nytimes.com/2009/11/19/sexual-harassment-is-no-1-quality-of-life-offense-on-subways-police-say/.

Lemon, Alaina. "Talking Transit and Spectating Transition: The Moscow Metro." In *Altering States: Ethnographies of Transition in Eastern Europe and the Former Soviet Union*, edited by Daphne Berdahl, Matti Bunzl, and Martha Lampland, 15–39. Ann Arbor: University of Michigan Press, 2000. https://www.academia.edu/4564168/Talking_Transit_and_Spectating_Transition_The_Moscow_Metro.

Levine, Janey, Ann Vinson, and Deborah Wood. "Subway Behavior." In *People in Places: The Sociology of the Familiar*, edited by Arnold Birenbaum and Edward Sagarin, 208–16. New York: Praeger, 1973.

Lieberg, Mats. "Teenagers and Public Space." *Communication Research* 22, no. 6 (1995): 720–44.

Lipsky, Michael. *Street-Level Bureaucracy: Dilemmas of the Individual in Public Service*. New York: Russell Sage Foundation, 1980.

"List of Metro Systems." *Wikipedia*, January 15, 2015. http://en.wikipedia.org/w/index.php?title=List_of_metro_systems&oldid=642060241.

Lobo, Arun Peter, and Joseph J. Salvo. *The Newest New Yorkers, 2000: Immigrant New York in the New Millennium*. New York: Department of City Planning, Population Division, 2004.

——. *The Newest New Yorkers: Characteristics of the City's Foreign-born Population*. 2013 ed. New York: Department of City Planning, Office of Immigrant Affairs, 2013. https://www1.nyc.gov/site/planning/data-maps/nyc-population/newest-new-yorkers-2013.page.

Lofland, Lyn H. *The Public Realm: Exploring the City's Quintessential Social Territory*. Hawthorne, N.Y.: Aldine de Gruyter, 1998.

——. *A World of Strangers: Order and Action in Urban Public Space*. New York: Basic Books, 1973.

Logan, John R., and Harvey L. Molotch. *Urban Fortunes: The Political Economy of Place*. Berkeley: University of California Press, 2007.

Low, Setha M., Dana Taplin, and Suzanne Scheld. *Rethinking Urban Parks: Public Space and Cultural Diversity*. Austin: University of Texas Press, 2005.

Maines, David R. "Ecological and Negotiation Processes in New York Subways." *Journal of Social Psychology* 108, no. 1 (1979): 29–36.

——. "Tactile Relationships in the Subway as Affected by Racial, Sexual, and Crowded Seating Situations." *Environmental Psychology and Nonverbal Behavior* 2, no. 2 (1977): 100–108.

Malkki, Liisa. "News and Culture: Transitory Phenomena and the Fieldwork Tradition." In *Anthropological Locations: Boundaries and Grounds of a Field Science*, edited by Akhil Gupta and James Ferguson, 86–101. Berkeley: University of California Press, 1997.

Marchand, Roland. "The Designers Go to the Fair II: Norman Bel Geddes, the General Motors 'Futurama,' and the Visit to the Factory Transformed." *Design Issues* 8, no. 2 (1992): 23–40. doi: 10.2307/1511638.

Matthews, Hugh, Melanie Limb, and Mark Taylor. "Reclaiming the Street: The Discourse of Curfew." *Environment and Planning A* 31 (1999): 1713–30.

Matthews, Hugh, Mark Taylor, Barry Percy-Smith, and Melanie Limb. "The Unacceptable Flaneur." *Childhood* 7, no. 3 (2000): 279–94.

Matus, Kimberly. "I Was Groped on the Subway." *Opinionator* (blog). *New York Times*, May 13, 2013. http://opinionator.blogs.nytimes.com/2013/05/13/i-was-groped-on-the-subway/.

May, Emily, and Sam Carter. "MTA Must Crack Down on Epidemic of Subway Groping." *Daily News*, July 19, 2007. http://www.nydailynews.com/opinion/mta-crack-epidemic-subway-groping-article-1.348236.

Metropolitan Transportation Authority. "MTA Financial Plan." MTA, New York, November 2008.

Milgram, Stanley. "The Familiar Stranger: An Aspect of Urban Anonymity." In *The Individual in a Social World: Essays and Experiments*, 51–53. Reading, Mass.: Addison-Wesley, 1977.

Milgram, Stanley, and John Sabini. "On Maintaining Urban Norms: A Field Experiment in the Subway." In *Advances in Environmental Psychology*, edited by Andrew Baum, Jerome E. Singer, and Stuart Valins, 1:34–40. Hillsdale, N.J.: Erlbaum, 1978.

Miyares, Ines M. "From Exclusionary Covenant to Ethnic Hyperdiversity in Jackson Heights, Queens." *Geographical Review* 94, no. 4 (2004): 462–83.

Mollenkopf, John H. *The Contested City*. Princeton, N.J.: Princeton University Press, 1983.

——. *A Phoenix in the Ashes: The Rise and Fall of the Koch Coalition in New York City Politics*. Princeton, N.J.: Princeton University Press, 1994.

Molotch, Harvey. *Against Security: How We Go Wrong at Airports, Subways, and Other Sites of Ambiguous Danger*. Princeton, N.J.: Princeton University Press, 2012.

Moore, Mark, and David Eddy Spicer. *The New York City Transit Authority Station Manager Program*. Cambridge, Mass.: John F. Kennedy School of Government, 1995. http://www.thecasecentre.org/educators/products/view?id=7607.

Nelson, Dean. "Rape Cases in Delhi Double After Gang Rape of Student on Bus." *Telegraph* (London), October 31, 2013. http://www.telegraph.co.uk/news/worldnews/asia/india/10417749/Rape-cases-in-Delhi-double-after-gang-rape-of-student-on-bus.html.

Neuman, William. "Between-Cars Crackdown Adds to Arrests on Subways." *New York Times*, March 27, 2007. http://www.nytimes.com/2007/03/27/nyregion/27crime.html.

Newman, Andy. "Finding Stress, and Some Friction." *New York Times*, March 29, 2005. http://www.nytimes.com/2005/03/29/nyregion/29scientology.html.

Norris, Pippa. *Digital Divide: Civic Engagement, Information Poverty, and the Internet Worldwide*. New York: Cambridge University Press, 2001.

Ocejo, Richard E. *Upscaling Downtown: From Bowery Saloons to Cocktail Bars in New York City*. Princeton, N.J.: Princeton University Press, 2014.

Ocejo, Richard E., and Stéphane Tonnelat. "Subway Diaries: How People Experience and Practice Riding the Train." *Ethnography*, November 17, 2014. doi: 10.1177/1466138113491171.

O'Connor, Anahad, and Terry Pristin. "Bloomberg Unveils Plan to Redevelop Willets Point." *New York Times*, May 1, 2007. http://www.nytimes.com/2007/05/01/nyregion/01cnd-willets.html.

Paddock, Barry, and Sarah Ryley. "Exclusive: Arrests for Transit Fare Evasion Surge in Recent Years, Putting It Among City's Top Offenses Leading to Jail: *Daily News* Analysis." *Daily News*, August 18, 2004. http://www.nydailynews.com/new-york/nyc-crime/fare-evasion-arrests-surge-years-article-1.1906667.

Paravel, Véréna, and J. P. Sniadecki. *Foreign Parts* [documentary film]. New York: Kino International, 2010.

Park, Robert Ezra, Ernest W. Burgess, and Roderick D. McKenzie. *The City*. Chicago: University of Chicago Press, 1967.

Pearlman, Jeff. "At Full Blast." *CNN/Sports Illustrated*, December 23, 1999. http://sport sillustrated.cnn.com/features/cover/news/1999/12/22/rocker/.

Pérez-Peña, Richard. "Businesses Tally Losses from Strike." *New York Times*, December 24, 2005. http://www.nytimes.com/2005/12/24/nyregion/nyregionspecial3 /24fallout.html.

Petiteau, Jean-Yves, and Élisabeth Pasquier. "La méthode des itineraires: Recits et parcours." In *L'espace urbain en méthodes*, edited by Michèle Grosjean and Jean-Paul Thibaud, 63–78. Collection Eupalinos. Marseille: Éditions parenthèses, 2001.

Piliavin, Irving, M., Judith Rodin, and Jane A. Piliavin. "Good Samaritanism: An Underground Phenomenon?" *Journal of Personality and Social Psychology* 13, no. 4 (1969): 289–99.

Pink, Sarah. "An Urban Tour: The Sensory Sociality of Ethnographic Place-Making." *Ethnography* 9, no. 2 (2008): 175–96.

Plunz, Richard. *A History of Housing in New York City*. New York: Columbia University Press, 1990.

Quéré, Louis, and Dietrich Brezger. "L'étrangeté mutuelle des passants: Le mode de coexistence du public urbain." *Annales de la recherche urbaine*, nos. 57–58 (1992): 89–99.

Rankine, Claudia. *Citizen: An American Lyric*. Minneapolis: Graywolf Press, 2014.

Raskin, Joseph B. *The Routes Not Taken: A Trip Through New York City's Unbuilt Subway System*. New York: Fordham University Press, 2013.

Ravitch, Richard. "Report to Governor David A. Paterson." Commission on Metropolitan Transportation Authority Financing, New York, 2008.

Rawls, Anne Warfield. "The Interaction Order Sui Generis: Goffman's Contribution to Social Theory." *Sociological Theory* 5, no. 2 (1987): 136–49. doi: 10.2307/201935.

Riis, Jacob August. *How the Other Half Lives: Studies Among the Tenements of New York*. 1890. Reprint, New York: Penguin, 1997.

Rivoli, Dan. "Subway Riders Offer Their Tips for Subway Travel." *amNew York*, March 9, 2014. http://amny.com/transit/subway-riders-offer-their-tips-for-subway-travel -1.7335755.

Roberts, Sam. *Grand Central: How a Train Station Transformed America*. New York: Grand Central Publishing, 2013.

Robin, Joshua. "MTA Fails to Pass Subway Photo Ban." *Newsday*, March 14, 2005.

Ryley, Sarah, and Pete Donohue. "How Safe Is Your Subway?" *Daily News*, June 22, 2014. http://www.nydailynews.com/new-york/nyc-crime/daily-news-analysis-reveals -crime-rankings-city-subway-system-article-1.1836918.

Sacks, Harvey. "Lecture Eleven on Exchanging Glances." *Human Studies*, 1964–1965 Lectures, 12, no. 3–4 (1989): 333–48.

Sadana, Rashmi. "The Metro and the Street." *Seminar*, no. 646 (2012): 16–20.

——. "On the Delhi Metro: An Ethnographic View." *Economic and Political Weekly*, November 13–19, 2010, 77–83.

Sanjek, Roger. "Color-Full Before Color Blind: The Emergence of Multiracial Neighborhood Politics in Queens, New York City." *American Anthropologist* 102, no. 4 (2000): 762–72.

——. *The Future of Us All: Race and Neighborhood Politics in New York City*. Ithaca, N.Y.: Cornell University Press, 1998.

Santora, Marc. "Woman Is Held in Death of Man Pushed onto Subway Tracks in Queens." *New York Times*, December 29, 2012. http://www.nytimes.com/2012/12/30/nyregion/woman-is-held-in-death-of-man-pushed-onto-subway-tracks-in-queens.html.

Santos, Fernanda. "A Prime Retail Spot, but No Takers." *City Room* (blog). *New York Times*, November 8, 2010. http://cityroom.blogs.nytimes.com/2010/11/08/a-prime-retail-spot-but-no-takers/.

Saturno, Carol. "La Gare de l'est et les guides de Paris, un siècle de modes d'emploi." In *Villes en gares*, edited by Isaac Joseph, 94–110. La Tour d'Aigues: Éditions de l'Aube, 1999.

Schaller, Bruce. *Mode Shift in the 1990s: How Subway and Bus Ridership Outpaced the Auto in Market Share Gains in New York City*. New York: Schaller Consulting, August 8, 2001.

Scherer, Klaus R., Angela Schorr, and Tom Johnstone. *Appraisal Processes in Emotion: Theory, Methods, Research*. New York: Oxford University Press, 2001. https://books.google.com/books?hl=en&lr=&id=IWLnBwAAQBAJ&oi=fnd&pg=PT14&dq=appraisal+theory+of+emotions+scherer&ots=tdtTKO8PSX&sig=3XSUSt_GY8B-pwwJiLz9ODi5vIE.

Schulz, Dorothy M., and Susan Gilbert. "Women and Transit Security: A New Look at an Old Issue." In *Women's Travel Issues, Proceedings from the Second National Conference*, 551–62. Washington, D.C.: Federal Highway Administration, 1996.

Schutz, Alfred. *Alfred Schutz on Phenomenology and Social Relations*. Edited by Helmut R. Wagner. Chicago: University of Chicago Press, 1970.

Scott, Janny, and Sewell Chan. "Transit Strike into 2nd Day; Stakes Climb." *New York Times*, December 22, 2005. http://www.nytimes.com/2005/12/22/nyregion/nyregionspecial3/22strike.html.

Scott, Joan W. "The Evidence of Experience." *Critical Inquiry* 17, no. 4 (1991): 773–97.

——. "The Tip of the Volcano." *Comparative Studies in Society and History* 35, no. 2 (1993): 438–43.

Scott Smith, Russell. "Onan the Vegetarian: The Story of a Raw-Food Guru Turned 'Subway Perv.'" *New York*, April 10, 2006. http://nymag.com/news/features/16576/index2.html.

Segrave, Kerry. *Policewomen: A History*. Jefferson, N.C.: McFarland, 1995.

Sheller, Mimi, and John Urry. "The New Mobilities Paradigm." *Environment and Planning A* 38, no. 2 (2006): 207–26.

Shuman, Amy. *Storytelling Rights: The Uses of Oral and Written Texts by Urban Adolescents*. New York: Cambridge University Press, 1986.

Simmel, Georg. "The Metropolis and Mental Life." 1903. In *The Sociology of Georg Simmel*, translated and edited by Kurt Wolff, 409–24. New York: Free Press, 1950.

——. *The Sociology of Georg Simmel*. Translated and edited by Kurt Wolff. New York: Free Press, 1950.

Small, Mario Luis. "'How Many Cases Do I Need?': On Science and the Logic of Case Selection in Field-Based Research." *Ethnography* 10, no. 1 (2009): 5–38.

Smith, Martha J., and Ronald V. Clarke. "Crime and Public Transport." *Crime and Justice* 27 (2000): 169–233.

Snyder, Robert W. *Transit Talk: New York's Bus and Subway Workers Tell Their Stories.* New York: New York Transit Museum; New Brunswick, N.J.: Rutgers University Press, 1997.

Sparberg, Andrew J. *From a Nickel to a Token: The Journey from Board of Transportation to MTA.* New York: Fordham University Press, 2016.

Stalter, Sunny. "The Subway Crush: Making Contact in New York City Subway Songs, 1904–1915." *Journal of American Culture* 34, no. 4 (2011): 321–31. doi: 10.1111/j.1542 -734X.2011.00783.x.

Stalter-Pace, Sunny. "Underground Theater: Theorizing Mobility Through Modern Subway Dramas." *Transfers* 5, no. 3 (2015): 4–22. doi: 10.3167/TRANS.2015.050302.

Star, Susan Leigh. "The Ethnography of Infrastructure." *American Behavioral Scientist* 43, no. 3 (1999): 377–91. doi: 10.1177/00027649921955326.

Steinhauer, Jennifer. "Citywide Strike Halts New York Subways and Buses." *New York Times*, December 21, 2005. http://www.nytimes.com/2005/12/21/nyregion/nyregions pecial3/21strike.html.

Stoudt, Brett G., Michelle Fine, and Madeline Fox. "Growing Up Policed in the Age of Aggressive Policing Policies." *New York Law School Law Review* 56 (2011): 1331.

Swalec, Andrea. "'Snackman' Who Stopped Subway Fight Now Has His Own Bat-Symbol." April 11, 2012. DNAinfo New York, http://www.dnainfo.com/new-york /20120411/greenwich-village-soho/snackman-who-stopped-subway-fight-now-has -his-own-bat-symbol/.

Swerdlow, Marian. *Underground Woman: My Four Years as a New York City Subway Conductor.* Philadelphia: Temple University Press, 1998.

Symes, Colin. "Coaching and Training: An Ethnography of Student Commuting on Sydney's Suburban Trains." *Mobilities* 2, no. 3 (2007): 443–61. doi: 10.1080/ 17450100701597434.

Tanenbaum, Susie J. *Underground Harmonies: New York City Subway Music and Its Implications for Public Space.* Ithaca, N.Y.: Cornell University Press, 1996.

Tarde, Gabriel. *L'opinion et la foule.* Paris: Felix Alcan, 1901.

Tavory, Ido. *Summoned: Identification and Religious Life in a Jewish Neighborhood.* Chicago: University of Chicago Press, 2016.

Teaford, Jon C. *The Rough Road to Renaissance: Urban Revitalization in America, 1940–1985.* Baltimore: Johns Hopkins University Press, 1990.

Thibaud, Jean-Paul. "La méthode des parcours commentés." In *L'espace urbain en méthodes*, edited by Michèle Grosjean and Jean-Paul Thibaud, 79–100. Collection Eupalinos. Marseille: Éditions parenthèses, 2001.

Thompson, John Brookshire. *Political Scandal: Power and Visibility in the Media Age.* Cambridge: Polity Press, 2000.

Thrasher, Frederic M. *The Gang: A Study of 1,313 Gangs in Chicago.* Chicago: University of Chicago Press, 1927.

Todd, Charlie. "No Pants 2k8 at Improv Everywhere." *Improv Everywhere*, January 16, 2008. http://improveverywhere.com/2008/01/16/no-pants-2k8/.

Transit Adjudication Bureau. "Rules of Conduct & Fines." Metropolitan Transportation Authority, New York. http://web.mta.info/nyct/rules/rules.htm.

Tuckel, Peter, William Milczarski, and Michael Benediktsson. "Etiquette of Riders on New York City Subways." An Observational Study Conducted by Students at

Hunter College, The City University of New York, Spring 2016. http://silo-public. hunter.cuny.edu/798320a76b1c330347bb7155d717c86bdf278c0f/Behavior-of-New-York -City-Subway-Riders_v.8.pdf.

Turner, Roy, ed. *Ethnomethodology*. New York: Penguin, 1974.

Union internationale des transports publics (UITP). "Statistics Brief: World Metro Figures." October 2014. http://www.uitp.org/sites/default/files/cck-focus-papers-files /Metro%20report%20Stat%20brief-web_oct2014.pdf.

Urry, John. *Mobilities*. Cambridge: Polity Press, 2007.

Valentine, Gill. *Public Space and the Culture of Childhood*. Burlington, Vt.: Ashgate, 2004.

Walzer, Michael. *What It Means to Be an American: Essays on the American Experience*. New York: Marsilio, 1996.

Warren, Roxanne. "Subway Fares Rise, as Do Riders' Gripes." *New York Times*, March 24, 2015. http://www.nytimes.com/2015/03/24/opinion/subway-fares-rise-as-do-rid ers-gripes.html.

West, Candace, and Don H. Zimmerman. "Doing Gender." *Gender & Society* 1, no. 2 (1987): 125–51. doi: 10.1177/0891243287001002002.

Whitehead, Colson. *The Colossus of New York: A City in Thirteen Parts*. New York: Anchor Books, 2004.

Whyte, William H. *The Social Life of Small Urban Spaces*. Washington, D.C.: Conservation Foundation, 1980.

Wieder, D. Lawrence. "Telling the Code." In *Ethnomethodology*, edited by Roy Turner, 144–72. New York: Penguin, 1974.

Williams, Terry, and William Kornblum. *Growing Up Poor*. Lexington, Mass.: Lexington Books, 1985.

Winkel, Gary H., and D. Geoffrey Hayward. "Some Major Causes of Congestion in Subway Stations. Research Report to the Transit / Land Use Committee." Environmental Psychology Program, City University of New York, 1971.

Wirth, Louis. "Rural-Urban Differences." In *Classic Essays on the Culture of Cities*, edited by Richard Sennett, 165–70. New York: Appleton-Century-Crofts, 1969.

——. "Urbanism as a Way of Life." *American Journal of Sociology* 44, no. 1 (1938): 1–24.

Yoder, Janice D., Mary Hogue, Robert Newman, Linda Metz, and Tonya LaVigne. "Exploring Moderators of Gender Differences: Contextual Differences in Door-Holding Behavior." *Journal of Applied Social Psychology* 32, no. 8 (2002): 1682–86. doi: 10.1111 /j.1559-1816.2002.tb02769.x.

Zaporozhets, Oksana. "Becoming a Subway User: Managing Affects and Experiences." SSRN Scholarly Paper. Social Science Research Network, Rochester, N.Y., May 6, 2014. http://papers.ssrn.com/abstract=2433951.

Ziegler, Garrett. "Subjects and Subways: The Politics of the Third Rail." *Space and Culture* 7, no. 3 (2004): 283–301.

Zimmerman, Don H., and D. Lawrence Wieder. "The Diary: Diary-Interview Method." *Journal of Contemporary Ethnography* 5, no. 4 (1977): 479–98.

Zraick, Karen. "A Personal Story of Sexual Harassment." *City Room* (blog). *New York Times*, November 10, 2010. http://cityroom.blogs.nytimes.com/2010/11/10/a-personal -story-of-sexual-harassment/.

Index